NATIONAL SELF-DETERMINATION AND JUSTICE IN MULTINATIONAL STATES

STUDIES IN GLOBAL JUSTICE

VOLUME 5

Aims and Scope

In today's world, national borders seem irrelevant when it comes to international crime and terrorism. Likewise, human rights, poverty, inequality, democracy, development, trade, bioethics, hunger, war and peace are all issues of global rather than national justice. The fact that mass demonstrations are organized whenever the world's governments and politicians gather to discuss such major international issues is testimony to a widespread appeal for justice around the world.

Discussions of global justice are not limited to the fields of political philosophy and political theory. In fact, research concerning global justice quite often requires an interdisciplinary approach. It involves aspects of ethics, law, human rights, international relations, sociology, economics, public health, and ecology. Springer's new series *Studies in Global Justice* up that interdisciplinary perspective. The series brings together outstanding monographs and anthologies that deal with both basic normative theorizing and its institutional applications. The volumes in the series discuss such aspects of global justice as the scope of social justice, the moral significance of borders, global inequality and poverty, the justification and content of human rights, the aims and methods of development, global environmental justice, global bioethics, the global institutional order and the justice of intervention and war.

Volumes in this series will prove of great relevance to researchers, educators and students, as well as politicians, policy-makers and government officials.

For further volumes:
http://www.springer.com/series/6958

National Self-Determination and Justice in Multinational States

ANNA MOLTCHANOVA
Carleton College, Northfield, MN, U.S.A.

Springer

Anna Moltchanova
Carleton College
Department of Philosophy
1 North College Street
Northfield MN 55057
USA
amoltcha@carleton.edu

ISSN 1871-0409
ISBN 978-90-481-2690-3 e-ISBN 978-90-481-2691-0
DOI 10.1007/978-90-481-2691-0
Springer Dordrecht Heidelberg London New York

Library of Congress Control Number: 2009926812

Printed on acid-free paper

Springer is part of Springer Science+Business Media (www.springer.com)

Contents

Introduction

Centers of political and military influence in world politics change, as the fading away of the bipolar arrangement of the Cold War has made clear. But regardless of whether one or two great powers or a coalition of states dominates international politics, there ought to be a set of norms that allows us to evaluate the actions of governments and individuals in the international arena from a moral standpoint.[1] Labeling an action or a policy as morally wrong cannot prevent it, of course, but moral norms have some power to shape individual and group actions, even if these actions consciously counter the norms. When both the citizens of a state and outsiders are able to evaluate the moral status of state actors by reference to an established moral ideal, they can find a way to mobilize around the moral ideal and make it known to those who violate that ideal that their actions are wrong. Establishing a moral foundation for international relations would also demand consistency: if actions are to be prohibited for one type of group actors and allowed for others, the norms behind these regulations would need to be aligned.

From a moral standpoint, human rights are a set of inviolable standards of international and domestic politics. Many governments of the world fail to respect them, however, and individual enjoyment of this basic entitlement depends on what group one belongs to, which is itself a function of the vagaries of personal and societal history. The country one is born into, its geographical location and political and economic fortunes, often are not and cannot be chosen. Some may say that because all individuals enjoy benefits or are denied benefits on the basis of their group membership, the goal of the international community should be to minimize the influence of the historical contingencies that determine group membership and bridge the gap separating individuals around the globe from the pursuit of a decent life. If we wish to do away with the inequality of persons worldwide, however, we must find a principled way to determine what contingencies ought to be addressed and under what circumstances. This requires a set of norms subsidiary to the universal standard of human rights but nonetheless moral in nature.

Determining under what circumstances national belonging matters to the exercise of human rights enables us to attend to a number of factors relevant to individual quality of life: being Croatian or Serbian does not matter that much in the sense of affecting one's political activity if one lives in Canada or the United States, for example, but it matters a great deal if one lives in Bosnia. More important, if we treat individuals as moral agents, not simply as moral recipients, we need to account for their preferences for group membership and consider the nature of their present engagement with the group under which they live and whether it is voluntary. Finally, every contingent framework can easily acquire normative features if considered in terms of the relations of individuals. Being born in a certain territory and enjoying remaining there is contingent. If others claim the territory as their own, then one's decision to remain there or, even more, one's claim to possess a right to do so is a contingent event that acquires a normative dimension. When individuals advance competing or conflicting claims—any claims that affect others—they may explicitly support the claims using a norm or standard that endorses the kind of relationship to others that they wish to maintain or achieve. This background norm or standard needs to be evaluated at least in relation to the standard used by the other party or parties against whom their claim is advanced. If competing claims to territory are not made with explicit reference to a standard, the claims' very advancement implies that the individuals who advance them rank their own entitlement higher than that of others. Thus, the basis for the entitlement to the right to the territory or its absence is moral in nature.

That individuals' preferences to be included in the group of their choice ought to be respected does not imply that groups should be unimpeded in the aspects of their functioning that violate their members' human rights. Specifying what facet of group existence must be regulated to safeguard group members' human rights requires us to pay special attention to group constitution. Groups are constituted through the modes of their members' interaction. To alter a group's influence on its members, we need to alter the mode of their interaction, and for a change to be lasting, group members must cooperate and embrace it. An effective change cannot be produced by a third party alone, even if it is motivated by the quest for justice. It needs to engage the group members on the right terms. Determining what these terms are is the task of a theory of international justice.

In this book, I propose an element of such a theory, focusing on membership in national groups. The basic intuition that I develop and defend in this book is that national groups are collective agents (or "group agents") of a certain kind. Given that group agents may take shape or interact in ways that threaten the rights of members or nonmembers, we need to determine which modes of organization are acceptable and on what terms groups agents should interact. Because groups formulate their demands upon others using the discourse of rights, even engaging in war over these "rights" in the worst-case scenario, we need to define a principled basis for group entitlements in conflicts between national groups. Only a set of norms concerning groups' status in relation to the rest of the world can provide the international community with an idea of the proper state of affairs to which the warring groups ought to be restored. This is not a simple task, because warring groups often aspire to control a contested territory. For the sake of world peace, such territories need to be governed efficiently and justly, and setting the terms of acceptable group interaction is vital to achieving this goal. One precondition for encouraging a group to cooperate, I argue in this book, is to ensure that its status as a world actor or within its political community is determined in accordance with the particular shared good around which the group is organized, whether it be territory, language, religion, culture, political rights, or something else.

Substate nationalism, especially in the past fifteen years, has noticeably affected the political and territorial stability of many countries, both democratic and democratizing. The United Kingdom and Fiji, Spain and Russia, Canada and the former Yugoslavia, and many other states have encountered problems, from political crisis to long-lasting asymmetrical warfare, caused by stateless national groups' advancing self-determination claims. Because most states are multinational—that is, they have more than one national group living within their boundaries—the challenge of accommodating multiple claims to self-determination within a single territory is unlikely to diminish in the future. It would be impractical for every national group to acquire a state of its own, and international law does not normally permit stateless national groups to secede, yet they are usually not willing to give up their claims to self-determination, especially given the high value placed on the acquisition of independent statehood, which is normally associated with the realization of self-determination in the current international context.

Secessionist movements are a typical but extreme challenge to the stability and territorial integrity of multinational states. The pursuit of self-determination by secessionist national groups often leads to protracted conflicts accompanied by severe deterioration in the political and economic situations of secessionist regions, sometimes leading to total paralysis and the groups' failure to effectively govern themselves. We have seen such a situation develop in Chechnya, for example. A widely accepted framework for the consideration of such conflicts that is based on the norms of international law regards wars of secession as matters internal to the host states or, if more than one state is concerned, as matters to be dealt with by the recognized state units involved. The secessionist claims of Abkhazia and Southern Ossetia, for example, have been treated as matters internal to Georgia or, when there is Russian covert involvement, placed in the context of relations between Russia and Georgia. This perspective treats Georgia as the legitimate state in the conflict because Georgia was a union-level national republic in the former USSR, while Abkhazia and South Ossetia were its autonomous national republics. This historical classification established a hierarchy that continues to be respected by international law. But the very ranking presupposes that the ranked units are separate *national* groups, and this important constitutive feature should figure in the perspective on the conflict between Abkhasia and Georgia or Southern Ossetia and Georgia taken by the international community.

In addition to secessionist claims, federations currently face a number of other problems related to substate groups. The advantages and prerogatives that minority nations can acquire within a federal system are affected by the internal composition of their federal state. Many federations are mixed: they contain national and territorial subjects. The Russian Federation, for example, includes both territorial-administrative and national units.[2] All eighty-nine subjects of the Russian Federation were considered equal in the federal treaty signed after the fall of the Soviet Union. In reality, however, the status of the national and territorial-administrative units is different. Many of the twenty-one national republics have declared themselves to be sovereign states within the federation.[3] "Sovereign" here has a specific and historically defined meaning. The former Soviet (union-level) republics nominally retained their sovereignty through the constitutional right of exit. Others (non-union-level republics) only qualified as national minorities with various levels of self-government (as autonomous republics, regions, and districts) within the boundaries of the union-level republics and were not sovereign.

Should territorial and national subjects in federal states receive differential treatment? The clear but hierarchical definition of various national groups in the former USSR constructed the official evaluation of their status as just, but it was not always perceived as such by the groups themselves. The hierarchy of nationalities, a cornerstone of Soviet national policy, was clearly arbitrary (Armenia, for example, was a union republic, while Bashkortostan, which is comparable in size, was only an autonomous republic). Mikhail Gorbachev, just before the fall of the Soviet Union, tried to elevate the status of some autonomous republics to the union republic level and thus acknowledge their sovereignty. On April 26, 1990, the Supreme Council of the USSR issued a law on "the division of powers between the USSR and the subjects of the federation" that gave equal legal status to union-level and autonomous republics. The latter acquired a right to interact with the federal authority directly, rather than through their host union republics. The autonomous districts and regions, still acknowledged by the Soviets to be a lower level of national identity, were now required to have treaty-based relations with their republics, which elevated their status as national groups.[4] While this move was prompted by the autonomous republics' desire to sign the USSR treaty, Boris Yeltsin wanted them to sign the Russian federal treaty instead. In the end, the USSR fell apart, and the republics signed the Russian Federation's federal treaty.[5] Thus, when the USSR was disbanded, the former autonomous republics of the Soviet Russian Federation became the national republics in the present federation. Their constitutions demand a significant degree of independence from the Russian federal state: Tatarstan's constitution considers the federal law void if it contradicts treaties the republic has signed with other subjects of the federation, while the constitution of Sakha grants its legislature the right to ratify federal laws before they acquire force in the republic.[6] The territorial-administrative units (49 *oblasts,* 6 *krai*, and 2 cities), on the other hand, do not have the statelike status of the national republics in either internal or international relations, and they perceive that the sovereignty of the republics puts them in an unequal position in the federal state.[7] In the course of the 1990s, some of them attempted to elevate their status by declaring themselves republics. Adding to the confusion, the Federal Constitution says that neither the federal treaty nor the republics' own constitutions determine their status and that the republics are not sovereign.[8] Thus, what the groups that perceive themselves as national can in principle claim and how they can justifiably relate to the territorial units are open questions.

As the example of the Russian Federation demonstrates, while historical factors such as power asymmetries and the role of previous political leadership causally define groups' present status, the historical demarcation of groups is dynamic and often unhelpful in identifying group agents in present-day conflicts. Moreover, the intentions of group agents adjust to and often escalate based upon their officially recognized status.

In addition to the status struggle with the federal state and the territorial districts, the national republics of the Russian Federation inherited the problem of "substate" nationalities, wherein formerly autonomous districts and regions have become their national minorities.[9] What needs to be determined is, first, whether there is any difference in principle between territorial and national subjects of federations that can justify the special status of national republics in the Russian Federation and, second, whether differences in size and historical standing among national groups in a federal state, such as the present division into national republics and national minorities in the Russian Federation, warrant differential treatment based solely on these factors.

One approach to national minorities is offered by the Council of Europe's Framework Convention for the Protection of National Minorities. It introduces norms for the equal treatment of individuals from both national minorities and majorities before the law and in economic, political, and cultural spheres. In this document, the essential elements of national minorities' identity are considered to be religion, traditions, language, and cultural heritage. The rights that the convention aims to promote are given to individuals and not to groups, although it acknowledges that individuals can enjoy their rights "in community with others."[10] The convention does not address self-determination claims, however, and thus it does not provide a fully adequate response to the demands of minorities.

To settle problems related to the status of various groups presently referred to as "national" in relation to one another and to arbitrate the various claims of minority national groups, including the claim to self-determination, we need to decide which groups possess a moral right to self-determination. Substate groups' perception of unjust treatment is warranted only if substate and state-endowed national groups are similar kinds of communities—if, in other words, both are "nations" with a moral right to self-determination. And even if substate groups are in principle entitled to the same treatment with respect to self-determination as state-endowed groups, it may still be the case that they cannot be afforded that treatment due to pragmatic limitations. If so, the basis for the denial of the exercise of the right to self-determination would be different from what it would be if the group did not possess the right at all, and thus being denied the right may entitle the group to some form of compensation. In short, the regulation of self-determination claims on a moral basis requires us to define nationhood and to explain the moral entitlements of national groups in relation to self-determination by specifying which groups are the subjects of the right to self-determination and how they may exercise that right, particularly in regard to statehood.

The very different international status and privileges presently enjoyed by stateless and state-endowed groups provide a difficult setting for the regulation of their relations. State-endowed nations are full members of the international community and have control over their political futures, whereas non-state national groups do not have an internationally recognized legal right to self-determination unless they are occupied or colonized.[11] They are not even considered nations according to the prevalent understanding of the term in international relations, which associates "nation" with "state." There are no legal international means for addressing a minority's claim to self-determination except indirectly through an appeal to the principles of human rights. Once human rights are violated, however, it is usually too late to resolve conflict by peaceful means.

To address destabilizing self-determination claims, we must regulate the behavior of substate groups with respect to one another and to their host states. Norms exist to limit the behavior of collective agents in relation to individuals; the set of universally accepted human rights provides a basic framework. There is a lacuna in international law, however, in the regulation of the behavior of groups toward other groups, with the exception of relations among states. International law does not define the status or powers that non-state groups that claim to be nations but reside within multinational states should have in relation to other groups, their citizens, or their own national minorities.

Solving the self-determination problem can be seen as a purely practical exercise: multinational states' territorial integrity can better be preserved if an improved set of measures is put in place to ensure the enforcement of the present norms of international law, which protect the territorial integrity of states and allow secession only in exceptional circumstances. A strict adherence to current norms, however, will not eliminate tensions introduced by the norms themselves. A non-state group's claim to self-determination is illegal if unsupported by its host state, because the claim violates the host state's sovereignty and territorial integrity. Thus, the international system is organized in such a way that it poses a dilemma to groups that advance claims to self-determination (unless they are occupied or colonized): they can either follow the rules and give up their claims or break the rules and try to secede, which usually leads to violent conflict. The first option is designed to maintain the current formal order of international society, which continues to be provided by the collectivity of sovereign states.[12] The second option is backed up by the existing moral right of all peoples to self-determination but is not straightforwardly practicable in the terms of an international system that associates the exercise of self-determination with the acquisition of independent statehood.

A state-centered attitude, while motivated by practical considerations of stability and supported by the current principles of international law, is not, in the end, a practical one, because it does not resolve conflicts, and to some extent it even encourages them. While there is simply no good normative explanation for why stateless national minorities' exercise of the right to self-determination should be second to that of groups with states of their own, or for why stateless groups are not entitled—or are significantly less entitled than state-endowed groups—to control their future political status, it may be said that, given the costs of accommodation, stateless groups cannot be granted the right to self-determination for practical reasons. But restricting the exercise of the right to self-determination by substate groups could not be justified pragmatically on the basis of the need to preserve the stability and territorial integrity of multinational states if an approach were developed that served this need while granting moral claims to substate groups. This book suggests such an approach to the entitlements of national groups, which I will call the "nations approach." I begin by considering what guidance the current international norms provide for the regulation of relations among national groups and briefly review various theoretical approaches to self-determination and nationhood in the first chapter. I argue that we cannot reduce the right to self-determination of a group to the individual rights of group members and that we need to differentiate self-determination from other types of group entitlement.

The existence of the collective legal right to self-determination is commonly acknowledged, but the notion that collectives have moral rights is often contested. On one side of the debate is the claim that moral rights can inhere only in individuals and that, at most, collectives can acquire "derivative" moral rights, which belong to individuals but can be exercised by individuals only through their participation in a group. Using this reasoning, the right to be educated in French in Manitoba belongs to individual Francophone Manitobans, but it cannot be exercised unless there are a sufficient number of Francophone children present in a given area who warrant the right of the Francophone minority to receive instruction in French schools.[13] On the other side of the debate is the claim that moral rights can belong to collectives as such as "primary" collective rights.[14] In line with the spirit of this position, Nunavut, an autonomous Inuit territory in Canada, was created in recognition of the moral right of the Inuit people to self-government. Reversing the viewpoints in the two examples, could Nunavut's autonomy derive from its individual members' right to democratic self-governance? And could the right to be educated in French belong to the Francophone citizens of Manitoba as a group?

I address these questions in the second chapter, wherein I distinguish between the two types of group moral rights and argue that the type of group entitlement can be determined by how a group is constituted in relation to non-members. All group rights belong to collective agents sharing in the good that the right in question promotes. I argue that only collective agents constituted so that they are capable of exercising equal freedom can have a primary moral right. A collective right to self-determination can be primary because self-determination concerns the relation of a collective to other collectives as free equals. Collective moral rights of groups organized around such shared goods as language, culture, or religion are derivative because these groups are identified by the circumstances of their inclusion in the host self-determining communities and do not have the capacity for equal freedom. I argue that self-determination is an important shared good to which certain group agents have a moral right.

I define the subjects of the right to self-determination in Chapter 3, in which I introduce a new definition of nationhood. A number of conceptions of nationhood have recently been advanced,[15] and some theorists argue that the very notion is amorphous and passé.[16] I define "nationhood" as a political culture shared by the members of a group with the collective end of maintaining or acquiring effective agency of a certain kind. Nations are organized around the ideal of self-determination: the members of a nation believe that membership in the group defines the bounds within which political authority can originate meaningfully for those the group governs. Finally, for a political culture to characterize a national group, the group's members have to identify with that culture. By focusing on political culture,

I capture how national groups relate to one another and provide a conception of nationhood that reflects the self- and mutual understanding of the members of a national group.

The present international community's inability to manage issues of substate nationalism affects not only societies with established democratic traditions and clearly defined nations but also newly democratizing countries in all parts of the world. Regulating relations among national groups in transitional societies is important for democratization. The scholarship on minority nationalism has paid little attention, however, to the instability of national identities in transitional societies. I extend the theory of nationhood to account for the presence of changeable or unknown national identities in transitional and oppressive societies in Chapter 4, in which I introduce the concepts of "potential" and "vacuous" political cultures to demonstrate how my definition of nationhood can be applied in such societies. A vacuous culture represents official norms and political goals rather than societal values and beliefs. Citizens usually do not identify with a vacuous political culture. Instead, they relate to often-fragmented attitudes toward or beliefs about politics that are not fully expressed or even articulated. These beliefs and attitudes reflect a potential political culture, which coexists with the vacuous culture. The existence of vacuous political cultures explains why self-identification with a political culture is so important to my definition of nationhood. The presence of a vacuous culture tells us that we should pay attention to changing or murkily expressed national identities and that in some circumstances we should suspend our judgment concerning the national makeup of a society. Although the notion of political culture does not produce a theory of nationhood that has the unfailing capacity to identify all groups that qualify as nations in transitional societies, defining the terms of interaction for any national groups that might emerge during the transition to democracy in advance, even before national identities crystallize, could help control the newly formed nations' relations and thereby facilitate peaceful political changes in transitional periods. I conclude Chapter 4 by formulating a general strategy for transition based on a set of normative guidelines about the treatment of substate national groups.

I next defend in Chapter 5 that national communities have a moral right to self-determination and that the just treatment of substate national groups requires the equality of different national groups to be the norm governing the treatment of self-determination claims. Because I do not associate nationhood or self-determination with statehood, my approach to self-determination can accommodate the pragmatic limitations on normative ideals posed by the requirements of security and stability. I argue that the right to national self-determination must go beyond self-government but to stop short of statehood, and thus I introduce a modified right to self-determination, which states that all national groups have an equal right to self-determination provided that the realization of the right does not require the acquisition of independent statehood as its necessary condition. It is unjust not to allow national communities to live according to their internal constitutions provided they do not harm others. National groups should be given an opportunity equal to those of other members of their host multinational states to determine their future political status within these states.

Many treatments of self-determination concentrate on conditions for secession, a much-debated topic in recent scholarship. Presently, a national group has the right to secede from a state if the state is subjecting the group to colonization or illegal occupation. A common approach to secession allows secession also if the host state is guilty of gross violations of human rights.[17] This approach, however, ignores states that respect human rights but harbor competing claims to self-determination. The modified right requires that states respect not only human rights but also the equal right of the national groups within their territory to self-determination. Substate national groups can secede either by mutual agreement with other national groups present within the territory of a multinational state after their equality within the state has been achieved or if they are persistently denied the right to exercise self-determination on an equal basis with other groups within the state.

Since the modified right to self-determination can be afforded in an equitable fashion to all national groups without breaking up existing states, it has the potential to become a universal legal right. The current international system is prone to conflict partly because it treats similar groups unequally. Expanding the sphere of international regulation to include national groups within multinational states could help improve the stability of such states by establishing norms for the just treatment of national groups within these states. The idea behind this approach is that normalizing relationships among groups is most effective when it takes into consideration groups' motivations for acting, which allows it to address instability associated with their behavior. This book suggests a positive theory of self-determination—the nations approach—that aims to foster the systematic regulation of relations of self-determination among national groups rather than simply specify conditions for secession. This approach would preserve the territorial integrity of multinational states better than alternative proposals that make respect for human rights the only criterion for multinational states' legitimacy.

Ultimately, I contend that the nations approach, which promotes equal access to self-determination for minority and majority nations within their host states, is not only justified but also can be implemented and will improve the stability and preserve the territorial integrity of multinational states. In Chapter 6, I discuss which principles for the institutional arrangement of multinational states properly address the self-determination claims of national minorities, and thus which principles can be put into place for the implementation of the modified right to self-determination. I also consider a number of challenges that substate self-determination poses for multinational federations. I argue that the employment of my nations approach to self-determination will have positive consequences for international peace. If this approach were to become an accepted part of the international legal framework, it would undermine the moral basis of justifications for asymmetrical warfare, provide incentives for non-state groups to participate in negotiations, and help them transform themselves into responsible members of the international community. I demonstrate that since the norms for the regulation of self-determination that I propose respect the principle of territorial integrity, these norms have a good chance of being accepted by the members of the international community. The modified right embedded in the nations approach would afford substate groups the equal status with respect to self-determination that they desire and serve their host states' interest in stability. This would facilitate the voluntary compliance of the collective agents holding the modified right to self-determination—both state-endowed and substate—with the requirements it places upon them to qualify for membership in the international community. I consider various approaches to the empirical effects of implementing theories like mine and conclude that the approach to self-determination I propose would provide the most stable and morally appealing arrangement of multinational states and therefore is consequentially beneficial. The introduction of the modified right to self-determination would help to alter stateless groups' goals for achieving self-determination by demoting the status of statehood. Rather than compete for a state of their own, their goal would become to cooperate within their host states, which they would share with a number of national groups in an equal relationship, creating conditions for peace within the boundaries of multinational states.

Readers fairly familiar with the various theoretical approaches to self-determination may choose to skip Chapter 1, which highlights the differences of these approaches with my approach. Those readers who are more interested in the practical applications of my theory may want to skip Chapter 3, in which I defend my definition of nationhood.

Notes

1. Allen Buchanan argues persuasively for the need for a moral theory of international law in *Justice, Legitimacy, and Self-Determination: Moral Foundations for International Law* (Oxford: Oxford University Press, 2004). Michael Walzer engages in a deeply moral discussion of conventions of war in *Just and Unjust Wars: A Moral Argument with Historical Illustrations*, 3rd ed. (New York: Basic, 2000). For a good discussion of the need for normative theorizing, see Allen Buchanan and David Golove, "Philosopy of International Law," in *The Oxford Handbook of Jurisprudence and Philosophy of Law*, ed. J. Coleman and S. Shapiro (Oxford: Oxford University Press, 2003), pp. 868–934.
2. There is a similar tension between federal subjects in Canada, where Quebec's demands for special recognition are deemed excessive by the other provinces, which view Quebec on a par with themselves and not as a different type of federal subject.
3. A. N. Arinin, "Rossiiskaja Gosudarstvennost' i problemi federalizma," in *Issledovania po prikladnoi I neotlozhnoi etnologii*, no. 105 (Moscow: Institut etnologii i antropologii RAN), p. 9.
4. Ibid., p. 19.
5. Ibid., p. 9.
6. L. M. Drobizheva, A. R. Aklaev, V. V. Koroteeva, and G. U. Soladtova *Democratizatsiia i obrazi nationalizma v Rossiiskoi Federatsii 90-x godov* (Moscow: Misl', 1996), p. 169.
7. V. A. Mikhailov, *Natsional'naja Politika Rossii: istoria I sovremennost* (Moscow: Pusskii mir, 1997), pp. 383–85.
8. Drobizheva, Aklaev, Koroteeva, and Soladtova, *Democratizatsiia*, p. 186.
9. The situation is also complicated by the fact that many title nationalities in the national republics of the federation are not even majorities in the territories named after them. The overall percentage of the title nationalities in the republics is 42.4 percent, though some republics have the title nationality as a majority, including Dagestan (80.2%), Chuvashia (67.8%), Tuva

(64.3%), Kabardino-Balkaria (57.6%), and North Ossetia (52.9%). See M. Guboglo, *Mozhet li dvuglavii oriol letat's odnim krilom? Pazmishlenia o zakonotvorchestve v sphere ehnogosudarstvennikh otnoshenii* (Moscow: Russian Academy of Sciences, 2000), p. 84.

10. Council of Europe, Framework Convention for the Protection of National Minorities, Strasbourg, 1.II.1995, CETS no. 157, http://conventions.coe.int/ Treaty/en/Treaties/Html/157.htm, art. 4.1, 4.2, 5.1, 3.2.
11. The UN Charter acknowledges that "all peoples have a right to self-determination," but that right is limited in the current international law to occupied and colonized national groups. Cassese states, for example, that self-determination is firmly entrenched in the corpus of international general rules in three areas only: as an anticolonialist standard, as a ban on foreign military occupation, and as a standard requiring racial groups be given full access to government. See *Self-Determination of Peoples: A Legal Reappraisal* (New York: Cambridge University Press, 1995), p. 319. For another argument supporting this interpretation, see Hurst Hannum, *Autonomy, Sovereignty, and Self-Determination: The Accommodation of Conflicting Rights* (Philadelphia: University of Pennsylvania Press, 1996).
12. For more on this argument, see James Mayall, "Sovereignty, Nationalism, and Self-Determination," *Political Studies* 47 (1999): 474–502.
13. Canadian Charter of Rights and Freedoms, art. 23.
14. Bhikhu Parekh considers religious, cultural, and linguistic rights to be primary collective rights. See *Rethinking Multiculturalism: Cultural Diversity and Political Theory* (Cambridge, MA: Harvard University Press, 2000), pp. 213–19. Michael McDonald argues that there is a need for primary collective rights based on the possession of significant collective goods. See "The Personless Paradigm," *University of Toronto Law Journal* 37, no. 2 (Spring 1987): 223.
15. See David Miller, *On Nationality* (Oxford: Oxford University Press, 1995); Yael Tamir, *Liberal Nationalism* (Princeton: Princeton University Press, 1993); Margaret Canovan, *Nationhood and Political Theory* (Cheltenham, UK: Edward Elgar, 1996).
16. See Rogers Brubaker, *Nationalism Reframed: Nationhood and the National Question in the New Europe* (Cambridge: Cambridge University Press, 1996).
17. Allen Buchanan, "Recognitional Legitimacy and the State System," *Philosophy and Public Affairs* 28, no. 1 (Winter 1999), pp. 46–78, p. 55.

Chapter 1
Multinational States and Moral Theories of International Legal Doctrine

When those of us armed with a typical liberal sense of right and wrong read historical accounts of liberation movements directed against either domestic tyrants or colonizers, we intuitively agree that the oppressed peoples deserved their freedom, because they deserved to govern themselves. But what lies behind our intuition? How do we establish that the oppressed are a people and explain why they deserve this freedom? Furthermore, groups with internationally recognized governments sometimes oppress their members in the name of their right to self-determination, as do groups whose internal organization is neither properly institutionalized nor internationally endorsed. Thus while self-determination, especially qualified as a "moral" right, may seem fine as a general rule, in its application it is potentially dangerous and destabilizing, and even contrary to human rights. The questions that need to be answered to unpack our intuition concerning self-determination are very basic: Does a moral right to self-determination exist? If so, who holds the right? This chapter begins to examine these questions by first considering the current international norms that control self-determination and then looking at the various theories that attempt to provide a moral foundation for the regulation of relations among different types of national groups. In the course of this brief survey, I discuss the ways in which major theoretical accounts of self-determination can be modified to deal with substate nationalism and identify the areas in which my approach to nationhood and self-determination can be particularly useful. I continue the discussion concerning who holds group rights in the next chapter.

Current International Norms

Both the Charter of the United Nations and several subsequent UN documents identify the moral right of "all peoples to self-determination." The United Nations was created in part to "develop friendly relations among nations based on respect for the principle of equal rights and self-determination of peoples."[1] UN resolution 1514, the International Covenant on Civil and Political Rights, and the International Covenant on Economic, Social and Cultural Rights reiterate that "all peoples have the right to self-determination" and that "by virtue of that right they freely

A. Moltchanova, *National Self-Determination and Justice in Multinational States*, Studies in Global Justice 5, DOI 10.1007/978-90-481-2691-0_1,

determine their political status and freely pursue their economic, social and cultural development."[2]

Although these formulations do not specify what kinds of national groups qualify for the right to self-determination—"people" is not clearly defined and does not in principle exclude substate national groups from the entitlement—only a limited number of national groups are acknowledged to have the legal right to self-determination in the current international system. International law understands the right to self-determination as the right to be free from external occupation and colonization. This understanding excludes the self-determination claims of many substate national groups. The self-determination claims of national groups on the territory of the Russian Federation, such as Dagestan, Mordovia, or Tatarstan, for example, are excluded from consideration under the present interpretation of the right to self-determination, whereas the Baltic republics were considered to have this right due to their unjust occupation by the Soviet regime.

National groups currently qualify for the right to self-determination not according to a principle or a norm but as a result of the vagaries of history. In terms of their qualification for the right to self-determination, the difference between the peoples of Tatarstan and the Baltic republic of Estonia—two peoples who each have institutions of political self-government and a sense of national identity—lies in the Estonians' prior possession of an independent state. This is a contingent historical factor that does not *morally* justify the allocation of the right to self-determination to Estonia and not to Tatarstan. The legal right to self-determination is in fact not backed by a moral justification for what stateless groups perceive to be the unfair limitation on the subjects of the right, the enjoyment of which is distributed in a way that is rather arbitrary. Tatarstan could take a broad historical approach and trace its political institutions to the times of the Golden Horde, when the Khanate of Kazan was independent of Russia before being defeated by Ivan the Terrible in the late fifteenth century. In reply, the international community might insist that only those self-governing institutions that existed following the Peace of Westphalia can claim to have a historical lineage that justifies their right to self-determination. But if that is the case, why is one historical dividing line relevant while another is not? This study does not refer to historical timelines to define nations on the basis of when they formed but provides a definition that identifies nations based on the presence of a particular kind of collective agent. The right to self-determination is grounded in the moral entitlement of this type of collective agent, as well as in the need to regulate relations among national groups that act based on their perception of themselves as agents of this type.

It is difficult for the international community to affect states' behavior toward national minorities within the current system. With the exception of violations of internationally recognized individual rights (human rights and some rights guaranteed by treaties, such as the European Framework Convention), rules governing the treatment of minorities remain within the domestic jurisdiction of their host states. The charter of the United Nations states that "nothing contained in the present Charter shall authorize the United Nations to intervene in matters which are essentially within the domestic jurisdiction of any state or shall require the Members to submit such matters to settlement under the present Charter."[3] There is no law that specifies the duties of states even to provide autonomy to minorities beyond the limited rights to practice their religions and cultures and to use their languages. The international community's reluctance to establish universal duties regarding the autonomy of national minorities leaves the self-determination claims of national groups largely unaddressed.[4] The concluding document of the Copenhagen meeting of the Helsinki Commission's Conference on the Human Dimension, for example, concerns the rights of persons belonging to minorities to establish and maintain their own educational, cultural, and religious institutions, organizations, or associations. It does not deal with political rights, such as self-determination, which often constitute the chief concern of ethnic minorities.[5] The very couching of disputes between states and stateless national groups as "minority disputes" is not helpful to the development of international legal norms for their resolution.

Since substate groups are not proper members of the international community—they are not, for example, members of the UN or parties to the International Court of Justice[6]—they cannot use the same means to pursue and defend their interests as state-endowed national groups can. Stateless national groups cannot legitimately wage a war of self-defense when their political community is in danger, though legally self-determining political entities can. Substate groups' status with respect to self-determination, except for a handful of cases that fall under current international regulations, is covered by international legal norms only negatively: most national groups are prohibited to act so as to exercise self-determination.

The current association of the exercise of self-determination with some form of independent statehood fosters the creation of multinational states that are neither stable nor politically flourishing. It shapes the aspirations of substate national groups in terms of the limited right to self-determination. These aspirations to acquire the rare good of self-determination, which endows a selected few nations with the prerogative of sovereignty, are bound to be frustrated and to complicate stateless groups' relations with their state-endowed host nations. The absence of international norms regulating the status of substate national groups with respect to their host multinational states does not help to resolve internal conflicts within these states and adds to the challenge of protecting national minorities. In the absence of a moral and legal framework that justifies actions taken by the international community to resolve conflicts among national groups, this community is often helpless to stop states from taking aggressive action against national minority groups within their territory or to prevent the belligerent actions taken by national minorities. Before the international community can attempt to regulate the behavior of national groups, it needs to determine substate groups' entitlements with respect to self-determination in order to define what laws stateless national groups and their host states ought to (or need not to) comply with. Thus, while the present world system is centered on sustaining peaceful relations among states, which is certainly necessary to maintain universal peace, it is deficient with respect to the preservation of peace *within* states.

The prospects for the implementation of the normative ideal of the equality of self-determination of all peoples contained in the UN Charter depend on how the terms of this important clause are defined. The current state system has a limited capacity to accommodate self-determination claims if the exercise of self-determination is equated with the acquisition of independent statehood (while all national groups are considered to be "peoples"). In this case, the normative ideal of equality faces insurmountable practical limitations, and the present international system lacks the ability to accommodate the majority of self-determination claims. The restrictive formulation of the legal right to self-determination, which defines its subjects with an eye only to a very selective set of historical circumstances, simply ignores relations between substate and state-endowed national groups with respect to self-determination claims. This formulation puts the limited legal right in tension with the normative moral ideal of equality of the UN Charter.[7] The modification of international legal norms is necessary to improve on the present approach to self-determination.

Moral Theories of International Legal Doctrine Concerning Self-Determination

Given the present tension between the moral and legal norms concerning self-determination and the infeasibility of granting sovereignty to all substate groups, a normative framework for addressing the challenges posed by substate national groups' claims needs to define the fair conditions for national groups' membership in their host states. Such a framework ties the question of whether substate groups should enjoy the right to self-determination to the justice of their treatment by their host multinational states; it, therefore, requires a moral theory of international legal doctrine and its corresponding institutions.

The extent to which a normative theory of multinational accommodation may be implemented is limited by what is possible in practice, and thus any normative theorizing about international law needs to attend to the realities of the current state-centered international system. We also need to pay attention, however, to the fact that states are not homogenous political communities and that one type of diversity among political communities within states runs along national lines. Within their borders, multinational states contain more than one political community that aspires to be self-determining. It is widely acknowledged that since there are many more national groups than there are possible states, breaking states up is destabilizing. It is simply prudent, therefore, to think of norms as they would govern federal arrangements rather than as they would govern terms of secession: accommodating stateless nations necessitates establishing norms of federation building.

One theory of the substate accommodation of self-determination is offered by Margaret Moore, who treats national groups as moral communities and argues that the strongest claim they can make to be accommodated within multinational states is the claim to fair treatment.[8] I agree that fairness should play an important role in designing a set of international legal norms to prescribe how national minorities ought to be treated by their host states. It is hard to predict whether making the legal standards of interaction between stateless and state-endowed groups conform to moral norms of fairness will solve the problem of conflicting self-determination claims on its own, but it is certainly true that morally unjustifiable legal norms have lesser force. To *be* a legal system, the international legal system needs to be coherent and clear in its principles. Norms that prescribe treating similar subjects differently are likely to be difficult to enforce. Even a very generous accommodation based on existing principles, such as autonomy within the host state—an accommodation proposed by many theories of federalism—countenances inequalities between state-endowed and stateless nations if the host state is considered the possession of the majority nation and not of the stateless minority nation. When legal norms resonate with existing tensions, moreover, they contribute to the instability of multinational states. Thus, a theory of federalism that prescribes the norms for a fair federal arrangement also needs to have an international normative dimension that describes a fair status for all national groups in relation to one another.

A critic might say that we can deal with stateless groups' problems on a case-by-case basis rather than by determining norms to define their status and entitlements in advance. But such an approach would be a compromise, the result of an inability to establish a set of norms.[9] If it is possible to establish norms of what Allen Buchanan and David Golove call "transnational justice," compromise is unnecessary. In this book, I define such norms and show that pragmatic limitations on the exercise of the right to self-determination by substate groups can be largely overcome if self-determination is disassociated from statehood. I argue that the requirement of treating substate national groups justly should be primarily concerned with the satisfaction of their self-determination claims *within* their host multinational states and only secondarily with the conditions of secession. This approach is sound, of course, only if non-state groups have a moral right to self-determination. Thus, we need to consider whether national groups deserve a right to self-determination on moral grounds and, if so, whether the international community has the corresponding moral duty to make sure that multinational states properly respond to their substate groups' claims.

Below, I examine two major perspectives on the justification of group rights. The first holds that the right to self-determination can be reduced to the individual rights of group members, while the second considers self-determination as a group right. I will deal with different approaches to this second perspective on group rights in the next chapter.

Individual Rights-Based Theories

Theoretical approaches to the self-determination of minorities range widely, from ignoring them under the rubric of "equal citizenship for all" to granting them the right to secede. A number of theorists argue that self-determination claims should not be singled out and can be dealt with on the basis of respect for individual rights.[10] According to theories that ground the right to self-determination in individual rights, members of national groups express preferences related to their identity in the process of participating politically in their larger society, and these preferences are satisfied by the state through its regular means of satisfying all individual preferences. We can therefore provide equality of identity to citizens by ensuring their equal individual participation in politics. Two considerations make the individual rights-based approach questionable when applied to minority groups' self-determination claims, however. The first has to do with the fact that the weight given to the minority preference varies according to how preferences are counted. If the preferences of a national minority are counted in the context of the larger state as a whole, the minority can easily be outvoted. If the preferences of minority group members are considered within a portion of the state territory where it is a majority, on the other hand, the existence of the group is implicitly supported. This situation is likely to result eventually in an open expression of the group's claim to self-determination and in its mobilization to achieve its goals. Such a mobilization ensures that the group's preferences are clearly expressed and, according to some models of the democratic process (e.g., deliberative democracy) ought to give those preferences significant political weight in the country's decision-making process. Therefore, the preferences of the individual members of a substate national group in a politically open host state are likely either not to be accommodated at all, if the group is dispersed, or, if the group is concentrated in a single territory, to be expressed as group preferences that ought to be treated as such.

The second important consideration in assessing the individual rights-based approach is that self-determination claims primarily have to do with how members of a political community define the boundaries of that community, and this translates for the members of a minority group into the question of whether to belong to the larger community at all. If individual rights given to minority members within a host community are premised on the notion that the larger community is the political community of their choice, these rights will be inadequate to address the preferences of the members of a minority group who wish to change their political status within the larger community or to exit. If individual rights are given to the minority members *in their capacity as national group members*, on the other hand, this may have implications for the political reorganization of the state that need to be considered. Hence, the point at which a minority groups mobilizes to express its claim to self-determination is the starting point of my inquiry concerning the terms of accommodation for conflicting self-determination claims in a multinational state.

Allen Buchanan suggests that there is nothing special about national identity that distinguishes it from other identities associated with various comprehensive conceptions of the good and with individual projects that citizens perceive as extending across their whole lives. He argues that a society characterized by "dynamic pluralism" is composed of numerous groups of individuals with such projects. This pluralism is "dynamic" because individual allegiances change and can be multiple. Hence, "singling out nations as such as being entitled to self-government is nothing less than a public expression of conviction that allegiances and identities have a single, true rank order of value, with nationality reposing at the summit."[11] Disagreeing with such an ordering, Buchanan goes on to uncouple self-determination from both statehood and nationhood. I agree with Buchanan that there is no inherent need for self-determination claims to be accommodated through the acquisition of independent statehood and that secession should be allowed only under exceptional circumstances. I believe, however, that there is an essential connection between nationhood and self-determination.

Buchanan's discussion of autonomy arrangements is indicative of the difficulties that his refusal to admit this connection presents. Buchanan argues that self-determination can be realized through autonomy arrangements within a host state. The conditions of autonomy that could be supported by his conception of "transnational justice," however, cover a very limited range of claims to self-determination. According to Buchanan, arrangements ought to be made for groups only if (1) they have the right to secede but decide to stay, (2) their autonomy arrangements or their individual members' rights have been violated by the state, or (3) they are indigenous groups for whom autonomy would rectify past injustices and their ongoing effects. While the first and the last conditions seem to be sensible bases for entitlement to autonomy, they still require an explanation of the basis for determining the terms of fair inclusion. Moreover, self-determination is the capacity of a group to determine its future political status, while self-government is the capacity of a group to make and apply rules within the parameters of its existing political status. It is important to ask whether granting self-government to the groups in question (as distinct from self-determination) constitutes a fair arrangement. By disassociating nationhood from self-determination, Buchanan avoids answering the question of what national communities and their members are entitled to.

Concerning Buchanan's second condition for autonomy, it is necessary to clarify what obtaining self-government has to do with protecting against the violation of individual rights. If self-government takes the oppressed out of the sphere of influence of the oppressor or punishes the state by making it relinquish at least some of its power over the group's members, could it be given to an ethnic minority or to women in a state that oppresses them? If the violation of human rights signals a circumstance in which a group that is prima facie entitled to self-government can finally exercise it, the characteristics of this kind of group and its corresponding entitlement, again, need to be specified.

The "equal citizenship for all" approach to self-determination assumes that the boundaries of political communities are self-evident, that they do not require explanation. While I agree that geographic boundaries ought to be changed as little as possible, I would argue that the institutional structure of multinational states requires justification in terms of political legitimacy. If an autonomy arrangement that has been violated is bound to be restored, as happened in Kosovo after Serbia abolished its autonomy, a theory like Buchanan's, which deals with the legitimacy of states, needs to explain what norms underlay the autonomy arrangement in the first place and whether they made that arrangement just. If the autonomy arrangement is not just, furthermore, we need to explain what could make it just in the future. Acknowledging that under some circumstances some political communities can exercise self-government implicitly validates the value of these communities unless the restoration of autonomy to a national group is viewed by Buchanan as due to the group merely by virtue of a political deal struck between the government of the state and the past group leadership, thus respecting the terms of a prior contract or treaty. The latter would designate one circumstance under which a restoration of autonomy may be in order, but we can enjoin such a restoration only if we carefully examine the makeup of the community in question. That a nation was artificially constructed in the past in what had been an autonomous area, as happened in the former Checheno-Ingushetia in the USSR, whose two national groups were conjoined in one political space without their consent, does not warrant the restoration of the area's autonomy unless the group in question (the Chechen-Ingush national composite in my example) requests it. This brings us back to considering the importance of the meaning of the limits of political communities to their members. By glossing over this, Buchanan's approach countenances violations of the collective right of national minorities to self-determination when no prior autonomy agreement existed. Even when considered in purely pragmatic terms, states' failure to satisfy substate groups' aspirations for self-determination is these groups' main point of contention, and multinational states are prone to conflict when they ignore that aspiration.

If the endorsement of the government by those it governs is not a factor in the consideration of whether an autonomy agreement is required and, should it be required, what its terms ought to be, the legitimacy of the state is questionable from the point of view of the minority group, and this fact alone violates the right to equal treatment of individuals who belong to minorities. For even if, in the best-case scenario, a national minority acquires an autonomy arrangement but this arrangement gives it a status inferior to that of the majority nation with respect to self-determination, the minority members' preference for self-determination has still been given less weight than the preference of the members of the majority, which violates the norm of the equality of individuals with respect to their membership in the larger state. This is so because the right to self-determination, in part, concerns the ability of the members of a substate group to have a say, as a group, in *whether* to be members of the host state—not merely in the acceptable terms of inclusion in the host state when their membership in the host state cannot in principle be challenged and is a *fait accompli* from the point of view of the majority and the international community. A liberal commitment to respect individuals as persons in devising the principles of political association requires that these principles must be justifiable to everyone whom they are to bind.[12] Individuals from a minority national group cannot be said to have been treated equally by the state if their group does not receive proper accommodation within the state and if, as the result of this (as is often the case), their substate national membership is a handicap in the larger society, to which they do not want to belong.

Members of a national group may derive benefits from their group's inclusion in a multinational state that create obligations toward the state on their part.[13] Those obligations do not create their membership in the state, however, unless they cause the group to choose to belong to the state and to agree to the terms of membership. Therefore, respecting the individual, democratic rights of the members of a national group does not directly address the group's claim to self-determination. We must take into consideration the political status of national minorities in their host states if we are to avoid treating individuals from minorities differently than individuals from majorities with respect to their citizenship in the larger state.

The argument that national groups have a prima facie group right to self-determination on the basis of a consent theory of legitimacy is provided by Christopher Wellman. In his view, those groups whose members do not consent to membership in a state, instead advancing self-determination claims, have a right to secede.[14] This theory highlights members' consent as an important condition for both their proper membership in a state and the state's legitimacy from the point of view of its members. This account, however, can only tell us why each individual member of a minority group *is not* a proper member of the larger state; it does not describe what, if anything, would make them proper members. The members of a one-nation state that turns into a totalitarian regime through a coup d'état do not consent to be governed by their new leaders. They may not want to secede, however, preferring instead to change their government. Thus, when considering individual consent, we need to pay attention to the *shared goals of group members* in relation to political authority over them. So modified, the consent theory of secession would highlight an important aspect of nationhood: the existence of a collective that aspires to be governed by political authority that expresses the shared preferences of its members. Thus, we need to explain what self-determination has to do with the constitution of groups that are said to have the right, which I do in the next chapter.

In his more recent work, Wellman introduces an account of legitimacy not based on consent. He considers states as producers of essential political benefits and allows secessions that do not interfere with this production for either a secessionist group or the remainder state.[15] A state, nevertheless, can restrict a right to secede to groups of a certain size and further require that the interested parties demonstrate their ability to govern in a satisfactorily capable and just manner.[16] The latter is justified because states, according to Wellman, may permissibly coerce citizens to discharge duties they owe to others without these citizens' prior consent; in particular, it may prohibit the citizens' freedom of association if this freedom interferes with the state's ability to perform its requisite political functions. Wellman supports his view of legitimate coercion with an example: if B, morally speaking, owes A assistance, the state can legitimately coerce B to assist A without B's consent. He then generalizes from this example and concludes that a state can disallow any freedom of association that interferes with the state's ability to provide the political benefits essential to individuals in its territory. I agree with Wellman that legitimate states are owed respect, and that viable units' self-determination is to be respected; but his individualistic view of political membership misses some important details.

For example, the Russians who compactly populate Eastern Estonia can form a viable political unit, and the remainder state, should this unit secede, can perfectly fulfill its political functions. But there are many facts about the history of the region and the corresponding group identities that make the issue of secession in this area not as straightforward as that of finding geographically compact units that are also politically viable. Since both sides can appeal to the notion of harm resulting from either secession or its prohibition, it needs to be determined under which circumstances it is legitimate to prioritize state-wide membership over other group memberships, and under which circumstances a sub-state group's interests and intentions trump preferences of the remainder state.

Wellman claims that his account of legitimacy precludes impermissible coercion and exploitation.[17] To determine what actions are permissible in a state the citizenry of which is not homogenous, he needs to specify which political benefits are essential to individuals in light of what benefits should belong to them by virtue of their various group memberships. We cannot gauge political culture of a multinational or multicultural unit as an aggregate of an "average" citizen's beliefs and attitudes toward politics. This is because the political cultures that individuals espouse cannot be entirely divorced from the joint enjoyment of the collective good around which their group is constituted; furthermore, there exists a plurality of these goods in a multicultural state. Individuals have special attachments to cultures, languages, religions, and so on, and they can only enjoy many goods that are vital for their well-being as members of groups. The political benefits they are owed because of their membership in the larger state need to be adjusted accordingly. Thus, to make sure we have an explanation of what it means for a multicultural state to perform its requisite political functions well—and, correspondingly, when a group's actions amount to an impermissible coercion or exploitation of its compatriots—we need to first provide an account of differentiated group rights, or what groups are entitled to based on their constitution. Wellman doesn't provide such an account, and thus offers no ground for determining, in a principled manner, what citizens (and the state on their behalf) owe one another.

Wellman claims that "a group of citizens who are able and willing to perform the requisite political functions have a right to group self-determination."[18] Sometimes a group may be too small to become a viable independent state, and Wellman's account wouldn't consider the group as entitled to self-determination. For many groups, however, political efficiency is only part of the equation and membership in no other group but their own, rooted in their group history and its present intentionality will offer a proper milieu of political legitimacy. Not allowing such a group the freedom of association is unjust. If, contrary to Wellman's account, statehood is not considered to be a minimal level at which self-determination can and should be exercised, the group can still have control over its political future within its host state without struggling to form a state of its own.

Moreover, if we are dealing with a severely oppressed group that has had no political institutions of self-government but aspires to be self-determining, we cannot attest to the group's ability to self-govern. At the same time, the group's entitlements need to be determined, at least tentatively, before it is fully capable to provide its members with the enjoyment of self-determination, in order to guide the political transition which brings about the changes to the group's status. Wellman needs to provide a guide to group entitlements that goes beyond their de facto status to apply his theory to transitional societies.

Given that secession is not practicable as a universal mode of satisfying minority claims, we need a set of conditions that describes under what circumstances a state is justified in prohibiting secession—that is, what terms of agreement with a national group are to be considered fair. Many liberal theorists implicitly presuppose that the scheme of justice or fairness they design applies to a society whose members already think of themselves as a "people," who have a common life, and who are already interested in devising principles of political association. They assume that such individuals share enough to think of themselves as engaged in a common project and that they understand their bonds as setting them off from other people, since their aim is to live with one another, and not with everyone else, in political association.[19] John Rawls, for example, associates self-determination with peoples, not states, but he bypasses a debate about the justice or legitimacy of multinational states that contain several peoples within their territory.[20] Since most self-determination claims do in fact contest the limits of political communities, two questions arise: how to construe the terms of membership within a multinational state both for individual and collective agents and how to define the boundaries of political space that designate the limits of political communities meaningful to their individual members. Something other than just an account of individual preferences connected to membership is clearly required to determine the norms of fair arrangements for multinational states.

Group-Based Liberal Approaches

Will Kymlicka's theory of minority rights creates a much-improved version of the liberal theory of individuals' participation in groups by including cultural identity as a necessary condition of autonomy. Kymlicka's justification for this inclusion is based on the necessity of culture to belief revision: one's own culture provides a context for meaningful choice, and minority rights protecting group cultures can enlarge the freedom of their individual members.[21] He distinguishes three types of rights for minorities to account for moral, ethnic, and cultural (national) plurality: self-government rights for national minorities, polyethnic rights for immigrant groups, and special representation rights for women, sexual and racial minorities, religious groups, and the like.

In explaining why national minorities, unlike other types of minorities, are entitled to self-government, Kymlicka considers not culture but the shared attitudes of individuals from minority groups toward political authority, as represented by the institutional structures of the host society. National minority rights to self-government are the rights of differentiated citizenship, whereas the rights of ethnic immigrant groups exist to ensure that immigrants can exercise their citizenship in common with the rest of the society. Activities connected to immigrants' home cultures, for example, are funded by the state in order to promote the immigrants' integration in the larger society. Since immigrants migrate with an intention to integrate in the mainstream culture,[22] such support is often temporary, and the need for it is likely to disappear as immigrants' children and grandchildren mature. National minorities, unlike immigrant minorities, have institutions of self-government as well as territory. They are what Kymlicka calls "societal cultures," with a set of common economic, political, and educational institutions.[23] Mohawks in Canada, for example, are a national minority with a right to self-government, while the Greek community in Quebec is an immigrant group without such a right.

While it is clear that special rights are required for the proper accommodation of minorities and that culture provides an important context for belief revision, it is not entirely apparent that self-government rights are necessary for the protection of national minorities' culture on the basis of Kymlicka's argument alone. Basic conditions of belief revision, such as access to information and its reflective evaluation and freedom of expression and association, can be satisfied by institutions that guarantee the rights of the members of a minority culture to education, newspapers, theaters, a film board, and the other components necessary for examining and revising beliefs about value available to them in their own language. Granting political autonomy, on the other hand, has little to do with allowing access to belief revision. It has to do, rather, with establishing limits of political authority meaningful to the members of a national group that justify the mutually reduced influence between federal authorities and the national minority in particular areas of law, such as immigration, health care, trade, and so forth. Furthermore, if culture provides us with beliefs about the value of practices important to us, and if many immigrants reinterpret the societal culture they are supposed to assimilate into in the language of their previous societal culture's tradition, they may require self-government rights to recreate some of the self-governing institutions of their former culture in order to promote their autonomy. Or, conversely, members of national minorities may have a better chance of revising beliefs about value if they assimilate into the widely accessible and better financed system of culture of the larger society rather than remaining within their own system of culture.

I support the distinction Kymlicka makes between the rights of national and other types of minorities, but it needs to be clarified. Unless we pay special attention to the *political cultures* of substate groups and the modes of collective mobilization associated with these cultures, as well as corresponding individual intentions, it is hard to explain why assimilation is the wrong policy for national minorities but the right one for immigrants. Thus, we need to make it explicit that backing national minorities' self-government rights is their groups' possession of a political culture associated with the shared goal of achieving or maintaining self-determination. David Miller places a similar emphasis on the political aspects of national cultures. He argues that nations have a prima facie right to self-determination. Miller describes a nation as "a group of people who recognize one another as belonging to the same community, who acknowledge special obligations to one another, and who aspire to political autonomy—this by virtue of characteristics that they believe they share, typically a common history, attachment to a geographical place, and a public culture that differentiates them from their neighbors."[24] When Miller wants to distinguish between national and ethnic groups, he similarly emphasizes their members' intentions and points out that national groups make a claim to self-determination and create the appropriate organizations and institutions to fulfill that claim, while ethnic groups do not.[25] The elements of national culture that he isolates to distinguish between the entitlements of national and ethnic minorities are related to the political culture (and not the culture) of a collective agent that aspires to be self-determining.

A number of theorists criticize the distinction between polyethnic and self-government rights presented by Kymlicka. Some, like Joseph Carens, criticize

Kymlicka for the rigidity of the distinction, arguing that we should view minorities contextually based on their specific needs and situations.[26] Chaim Gans notices the difficulty of identifying which culture satisfies the freedom-based interest of individuals in culture: it is not clear whether it should be the culture of origin or the culture in which the individuals' endeavors are undertaken.[27] Kymlicka might answer such criticism by specifying the *type of culture* that is required for the right to self-government, making the move I indicate above. He does this implicitly when he acknowledges that a territorially concentrated immigrant group that mobilizes to demand institutions of self-government should in principle be able to receive the rights of differentiated citizenship.[28] This move also challenges David Hollinger's criticism that Kymlicka's distinction between national minorities and immigrants is abstract and based on the a posteriori legal circumstances of the groups' origin within a constitutional regime rather than their concrete behavior. I agree with Hollinger that we need to pay attention to the behavior of groups. However, Hollinger's alternative criterion for the distinction between ethnic and national groups requires clarification. He states that minority communities that are "historically continuous and . . . sharply separate from one another . . . are national minorities," and those that are "temporary and overlapping are other kinds of minorities."[29] Kymlicka's attention to the constitution of national groups with respect to societal cultures remains a superior criterion, because to make his distinctions Hollinger must consider what constitutes continuity and how to characterize the required degree of separation among communities.

The hierarchy of group rights and the very use of the concept of "nation" seem questionable to Iris Marion Young, who argues that African Americans, Indians in diaspora, refugees, guest workers, former colonial subjects, and Jews (prior to the establishment of Israel, at least) all fall, to various extents, outside of Kymlicka's categories.[30] She, like Carens, argues that a continuum model that provides more nuanced and complex arguments about what each cultural minority needs specifically would be superior.[31] Could such a continuum model be principled, however? Young writes, for example, that self-government rights can only be morally grounded as necessary to rectify injustice or promote greater justice. "It is possible," she states, "for a group to have self-government rights with respect to some issues and not others."[32] This approach does not seem problematic so long as we can epistemically reliably determine what issues are worthy of self-government, which requires, among other things, that we will know—and our understanding will reasonably correspond to—the group's own perception of what constitutes injustice with respect to the group or at least to its members. If we determine what constitutes injustice on an ad hoc basis, we leave too much to chance.[33] As Young would recognize, there are many forms of discrimination that only are visible at the group level. A race-neutral policy that has a racially disparate impact, such as geographically drawn school district lines that lead to de facto segregation, would not be defensible from the group perspective. Hence what appears as injustice to some, especially the group members, may appear as just treatment to others.[34]

Grounds for the differential treatment of groups need to include a set of principles specifying how to determine a group's basic entitlements. We also need to be able to determine if the aspects of a group's well-being that it wishes to promote are justifiable to the society from which the group expects to receive powers, privileges, or exemptions. Young thinks that introducing mutually exclusive categories of national and cultural/ethnic minorities for this purpose would be a misguided move.[35] In this book, I show that distinguishing between national and other types of minorities helps to set up a framework for the just inclusion of individuals in their multinational or multicultural states—the ideal that Young embraces. My approach provides guidelines for the determination of group entitlements based on the constitution of group agents. I give a definition of nationhood that allows us to decide questions like those that Young considers problematic for a "rigid" theory: whether Jews were a nation prior to the founding of the state of Israel or whether a group of African Americans who has lived in rural Alabama for generations is a nation.[36] I define nations as collective agents with a particular type of political culture that does not require the possession of the state but that is based upon the shared end of acquiring or maintaining effective agency in relation to the capacity of the group to control its own political future. Based on this definition, those Jews who shared a political culture based on the desire to acquire their own state were a nation prior to 1948. If African Americans of Alabama adopt this type of political culture, they would also have to be considered a nation, which is not the case at the moment. Thus, it is possible to maintain the distinction that Kymlicka introduces by considering nations as collective agents of a certain type.

A general framework for the determination of group entitlements based on the constitution of group agents is necessary also because we cannot assume that the current boundaries of existing multicultural societies are prima facie justified. The very notion of a multicultural society presupposes a set of defining features that identifies a group of people as a society. If these are lacking, the authoritative reach of the government over all of its territory and all of its citizens may be unjustifiable and the society would be better off, as far as justice is concerned, dividing into a number of independent political units. Defining the grounds for the membership of groups in a multicultural society creates the prospect of agreement on the issue of the larger society's organizing principles. Besides, without considering the entitlements of the groups present in a society, we cannot have a fair picture of how the larger society is constituted.

To determine minority groups' entitlements, we need to pay attention to the shared intentions of the group members regarding their political status in relation to state institutions—and thus to the type of political culture shared by the group. The right to self-government in the case of national minorities grows out of the shared goals and cooperative actions of the group members with respect to what they consider to be the desirable political expression of their group's internal organization (what Denise Réaume calls the "internal constitution" of the group).

I endorse Kymlicka's insight concerning the need for a principled, "rigid" basis for distinguishing among different types of group entitlements. But it is clear that closer attention to the constitution of group agents is warranted if we are to answer the range of criticisms above concerning differential group rights. In Chapter 2,

I argue that we can consider groups to be collective agents and that the entitlements and constitution of group agents are connected. That a group is a particular kind of collective agent enables us to identify it as a nation, and paying attention to the group constitution of both national and other types of minorities allows us to differentiate between types of groups, their entitlements, and changes in group identities.[37]

It is also important to consider how to determine whether a group's demands are truly constitutive of the group, that is, whether they correctly register the freely endorsed beliefs and intentions of group members or whether they are accidental or strategic. Explicitly considering the constitution of group agents allows us to evaluate whether the group's demands are justified.[38] Moreover, though the existence of groups is contingent and their membership and character can change, this does not mean that their constitution is not significant for the regulation of their relations with others, for it is precisely changes in their constitution that warrant a change in norms. Collective agents form intentions and engage in cooperative actions to fulfill these intentions. If a group that advances purely cultural claims later mobilizes as a self-determining group, its demands ought then to be dealt with accordingly. The question may be whether group agents of a particular kind should be allowed to exist, but this is precisely why we need to identify groups' constitution and assess their claims' authenticity and legitimacy to determine the answer to this question. This of course requires verification of whether the collective agent is what it claims to be. For example, strategic claims by political elites that are not endorsed by group members do not represent demands of the group. Or, in an oppressive society an official expression of group identity is not representative of the true make-up of society.

The presence of rules regulating the relations of group agents based on the evaluation of their mutual standing will certainly not prevent them from acting in violation of these rules, but the rules ought to exist to enable the evaluation of group behavior. The relevant questions are who has a particular right (the type of group and whether it is the group as a group or individuals that hold the right) and how it should be justified, as well as, in the case of self-determination, how it relates to territory.

Self-Determination, Territory, and the Continuity of Entitlement

Let us begin with the task of describing the holders of the right to self-determination. Can we say that national minorities represent a particular type of group that has a moral right to self-determination?

Avishai Margalit and Joseph Raz call a group relevant to the determination of the moral entitlement to self-government an "encompassing group."[39] The characteristics of the group that are relevant to a case for self-government and, ultimately, self-determination are quite complex and include the following aspects: The group is a big and anonymous community, with a common character and a common culture that encompass many, varied, and important aspects of life. Individuals grow up in the culture, and while membership in a group is in part a matter of mutual recognition, it is a matter of belonging, not achievement. Membership in the group is important for individual self-identification and is a collective good from which the right to self-determination derives. As such, it is a group right.[40]

Margalit and Raz's notion of encompassing group reflects the complexity of group constitution in relation to group entitlements. It is a complicated task, however, to justify the right to self-determination based on their notion of an encompassing group. They provide an instrumental argument for the right to self-determination that rests on an appreciation of the great importance that membership in and identification with encompassing groups has in the lives of individuals and on the importance of the prosperity and self-respect of such groups to the well-being of their members. That importance makes it reasonable to let the encompassing group that forms a substantial majority in a territory have the right to determine whether that territory should form an independent state in order to protect the culture and self-respect of the group, provided that the new state is likely to respect the fundamental interests of its inhabitants and provided that measures are adopted to prevent its creation from gravely damaging the just interests of other countries.[41] Margalit and Raz also state that the case for self-government applies to groups that are not in the majority anywhere, but that they do not have a right to self-determination.

This approach is sensitive to the realities of international relations and offers a strong alternative to individual-rights based approaches to the justification of group rights. Nevertheless, unless the meaning of self-determination as it applies to encompassing groups is clarified, Margalit and Raz's instrumental justification of the right to self-determination may yield some counterintuitive results. In the view of Margalit and Raz, numbers count in determining a group's entitlement to self-determination, for in the end the right to self-determination is applied to a territory. Thus, a substantial majority within a given territory is needed to ensure that the granting of independence to a group will not generate a problem larger in scale than the one it solves. It is important, however, to specify how we determine who is the relevant majority and what the relevant territory is. While Margalit and Raz relate the entitlement to self-government to the constitution of a particular type of group, it is not clear whether the right to self-determination is simply tied to any territory that the majority group deems suitable for itself. If the majority of 90% wants a given territory to be an independent state but there is a minority of 10% that considers itself a nation within this territory, is it justifiable to say that the minority in this case has no self-determination rights? Also, do present boundaries matter? Could the Russians in the eastern part of Estonia (where they were a majority of between 80 and 90%), for example, have obtained, after the fall of the Soviet Union, the right to self-govern? If Margalit and Raz would say that we ought to consider the whole of Estonia as the relevant territory, not only one part of it, this begs the question of the territory associated with the entitlement to self-determination, because it is not clear why historical borders are taken for granted prior to the determination of what encompassing communities exist within a territory. Assigning territories within already existing boundaries to their majority encompassing nations ignores the fact that the boundaries themselves are one contested issue that the identification of self-determining communities aims to resolve. Moreover, doing so means that everyone in the territory will be tied to the encompassing majority and that other, smaller encompassing cultures in the territory will be ignored. If Margalit and Raz would not think that the whole of Estonia is the relevant territory, on the other hand, then their theory is indeterminate, because the criterion they use to establish the entitlement to self-determination of a qualifying majority within a territory could lead to the same group's qualifying for the right when the territory is divided in one way and failing to qualify when it is divided differently.

Margalit and Raz's theory may work for defining the right to self-determination in a territory with one national group and possibly some non-national minorities. For more complicated cases where several national groups are mixed in one territory, however, some other means is needed to determine a group's qualification for the enjoyment of self-determination. We need to start with the identification of all political communities, regardless of their size, within the territory of the state. All national groups must be considered in defining a principled entitlement to self-determination if we are to prevent the strategic division of territories by majorities wherein only the majority encompassing group determines whether the territory it considers its own shall form an independent state. Then we need to determine how a state (if a single state is to exist for this territory) might be organized to protect all of the encompassing cultures. This does not necessarily guarantee that all groups will be able to exercise the right to self-determination in the same form, but pragmatic limitations on the enjoyment of the right should not interfere with the issue of moral entitlement.

According to Margalit and Raz, moreover, a group can lose its right to self-determination (even if it is entitled to restitution) after having been expelled from a territory in order to protect the existing inhabitants of the territory.[42] This outcome follows from their focus on territory in the definition of the right. It seems that Margalit and Raz tend to take existing boundaries for granted, regardless of their justice. Their account, however, creates a perfect case for the Russian domination of eastern Estonia after the fall of the USSR—a troubling outcome from a moral perspective.

There are additional problems with an approach like that of Margalit and Raz. It could motivate some communities to engage in wars of accession and then hold on to the conquered territory long enough to create an encompassing community that is loyal to them or to expand their encompassing community into the territory, thus claiming it for themselves. This situation could also cause expelled groups to mobilize aggressively and attempt to use force to reclaim their territory. Finally, their theory countenances a situation in which some individuals in the territory of a state count for more than others: they are protected both as individuals and as encompassing group members. This leads to the valuing of groups over individuals unless all groups within the territory of a state are given equal consideration. It could be that Margalit and Raz allow for the unequal treatment of individuals: so long as the basic minimal set of entitlements is assured for all, the discrepancy between the treatment afforded to the members of the encompassing group and the rest is irrelevant. But then their valuing of some groups over others is unexplained, given the careful attention it pays to the significance of encompassing groups. These difficulties arise because Margalit and Raz do not conceive of the bounds of encompassing groups as primarily defined in the groups' relations to others as political communities with certain goals and aspirations and do not consider the right to self-determination to be a basic right of all groups that are so constituted.

That Margalit and Raz combine the idea of the encompassing group with a restricted understanding of self-determination may be an impediment to extending their theory to difficult cases like that of the Kurds, who are an encompassing group but who are not in the majority in any current state. Margalit and Raz's approach needs to be clarified for cases of this sort. Perhaps Margalit and Raz can argue that Kurds have the right to self-government not as a cross-border group but *within* each state they inhabit. In this case, we need to explain how to apply the idea of encompassing Kurdish culture to each unit of the Kurdish self-government. In Chapter 3, I argue that we do not need an idea as broad as encompassing culture to determine the holders of the right to self-determination. Why is it that Americans and English-speaking Canadians do not share the same encompassing culture? It seems that their adherence to different political cultures is sufficient to differentiate between the two communities. I define nations in Chapter 3 based on the idea of political culture, and in the next chapter I argue that the type of group entitlement can be determined based on how the constitution of the group positions it in relation to non-members. The enjoyment of the right to self-determination does not have to be given up, moreover, if the right is modified so as to sever the connection between the right to self-determination and the right to statehood. Margalit and Raz seem to consider self-determination to mean sovereignty over a territory. What Jeff Noonan calls the "exclusionary logic of rights" applies to the right to self-determination in this territorial understanding: "A right ... necessarily ... excludes other groups or individuals from interfering with the exercise of the right," Noonan writes. If there is a dispute between two groups over certain property (like resources) wherein one group has control over the property the other lays claim to, using rights "does not address the problem—exclusion—but simply doubles it."[43]

The right to self-determination does not have to be exclusionary, because self-determination does not need to be associated with statehood or sovereignty over a territory, as Chaim Gans demonstrates. He provides a blueprint for sub- and inter-statist self-determination that can be shared by a number of groups in the same territory. I will discuss his approach to territory in more detail in Chapter 6. Gans also offers a non-instrumental justification of the right. He studies "cultural nationalism." By this, he means that members of a group sharing common history and societal culture have a fundamental, morally significant interest in adhering to their culture and in sustaining it for generations. He does not focus on "statist nationalism," or the interest of states in the homogeneity of their citizens. The groups relevant to self-determination for Gans are similar to Margalit and Raz's encompassing group.[44] Gans argues that a right to self-determination is not a right to a statist and territorial sovereignty.[45] Rather, a group has to be given a package of privileges, normally within the state that includes its homeland: self-government rights, special representation rights, and rights to cultural preservation. He advocates the possibility of a group's moving to a formative territory, such as a territory of primary importance in forming the historical identity of the group, and sharing self-determination there with groups already in place.[46] This presupposes that groups without current geodemographic conditions for self-determination can obtain it. I consider this a morally consistent outcome.

Gans defends cultural nationalism using two theses—the adherence thesis, which states that people have a basic interest in adhering to their culture, and the historical thesis, which holds that people also have a basic interest in recognizing and protecting the multigenerational dimension of their culture.[47] He also formulates the political thesis, which maintains that the two basic interests should be protected politically. Gans argues that Kymlicka's defense of national self-government based on the idea that an interest in culture is a prerequisite for people's freedom and identity cannot be used to defend the historical thesis, because Kymlicka's argument does not easily translate into the need for the generational continuity of culture.[48] First, the descendants are not "predisposed" to be attached to the culture of their parents and can satisfy their need for freedom within another culture. Likewise, these people's parents' desire to understand their children and share their world can also be fulfilled regardless of what culture the people choose.[49] In addition, an illiberal culture can impair the freedom and welfare of future generations, and the preservation of such a culture cannot be defended by Kymlicka's freedom-based argument. The approach that Gans proposes remedies these problems in the following way: people's ambition to undertake projects that will endure beyond their lifetime can be realized in a national culture. Thus, the endeavors people undertake have significance only within the existing and flourishing national culture, and people's interest in the meaningfulness of their endeavors justifies the historical dimension of nationalism.

The meaning of "endeavor" needs to be clarified, however. Why should children be interested in the endeavors of their ancestors? Gans seems to suggest that it is the interest of the existing members of a culture that counts. But then why do the aspirations of individuals concerning their membership in their group, considered from this angle, acquire more weight than when they are looked at from the point of view of the individual's interest in culture as a prerequisite for their freedom and identity, which Gans criticizes?

A difficult problem for Gans's approach is presented by cases in which the members of a culture want it to survive, but their belief in the persistence of the culture is mistaken because the culture has undergone a change. Consider what happened to Moldova: After the fall of the Soviet Union, the nation-building effort of Moldova, the former Soviet republic organized on Romanian territory annexed by the USSR in 1940, initially aimed at reunification with Romania but later changed focus to building an independent state. The mobilization of a national collective agent in Moldova reflected a shift in the meaning of its members' beliefs about national identity and the locus of political authority—and their corresponding political culture—from pan-Romanian to independent Moldovan. The nation-building strategy organized around independent Moldovan identity won out over the strategy of unification with Romania. The same historical events are now interpreted as belonging to two different national histories—Romanian and Moldovan.[50] Viewed from Gans's perspective, the inhabitants of Romania prior to the annexation of its part by the USSR shared a common history and societal culture and had a fundamental, morally significant interest in adhering to their culture and in sustaining it for generations. The inhabitants of the present Moldova have splintered from this cultural identity, however, due to a political rupture with the past. The Moldovan territory was part of a culture that pre-World War II Romanians endeavored to preserve. If a basic interest in preserving the multigenerational dimension of culture is not affected by the reduction in the scope of the territory a group aspires to control (that is, if we can still consider that the "branched" Romanian culture is preserved separately within present-day Romania and Moldova, with adjustments for the changes in the locus of political authority created by changes in boundaries), this interest is not affected by changes in membership either, and the cultural communities to be preserved acquire "fuzzy" boundaries. The strength of the "endeavor" argument is diminished under these conditions of indeterminacy. It is crucial for the argument to clearly delineate the conditions and boundaries of membership in a culture that is to be preserved if the argument is to fare better than freedom-based arguments in defending the basic interest in the intergenerational preservation of the culture. In other words, the culture associated with the endeavor has to be fairly determinate; it cannot be just *any* culture, for then the endeavor argument faces difficulties similar to those of the freedom-based arguments when they defend the importance of culture to individual interests.

The dynamic aspect of national identity is recognized by Gans when he discusses the case of Jews from India who no longer perceive Israel as their formative territory. He advocates limiting Israel's Law of Return, which presently grants the right to emigrate to Israel to any person of Jewish nationality. His conception of the Jewish nation is different from that of the Law of Return in significant ways, and it needs to be explained, given his culturalist account, how these conceptions can similarly refer to anything as significant as the life endeavors that are characteristic of a nation and who is to judge which of the conceptions of the Jewish nation—the one that includes or the one that excludes Jews from India—constitute it. Something more than his endeavor-based approach is needed to define the type of "community" relevant to the idea of self-determination. To reintroduce some determinacy to the picture, we can notice that it is, perhaps, the intentions of individuals standing in relation to one another as a community that matter, regardless of whether the future they envision for the community is attainable (or whether the past they attribute to it is factual). If we attend to the intentions of groups, we end up with not a historical thesis but an account of collective agency, or group agency.

As I discussed in this chapter, we cannot reduce group rights to individual rights, as doing so immediately requires us to clarify what group of individuals holds a particular right. The theories of group entitlement I considered in this chapter must identify with more precision why certain groups are eligible to enjoy self-determination if they are to be useful. The clarifications required of various approaches to justify granting self-determination to groups or to differentiate self-determination from other types of entitlement converge upon the idea that groups entitled to self-determination are agents of certain kind. I use the idea of group agency to discuss the meaning of group rights and differentiate between the right to self-determination and other group rights in light of the constitution of group agents in the next chapter.

Notes

1. *Charter of the United Nations* (San Francisco: UN Conference on International Organization, 1945), ch. 1, art. 1–2.
2. *Declaration on the Granting of Independence to Colonial Countries and People* (New York: General Assembly UN, 1960), A/RES/1514 (XV); *International Covenant on Civil and Political Rights* (New York: General Assembly UN, 1966), A/RES/2200A (XXI); *International Covenant on Economic, Social and Cultural Rights* (New York: General Assembly UN, 1966), A/RES/2200A (XXI).
3. *Charter of the United Nations*, ch. 1, art. 2, sec. 7.
4. For more discussion, see Steven R. Ratner, "Does International Law Matter in Preventing Ethnic Conflict?"*International Law and Politics* 32 (2000): 591–642.
5. CSCE, Copenhagen meeting of the Conference on the Human Dimension, June 29, 1990, 29 I.L.M. 1305.
6. The statute of the Court presupposes that "only states may be parties in cases before the Court." See *Statute of the International Court of Justice*, ch. 2, art. 34, sec. 1.
7. Benedict Kingsbury calls this clash a "fundamental conflict between values of justice and the hitherto dominant values of order." See his "Claims by Non-State Groups in International Law," *Cornell International Law Journal* 25 (1992): 481.
8. Margaret Moore, *The Ethics of Nationalism* (Oxford: Oxford University Press, 2001).
9. Kingsbury points out that *ad hoc* responses to claims of non-state groups when "no adequate normative or procedural framework has been established in advance result in a very limited compliance-pull and legitimacy of norms and procedures." See "Claims by Non-State Groups," p. 485.
10. For this account, see Buchanan, "Recognitional Legitimacy and the State System." James A. Graff argues, for example, that individual human rights alone can justify the creation of ethnoculturally based sovereign states or self-governing entities. See "Human Rights, Peoples, and the Right to Self-Determination," in *Group Rigths,* ed. J.Baker (Toronto: University Toronto Press, 1994), p. 213. Michael Hartney maintains that the idea of collective rights is not conducive to clear thinking and that the rights of individual members of communities to the preservation or protection of their communities suffice to defend those communities' interests. See "Some Confusions Concerning Collective Rights," in *The Rights of Minority Cultures*, ed. Will Kymlicka (Oxford: Oxford University Press), p. 221.
11. Allen Buchanan, "What's So Special About Nations?" in *Rethinking Nationalism*, ed. J. Couture, K. Nielsen, and M. Seymour (Calgary, Alberta: University of Calgary Press, 1996), p. 294.
12. Charles Larmore, "Political Liberalism," *Political Theory*, Vol. 18, no. 3 (August 1990), pp. 339–360, p. 351.
13. These obligations exist on the grounds of the "fair play" justification, by which the enjoyment of the benefits of a cooperative scheme is considered to generate an obligation to support the scheme. For a discussion of this argument, see A. John Simmons (1979), pp. 101–141.

14. Christopher H. Wellman, "A Defense of Secession and Political Self-Determination," *Philosophy and Public Affairs* 24, no. 2 (Spring 1995): pp. 142–171.
15. He argues that legitimate states should be owed respect, but so should, under certain circumstances, secessionist groups: "any group has a moral right to secede as long as its political divorce will leave it and the remainder state in a position to perform the requisite political functions." Christopher Wellman, *A Theory of Secession: The Case for Political Self-Determination* (Cambridge, New York: Cambridge University Press, 2005), p. 1.
16. Ibid., pp. 32 and 37.
17. Ibid., p. 19.
18. Ibid., p. 27.
19. Larmore, p. 352.
20. John Rawls, *The Law of Peoples* (Cambridge, MA Harvard University Press, 1999), pp. 23–27.
21. Will Kymlicka, *Multicultural Citizenship: A Liberal Theory of Minority Rights* (Oxford: Oxford University Press, 1995), p. 75.
22. This may not always be true: they may integrate out of economical necessity while wishing to maintain a national minority status.
23. Kymlicka, *Multicultural Citizenship*, p. 76. This culture, according to Ernest Gellner's description, is the one of mobile, educated, anonymous society, where individuals are subject to "random-seeming, entropic mobility and distribution." Gellner, *Nations and Nationalism* (Oxford: Basil Blackwell Publisher Limited, 1983), p. 64. "The members of such community are and must be mobile, and ready to shift from one activity to another, and must possess that generic training which enables them to follow the manuals or instructions of a new activity or occupation. In the course of their work they must constantly communicate with a large number of other men, with whom they frequently have no previous association, and with whom communication must consequently be explicit, rather than relying on context. They must also be able to communicate by means of written, impersonal, context-free, to-whom-it-may-concern type messages. Hence, these communications must be in the same shared and standardized linguistic medium and script" (Gellner, p. 35).
24. David Miller, "Secession and the Principle of Nationality," in *Rethinking Nationalism,* ed. J. Couture, K. Nielsen, and M. Seymour (Calgary, Alberta: University of Calgary Press, 1996), p. 266.
25. David Miller, *On Nationality*, p. 113.
26. Joseph H. Carens, "Liberalism and Culture," *Constellations* 4, no. 1 (April 1997): pp. 35–47.
27. Chaim Gans, *The Limits of Nationalism* (Cambridge: Cambridge University Press, 2003), p. 47.
28. This also answers Gerald Doppelt's challenge to the referral to historical reasoning in assigning entitlements to groups. According to Doppelt, if existing cultural identity and membership are what count for Kymlicka, it is hard to accept Kymlicka's history-based reasons for barring ethnic minorities from ever gaining the status and group rights appropriate to national minorities. Gerald Doppelt, "Is There a Multicultural Liberalism?" *Inquiry* 41, no. 2 (June 1998), pp. 223–248.
29. David A. Hollinger, "Not Universalists, Not Pluralists: The New Cosmopolitans Find Their Own Way," *Constellations* 8, no. 2 (2001): p. 244.
30. Iris Marion Young, "A Multicultural Continuum: A Critique of Will Kymlicka's Ethnic-Nation Dichotomy," *Constellations* 4, no. 1 (1997): pp. 48–53. Young writes: "According to Kymlicka, justice for national minorities requires self-government rights, the rights of the national minority to govern their own affairs within their own territory. ... Polyethnic rights, on the other hand, give special recognition to cultural minorities in order to compensate for the disadvantages they would otherwise have in political participation and economic opportunity in the larger society." See pp. 49–50.
31. Ibid., pp. 50–51.
32. Ibid., p. 53.

33. A policy dominated by an approach like Chandran Kukathas's, for instance, may not register group grievances correctly. He argues against group rights by saying that even among "generally" disadvantaged groups it is impossible to say that any particular member of a group is disadvantaged vis-à-vis the "dominant" group. Chandran Kukathas, "Cultural Rights Again: A Rejoinder to Kymlicka," *Political Theory* 20 (1992): pp. 674–80. Kukathas argues that "groups are not made up of equal persons and not all members of a group are unequal (in the relevant respects) to all those outside it." Thus: "To treat the group as a whole as 'less equal' to those outside with respect to, say, resources, would violate liberal equality to the extent that some group members are, in fact, better endowed with resources than some outsiders. It is because of the nature of 'groups' as associations of differently endowed individuals, whose memberships are not constant but in a state of flux, that liberal egalitarianism has... generally upheld individual rather than group equality—and individual rather than group rights." See pp. 674–75.
34. Another perspective that can interfere with Young's project and prevent it from correctly meting out justice with respect to groups is presented by James Nickel in a criticism of Kymlicka. Nickel makes a case for the indifference of the cultural context in protecting the freedom of individuals: "An adult does not need to continue to belong to her native culture, or even to any particular culture, in order to have options for choice or in order to retain and develop her capacity to form and revise beliefs about value." James W. Nickel, "The Value of Cultural Belonging: Expanding Kymlicka's Theory," *Dialogue* 33 (1994): 637. When actively pursued in the public political domain, this kind of approach, whether it is Nickel's indifference to the particularity of cultures or the individualistic anti-group perspective advanced by Kukathas, will allow Young to guarantee the defense of group membership only if there is a consistent and principled ground for the treatment of groups that counters it.
35. Young, "A Multicultural Continuum. . ." p. 51.
36. Ibid., p. 50.
37. Paying attention to group constitution for both national and other types of minorities also solves the problem Sujit Choudhry claims to exist for Kymlicka's account. He argues that Kymlicka's warrants for the distinction between immigrant and national minorities are based solely on what these groups actually demand. Sujit Choudhry, "National Minorities and Ethnic Immigrants: Liberalism's Political Sociology," *Journal of Political Philosophy* 10 (2002): 68.
38. Choudhry might object that then we assign normative significance to facts of political sociology. He argues that this would be akin to a naturalistic fallacy, wherein the fact that a given sociological condition exists proves any implied normative implications. Ibid., pp. 67–69. Choudhry does not distinguish the constitution of group agents from the institution of norms related to this constitution. Merely saying that agents can be defined by what they claim is not naturalistic fallacy, nor is saying that satisfying a definition of this type is a necessary condition for a certain type of entitlement. We ought to distinguish the constitution of agents and the evaluation of their entitlement based on what they are. It may be that Choudry is objecting to the institution of a set of norms that would systematically establish the entitlement of groups by type. I have already explained, however, why the ad hoc regulation of group relations is not satisfactory from a normative standpoint.
39. Avishai Margalit and Joseph Raz, "National Self-Determination," *Journal of Philosophy* 87, no. 9 (September 1990): p. 455.
40. Ibid., pp. 256–257.
41. Ibid., p. 457.
42. Ibid., p. 459.
43. Jeff Noonan, "Need Satisfaction and Group Conflict: Beyond a Rights-Based Approach," *Social Theory and Practice* 30 (2004): p. 182.
44. Gans, *Limits of Nationalism*, p. 1.
45. Ibid., p. 119.
46. Ibid., p. 108.

47. Ibid., p. 2.
48. Ibid., p. 39.
49. Ibid., p. 51.
50. For some good accounts of developments in Moldova after the fall of the Soviet Union, see Charles King, *The Moldovans: Romania, Russia, and the Politics of Culture* (Stanford: Hoover Institution Press, Stanford University, 2000); Charles King, *Post-Soviet Moldova: A Borderland in Transition*. (Iasi: Center for Romanian Studies, The Foundation for Romanian Culture and Studies, 1997); and Andrei Stoiciu, *Fiction et Réalité Identitaire: Le cas de la Bessarabie* (Montreal: Humanitas, 1995).

Chapter 2
Collective Agents and Group Moral Rights[1]

As I discussed in the introduction, the challenges posed by citizenship in pluralist societies and by claims to self-determination advanced in many parts of the world require a principled basis for determining the character and the entitlements of minority groups. While this book focuses on the entitlements of different national groups and what constitutes their just treatment, consideration of these issues requires that I go beyond the subject of my study to consider the constitution and entitlements not only of national groups but also of groups of other types. In this chapter, I distinguish between different types of group rights.

While the existence of collective legal rights is commonly acknowledged—the right to self-determination is an example—the notion that collectives have moral rights is often contested.[2] Scholars who deny the existence of group moral rights tend to argue that although collectives can certainly have legal agency, this agency has its basis exclusively in the moral rights of individuals. In the previous chapter, I explained why a position that derives group rights by counting individual preferences in a democratic fashion or by a straightforward summation of individual rights needs to be qualified concerning the nature of interactions among individuals that warrants considering a set of individuals as a group. Those scholars who recognize the existence of collective moral rights provide some account of how groups of individuals relevant to the rights in question are organized but still dispute what constitutes the holder of such rights: some claim that moral rights can inhere only in individuals and that collectives can, at most, acquire "derivative" moral rights; such rights are held individually, but individuals are capable of exercising them only as members of a group. Others argue that moral rights can belong to collectives as such; these are called "primary" collective rights.

In this chapter I consider the conditions under which primary collective moral rights exist and the difference, on this basis, between the right to self-determination and other minority rights. I develop a context-dependent account of collective agency to clarify what moral entitlements groups have. The theories of group rights I discuss in this chapter ascribe rights to groups by identifying corresponding collective goods or interests. I explain groups' entitlements by emphasizing that groups are collective *agents* organized around the constitutive collective goods shared by the members in a certain way. Thus I argue that group rights, whether derivative or

A. Moltchanova, *National Self-Determination and Justice in Multinational States*, Studies in Global Justice 5, DOI 10.1007/978-90-481-2691-0_2,

primary, belong only to collective agents, but primary and derivative rights belong to different types of collectives: the type of right a group possesses is determined by how the members of the group relate to non-members concerning the shared collective good in question and the features that constitute the group agents in these relations.

The argument below proceeds as follows: First, I establish that human groups, or collectives, can be agents, and I apply to collectives H. L. A. Hart's argument that the equal freedom of individuals is a necessary condition of their holding a primary moral right. A collective can be the subject of a primary moral right *only if* it is capable of being in a relation of equal freedom with respect to other collectives with similar claims. Following the lead of Philip Pettit, I assess the freedom of collective agents in terms of discursive control, which allows us to apply Hart's necessary condition to collective agents. I argue that the equal standing of agents required for primary moral rights presupposes that the constitutive characteristics of the group with the capacity to hold a primary right allow it to be in a relation of equal freedom with other groups of the same type. Groups that lack such constitutive characteristics can only hold derivative group rights.

In the second section, I first establish the difference between individual and group rights by considering the interactions of individuals who share a distinct characteristic in need of protection. I explain that group rights belong to sets of individuals who organize as collective agents around the shared characteristic that requires protection. Then I reexamine the distinction between primary and derivative group rights. Whether a right is primary or derivative depends on the constitution of the collective agent that would possess it. The constitution of a collective agent is defined for its members by its members in the context of the collective good around which the group is organized. I show that groups organized around the shared good of self-determination have the capacity to relate to other collectives as free equals and can possess primary rights and that religious, linguistic, and cultural communities derive group rights from individual rights to collective goods that do not require such equal freedom.[3]

In the third section, I answer the concerns of those who are unwilling to assign to groups an ontological status independent of thier members.

In the fourth section, I consider how the distinction between the two types of rights can be applied. I discuss the criteria that help us identify groups that are subjects of primary collective rights. Since primary collective rights may clash with individual rights, I consider how the two can be harmonized. I also argue that the application of the distinction between the two types of collective rights to the treatment of minorities underscores that the significance of the distinction goes beyond the satisfaction of the need for conceptual clarity.

Finally, in the last section of the chapter, I argue that self-determination is an important shared good to which certain group agents have a moral right. Self-determination brings significant benefits to the group agents that possess the right to it. In this chapter, I only deal with the benefits of self-determination that connect to its being a constitutive shared good for such groups. In Chapters 4 and 5, I consider the benefits of self-determination in a practical context.

Group Rights and Hart's Condition

Before I introduce H. L. A. Hart's necessary condition, I need to explain why his account, designed for individuals, can be extended to human groups and justifiably used for my purpose of classifying their moral rights. Moreover, given the traditional opposition of the will and interest accounts of rights, I also need to demonstrate on what basis I choose to use Hart's account commonly associated with the "will" theories of rights, rather than an interest-theory-based account. The will account distinguishes rights by the sort of agent they protect and sets up a necessary capacity condition for having rights.[4] It considers rights to provide normative protection for the existence of certain choices. The will account is traditionally opposed by the interest account of rights, which prioritizes the benefits of rights to their holders: to have a right is to have an interest important enough to justify holding others under a duty, regardless of whether one is an agent capable of full-blown action or choice. For example, a non-human contemplative creature that never acts (and never communicates) but merely ponders cannot have rights according to the will theory because it cannot exercise choice, while it can in terms of the interest theory if such rights would benefit it and provided that an aspect of its well-being protected by the right in question is deemed important enough.[5]

I begin by demonstrating that the opposition between the "interest" and "will" accounts of rights does not manifest itself when we deal with the rights of human groups.[6] As a result, when applied to groups, the will account of rights covers the same incidents as does the interest account. (Such a range of incidents would be covered, in case of human individuals, by the combination of the two accounts of rights.) While the interest account is implied by the will account (the capacity to choose presupposes in general the capacity to hold corresponding interests), I show below that to apply the interest account to groups for the purpose of identifying their rights, we need to consider groups as *collective agents*, and thus the interest account requires groups to satisfy the same capacity condition as does the will account. Since groups also ought to be considered as agents for the will account of rights, either account of the nature of rights qualifies groups for Hart's necessary condition as it is formulated for agents. This means that if a group, in the absence of external impediments, has no capability of exercising equal freedom with other similar agents, it cannot hold a primary moral right. Later in the section I employ Philip Pettit's account of freedom to defend this approach to the freedom of collectives.

Defining a necessary condition for the possession of primary rights does not preclude the possibility that group agents simply do not exist. In the process of establishing that the interests associated with group membership imply collective agency, I demonstrate that group agents do exist (as sets of individuals standing in a certain, relatively long-lasting, relation to one another). But even if the enjoyment of certain goods by a set of individuals under certain circumstances implies that the set is a collective agent, why do we need to consider groups from this perspective at all? I concluded in the previous chapter that other perspectives on group entitlements are lacking, and I will bolster this conclusion below. First, we cannot consider group rights as reducible to individual rights. Second, any account of group rights requires us to distinguish between different types of group entitlements, and this distinction can be made only if we pay attention to the constitution of group agents. Still, it could be the case that collective agents exist but do not have moral rights. This is precisely the question I am answering in this book. In this section, I consider what groups can hold a primary right and how their constitution distinguishes them from other collective agents that can have only derivative rights. In the last section of the chapter, I argue that self-determination is a moral right of certain groups based on their constitution.

Interest, Will, and Group Agency

To apply the interest account of rights to groups, we first need to explain how any group interest is constituted and then consider the interest in question from the point of view of rights, judging whether the interest in question is "important enough to generate duties." To attribute a shared collective interest to a group, we need to properly identify the bounds of the group and consider how the group members function in relation to the interest in question. And to judge the importance of any interest, whether group or individual, we need not only to consider the entity that has the interest in the context in which the interest is exhibited but also to assess the standing of the entity with respect to others with similar interests. My interest in hearing an opera may be very important to me, but it is important societally only if I require accommodation and only in relation to the accommodation afforded to or demanded by other members of my society with interests of a similar kind. Similarly, the importance of a group interest can only be judged in comparison to other kinds of interests and to similar interests of other groups. Thus, I consider how group members function with respect to non-members when engaged in interactions associated with a particular interest. In this section, I concentrate mostly on the formation of a group interest. I discuss how it can be compared to the interests of other groups through its constitution later in this chapter.

Some theorists deny that group interests exist. According to Michael Hartney, even the interest in group survival derives from the aggregate individual interest of a group's members in its survival.[7] I contend, however, that there is more to the collective interest of group members than the summation of majority preferences. The knowledge that a set of individuals constitutes a group does not derive from considering individuals as an aggregate unless we also consider how they relate to others. To know that a set of individuals is a group and to count the majority of this set, we need to look into how members recognize that shared membership in the group exists and define the shared interest corresponding to this membership. Individual interests concerning relations of individuals, like the interest in group survival, allow us to identify a set of individuals as a possible group.

We simply cannot tell if a collective interest exists if it is not expressed, and to be expressed, it needs to be shared in a particular way. The members of a group must believe that they belong to the group. What makes an individual's belief of membership in a group socially meaningful and allows her to relate to other individuals identified as co-members is a second-order belief (a belief about the beliefs of others) that other group members share a similar conviction that they belong to the group, while individuals outside of the perceived group do not. I may believe that I am a citizen of Atlantis, but I do not share this belief with others as part of the culture of any group, and thus my belief is not socially meaningful. I may believe that I am a Russian and still not be one, but such a belief is, in principle, socially meaningful, as a corresponding group of individuals exists who share membership in a group based on their belief of being Russian. There are various communities of Russian individuals around the globe, and the boundaries of these communities are determined by their members' shared beliefs about membership and their relationships to non-members: they can constitute a linguistic or cultural community in one part of the world and a national community in another. Thus, group interest and corresponding beliefs about membership are *knowingly shared* by the majority of the group's members, who, in their capacity as members, have clearly recognized particular interests as related to the group's existence.

Individuals relate to one another within a group through their shared beliefs and their corresponding knowledge that these beliefs are shared. The actions of members of a group in their capacity as members are performed in light of beliefs about group membership and are interdependent with respect to both other members and individuals outside the group, because group members' beliefs about the beliefs of others serve as partial reasons for these actions. The types of actions constitutive of membership differ widely from one group to another. The action of a member of the Russian community in Minnesota as a member will be different from the action of a citizen of the Russian Federation as a citizen (though one can be both, of course). It also should be noted that the fact that individuals engage in interdependent actions is not itself sufficient to identify their membership in a group: some interdependent actions can be inherently hostile, such as trying to preempt an attack by a person whom you believe wants to attack you and knows that you know about it.[8] The actions of members of a group in their capacity as members, then, are cooperative and not merely interdependent, because they are joint actions performed in pursuit of the continuous enjoyment of the collective goods that are constitutive of the group.

The relationship between Quebec and the rest of Canada may help illustrate the distinction between interdependent and cooperative actions in the creation of national agency. The consistent refusal of the rest of Canada to acknowledge Quebec as a distinct society heightens the salience of the boundary between Quebec and the rest of the country. Quebecers share what they perceive as a national identity. Non-Quebecers know that Quebec will not accept their rejection of Quebecers' belief about the nature and bounds of their membership in Quebec, and they also know that Quebecers are aware of their knowledge. Thus, the Canadian non-recognition of Quebec has been a repeated interdependent—but not cooperative—action. Likewise, Quebec's attempts to use language laws protecting the prominence of the French language in the public sphere as a means to maintain its identity have been perceived by non-Quebecers as polarizing. Quebecers knew that the rest of Canada would perceive the laws as violating the rights of non-Francophones when they passed them and that the rest of Canada knew that Quebec knew its actions would be met with this predictable reaction. Quebec thus also pursued interdependent but not cooperative actions with respect to the rest of Canada, contributing to a stricter demarcation of political space in Canada. Francophone Quebecers' efforts to maintain their language are cooperative, however, among themselves.

A group's members may discriminate against a subset of individuals within its midst. The beliefs and attitudes held by the members who are discriminated against are still accompanied, however, either by the conviction that they share membership with the rest of the group and that they resent the treatment afforded to them in part for this reason (and thus would want the rest of the group to cooperate by changing their behavior) or by the conviction that they belong to a separate group and aspire to leave the group that discriminates against them. A subset of cases involving discrimination includes situations in which the rules of membership themselves afford unequal standing and capacity to a group's members. Although the interactions of members of such a group based on beliefs of membership cannot be considered just, they still conform to what is seen as the identity-maintaining behavior of the group and to publicly accepted rules for action.

At a minimum, then, the members of a collective engage in actions supported by their group identity. They may also consciously aim to maintain the group identity. The consideration of group interest yields, therefore, that group members, when functioning together in relation to their collective interest, act and connect to one another in certain ways. We can say that they exhibit, as a group, the features of collective agency (and define themselves accordingly).

What are collective agents? There are different accounts of what groups constitute collective agents and of what evidence can be given in support of their existence. Pettit bases his account on the evidence that collective reasoning yields results different from the summation of the results of individual reasoning. He states that collective agents are discontinuous with the individuals who compose them; these agents form intentions discontinuously from the intentions of their members, and they act to fulfill these intentions.[9] Christopher McMahon defines a collective agent as a group of cooperatively disposed people that has made the choice of a cooperative scheme or of a procedure for selecting schemes.[10]

I consider collective agency as characterized not only by the irreducibility of the outcomes of the group's reasoning to the sum of individual decisions but also by the presence of a common set of beliefs having to do with membership, including corresponding collective interests. I agree with James Nickel that group identity and agency are closely related.[11] The agent may or may not have explicit purposes and procedures for collective decision making and action. A collective agent is neither an aggregate of its members nor an entity whose existence is independent of theirs, but rather a system of interactions of individual members who are fully aware that they share a sense of membership/identity in a particular context and, in the case of some agents, formulate and pursue goals as a collective, a whole. Collective interests cannot be defined, then, merely as aggregates of individual interests. This aspect of group existence is highlighted by the "social ontology" approach to group agency proposed by Carol Gould. A group, according to Gould, is a set of individuals who stand in a certain relation to each other, whether they share a common purpose, have a common intentionality, act together, or have a common interest. A group ceases to exist, she argues, when the relation no longer holds.[12] The consideration of a group interest, therefore, reveals the underlying structure of group agency.

The interests of groups, and correspondingly their bounds, cannot be defined by outsiders alone without being confirmed by the constitution and culture of the group. Suppose that Minnesota's legislature decides to consider Russian-speaking immigrants living in Minnesota as a group defined by its desire for access to Russian-speaking schools, even though Russian immigrants living in Minnesota have not expressed a desire for this access. The action of Minnesota's legislature does not amount to its having correctly identified the Russian immigrants as a group organized around the interest in Russian-language education: it may be that the immigrants in question are not a group agent or are a group agent organized around a different interest. In deciding what characterizes a group, we need to pay attention to what motivates group members to identify and to act as members of the group, and we must also attend to what they strive to realize through their actions. In other words, we need to base our judgment about the internal constitution and the boundaries of the group upon the insider perspective. In addition, we need to pay attention to the persistence of group agency. If we do not, any majority vote would constitute a group, but only a momentary one.

What if some individuals' status in a society changes their idea of group membership to accord with the way they are perceived by the rest of the society?[13] Can we say with certainty that a set of individuals who are not yet mobilized along the lines of a shared interest attached to their shared characteristic are not a group with its own constitution? Perhaps the Russian-speaking Minnesotans do not share an interest in Russian-language education for their children because the expectations of assimilation customarily directed at immigrants to the United States have caused them to expect only ESL classes to be provided. If they mobilize differently, they may become a minority that requires, to assure its just treatment, special public schools where the curriculum is taught in Russian, as well as special measures that support the immigrants' ambitions concerning the use of their language in the public sphere. While it is possible that groups that are currently not mobilized to demand group rights will mobilize in the future, we must rely on existing signs of the presence of collective agents and on presently expressed group interests. Certainly, in some political environments, a group's identity and its corresponding agency may not be actualized completely. But to be identified as a group, the members still need to have an understanding of themselves as a collective agent, even if they cannot act upon this understanding. They cannot be considered to be a group agent based only on the hypothetical idea that one day they might develop the corresponding type of identity that they do not now have.[14]

Finally, we need to be able to determine when individuals' interest in special treatment does not represent group interest and thus does not have a corresponding group agent. According to my approach, we have to determine whether individuals' interests associated with the protection of their distinct characteristic are shared in a way that constitutes a collective agent. Thus, we need to determine how the individuals in the set identified by the shared characteristics interact, including how they behave with respect to non-members. Members of a group agent will share second-order beliefs regarding membership and will engage in the corresponding interdependent cooperative actions, and individuals with common characteristics who do not share such beliefs or take such actions cannot be considered members of a group agent. The shared characteristics of group agents not only belong to each individual member but are also consistent with the members' beliefs about their collective goals and with their self-understanding. All students who have taken a 100-level course at a particular college can take a 200-level course, but these students do not have the group identity required for agency. Each student shares the characteristic of having taken a 100-level course, but these students do not share collective goals and do not self-identify as members of a collective of 100-level-course veterans. Nor do they consider their eligibility for 200-level courses to be a collective good or possess a corresponding collective interest in this eligibility, as each of them can take upper-level courses independently of the others, and none of them has the characteristic because the others have it. (It is irrelevant whether there has to be a minimum number of students for a course to be offered, as each can take a guided reading class instead. Even if taking classes is a group activity, the group is specific to a particular class and has nothing to do with all students eligible for 200-level courses).[15] A number of individuals who possess a moral right tied to an individual characteristic they share are normally not a collective agent. As I show in the next section, collective rights, whether derivative or primary, belong only to collective agents.[16]

Summing up, to define the collective interests of a group, we need to look at how membership in the group is defined by its members; to assess the relative importance of some collective interest, we must consider how the group is composed and how it functions with respect to non-members. We need to identify a set of shared and stable second-order beliefs held by group members (with which they also self-identify) concerning group identity and the group's relational properties. Such beliefs guide the members' cooperative interdependent actions in part by defining their shared goals, which at the least will include the preservation of their group identity. Hence, a group's collective interest cannot be defined without considering the situation and circumstances of the group as a collective agent. The reverse relationship also holds: collective agency by extension defines collective interest as going beyond individual interest by virtue of its constitution. We can now use Hart's necessary condition for moral rights, because we have determined that groups, for the purpose of rights, are agents in terms of both the will-based and the interest-based account of group rights.

Hart's Condition

Hart's necessary condition for the existence of moral rights is that all men have an equal moral right to freedom. Hart's condition must be reformulated if it is to apply to collectives, because not all collective agents are surrounded by relevantly similar collectives, and "all men" does not translate immediately into "all collectives." Hart's language must be made more specific about the rights in question: a necessary condition for the existence of a primary moral right is the equal freedom of the right-holders, if it is a general right, or, if it is a special right, of the right-holders and all other groups of the same type beyond the special relation governed by the right.

Not all moral rules presuppose equal freedom, but rights do. As Hart demonstrates, this is a consequence of the justification—required for the existence of moral rights—for why individuals can limit the freedom of others. The possessor of a moral right is conceived, according to Hart, as having a moral justification for limiting the freedom of another. He has this justification not because the action he is entitled to require of another has some moral quality in itself but simply because, in the circumstances, a certain distribution of human freedom can be maintained if he is, by his choice, allowed to determine how that other shall act.[17] The very notion of a general moral right presupposes the equal freedom of its subjects as a necessary condition, and Hart's challenge is to show that special rights also imply such equal freedom. In answer to this challenge, he first demonstrates that interference with the freedom of others is justified not by any special content of the actions the right-holders are entitled to but rather by the special right's background conditions, such as promises, consent, submission to mutual restrictions, and the like. The right arises from the special relationship of the parties, which ensues from their previous voluntary transactions.

An example may help to clarify Hart's point. If I promise to meet you at a coffee shop at 10 A.M. one morning, you have the moral right to demand that I be there at the promised time. You have the right, however, because I have promised to be there—my promise is the background condition to your special right—and not because my being there has any moral value independent of that promise. My presence at the coffee shop might comfort you before an important medical appointment. If so, this effect would be an additional reason for me to be there, and perhaps it even motivated me to make the promise in the first place, but it does not justify your limiting my freedom to be anyplace I wish at 10 A.M. on the agreed-upon morning. Your moral right is that I keep my promise. Rights can also be conferred based on consent or authorization. The voluntary transaction behind an authorization, to take another example, gives the authorized individual (and only this individual) the right to interfere within the sphere of her authority because she stands in a particular relationship to the authorizing person.

Finally, Hart argues that political obligations are based on the mutuality of restrictions—that the obligation to obey the rules is something distinct from "whatever other moral reasons there may be for obedience in terms of good consequences (e.g., the prevention of suffering)." "The obligation," Hart explains, "is due to the cooperating members of the society as such and not because they are human beings on whom it would be wrong to inflict suffering."[18] Hart looks for a principle that grounds all voluntary transactions among individuals as the basis formoral rights, and he concludes that the justification for interfering with another's freedom indirectly invokes that "all men have an equal right to be free."[19]

It is important that the moral justification for interference with another's freedom, even if only in relation to particular powers protected by the right in question, be connected to the general status of the parties with respect to one another. Claims to interfere that are based on the general character of activities or persons rather than on the mutual status of individuals engaged in free and reciprocal relations do not constitute justifications of a "right." Thus, moralistic or a racist interference with the freedom of others cannot be justified, because the submission it implies cannot be said to be owed or due to the individuals who interfere. No voluntary transactions have warranted the interference.

Even if Hart's argument is limited to (rational) moral agents, it still applies to collective agents provided that they exist and exhibit properties that are analogous to those of individual agents in the relevant respects.[20] The primary moral rights of collective agents can exist, therefore, only if (1) there are such entities as collective agents and (2) those entities have the capacity to preserve their equal freedom. This capacity does not need to be exercised for the necessary condition to obtain: an oppressed group that is capable, were it not for some particular circumstances, of maintaining equal freedom with other groups of the same kind may not be able to exercise this capacity and thus may not be free, but by virtue of its unrealized capacity it can in principle satisfy the necessary condition and thus qualify for holding a primary right.[21] I explained the conditions under which collective agents can be said to exist in the first part of this section. I will offer additional support for the view that assigns some ontological independence to group agents later on in this chapter when I answer some objections to this view. For now, I will establish that collectives can be equally free agents, because this capacity of group agents is required to ascribe primary rights to them.

The Freedom of Collective Agents

What does it mean for a collective agent to be free? In important ways, I follow Pettit's notion of freedom as discursive control. He argues that agents are free only if they can be centers of action, selfhood, and personhood, which requires that they possess exercisable discursive control.[22] Discursive control goes beyond rational control (the capacity to choose) and volitional control (the capacity to identify with one's choices). If an agent has volitional control, she identifies with her choices. The agent may, however, identify with her choices for reasons that are wrong for the constitution of her personhood. Under duress, individuals do not lose their capacity to choose, and they may even identify with their choices. When threatened with a beating, a woman may surrender her wallet willingly, but that does not mean that she has surrendered it freely: she makes her choice while being subjected to hostile coercion, that is, coercion that is not driven by the avowable interests of the coerced. Discursive control requires a particular standing or status in relation to others that is beneficial to an agent's personhood. To discourse is to reason together with others in the attempt to resolve a problem by reference to what all parties regard as "inferentially relevant considerations or reasons."[23] Discursive control, according to Pettit, involves both ratiocinative and relational aspects: an agent has to have the capacity both to participate in discourse and to enjoy discourse-friendly relationships.[24] A discourse-friendly relationship excludes hostile coercion but allows "friendly coercion." The exercise of freedom, when defined in terms of discursive control, requires the absence of arbitrary interference but not of interference that is controlled by the avowable interests of the coerced.

The purpose of Pettit's notion of discursive control is to surpass the limitations of defining freedom in terms of volitional control. I argue that in order to do so, the notion of discursive control requires an external limitation on discourse, such as the equality of status of the subjects of the discourse. Unless Pettit assumes that agents in a discourse possess equal standing guaranteed by a third party or by some externally imposed norms, existing society-related paradigms defining the agents' mutual status may adversely affect the discourse. Individuals who are free to engage in a discourse may also freely accept unequal status due to a prior habituation/acculturation or to diminished self-respect. In such cases, the acceptance of certain reasons given in the discourse as valid can be shared by the participants but may not properly describe the participants' freedom. For example, all participants may accept that a dominant person's interests have more weight in the group than that person's equal standing would allow. The problem here is not the way the dominated individuals think about themselves but that the way they think about themselves allows others to limit their freedom in ways otherwise unacceptable. Since discourse participants' interests may be defined so as not to exclude covert subjugation, there ought to be some external restriction defining terms of membership. Constraining discourse so that all parties have equal standing ensures that discourse participants can be free agents: their options will not be limited in advance of the discourse by the conditions of their inclusion in the society, and any limitations on their ability to control their future that result from the discourse will have to be negotiated based on the initial premise of their equal freedom.

Pettit understands the freedom of collective agents in the same way as that of individual agents. Accordingly, the freedom of collective agents involves not only the capacity to make collective decisions and act but also the capacity not to be dominated by others in a discourse and thus the possession of equal status in relation to other collective agents of the same kind. Collective agents may be unfree in two different ways: they may be capable of freedom "from the inside" but lack it due to external circumstances that prevent them from exercising the capacity, or they may lack the capacity altogether, as I will show is the case with linguistic minorities that do not aspire to be self-determining. In both cases, the collective agent lacks the capacity to maintain an equal standing in relation to other similar agents and therefore cannot be considered free, but in the former case it may qualify for a primary right. Each collective action and decision can entail collective responsibility with respect to its consequences, but the collective agent nevertheless cannot be considered free if it lacks the capacity to maintain an equal standing in relation to other similar agents.

Thus, although many groups are collective agents, in order to fulfill Hart's necessary condition, a group agent has to at least possess a capacity for equal freedom with other real or potential right-holders. It should be noted that satisfying this necessary condition for entitlement to a primary right does not imply that a group will be granted the entitlement, but a group that fails to satisfy the condition cannot hold a primary moral right. In the next section, I formulate the distinction between primary and derivative rights and illustrate this distinction by contrasting self-determining and linguistic collective agents.

Collective Moral Rights and the Constitution of Group Agents: Primary Versus Derivative Group Rights

The account of group moral rights as derivative states that group rights derive from the individually held rights of the members of a group because individuals are capable of exercising these rights only as members of the group. Raz, for example, considers collective rights to be individual rights arising out of aggregate individual interests in public goods (goods that serve individuals' interests as members of the group). A collective right, according to Raz, is more than a mere individual right, because the interest of no single member of the group in seeing the interest secured is sufficient to justify imposing duties on others.[25] Leslie Green emphasizes that duties corresponding to group rights are imposed on others not for the sake of the aggregate interest of group members in a public good, as Raz would suggest, but because of the special type of non-aggregate interest they exhibit: collective interest.[26] However, Green does not think that moral rights belong to collective agents.

The account of group moral rights as primary claims that groups as such can have rights. Bhikhu Parekh considers religious, cultural, and linguistic rights to be primary collective rights. Michael McDonald grounds such rights in significant collective goods.[27] Proponents of both "derivative" and "primary" accounts supporting the existence of moral group rights attribute collective rights to the existence of collective (also called "public" or "shared") goods—goods that serve individuals' interests as members of the group, such as language or culture. The public aspect of these goods' production or consumption or both is what is valuable about them, according to Denise Réaume, and thus there can be no individual rights—that is to say claims made independently of having membership in the group—to public goods. She calls collective rights to public goods claimed by a group against non-members "group rights."[28] (I will use "collective" and "group" rights interchangeably.) Hence, a primary group moral right belongs to a collective itself, while a derivative group moral right belongs to individuals, who are capable of exercising the right only as members of a group. As I will discuss shortly, both derivative and primary group rights are different from individual rights held due to a shared characteristic that is not connected to a shared good.

I am sympathetic to the two approaches to group moral rights. Each of the two accounts, "derivative" and "primary," provides, as I will show, an account of collective rights for a different type of group. In this section, I specify when each view is useful for identifying the valid rights claims of various groups. I argue that group rights are assigned only to collective agents and that the type of right granted to a group is based on the members' relations to non-members and the features that constitute the agents in this relation.

I agree with the view that group rights exist and cannot be reduced to individual rights, because we simply cannot explain some entitlements in terms of individual rights. Any attempt to identify group entitlements or maintain the conditions for groups' flourishing by means of a summation of the rights of their individual members implies an explanation of what type of individual interaction warrants counting these individuals as a group. As Raz points out, the interest of a single member cannot warrant the duty imposed on society in protecting a right to a collective good. Even identifying the nature of an interest as aggregate does not explain how many individuals will constitute a group of the size required to generate the duty. Additional criteria are needed to determine entitlement. I agree with Green that the interest in group rights has a special nature, but I argue that group rights belong to group agents—a conclusion with which he disagrees. I have shown that the interest and will accounts of rights cover the same range of incidents when applied to groups and that a right to collective interests is also the right of a group agent. I will show that what may help us distinguish between different types of entitlements is that individuals are organized in different types of groups based on how they interact. However, even individual rights are acquired through the interaction with a particular community in relation to which the rights are claimed. Therefore before I move on to the distinction between different types of group rights, I will first consider the distinction between individual and group rights.

The Distinction Between Holders of Individual and Group Rights

Brian Barry provides an account of group rights that distinguishes them from individual rights due to the fact that groups have the power of self-government. He thus pays attention to the modes of operation of groups and of individuals in relation to one another as members of groups. Barry distinguishes between two types of entitlements: an entitlement predicated over the group as a whole and an entitlement based on certain characteristics of individuals. The latter confers benefits on individuals rather than on a group as such, which is either a communal entity (like a family) or a corporate entity (like a church). I agree with Barry that characteristic-based individual rights can benefit individuals based on their membership in a group without turning their benefits into a group right.[29] For example, group members can enjoy individual immunity, like the right of Sikhs not to wear helmets, due to their membership in a group, but they acquire the right regardless of the actions of the other members of the group, as Barry points out. Even when the eligibility of individuals for a benefit is determined by judging their actions in reference to the actions of others qualified to benefit from the right, the right they possess is not always a group right. To use Barry's example, a quota scheme in which a given applicant's test score is ranked in comparison with the test scores of the other applicants eligible to enter within a quota generates only individual rights.

What kind of individual interaction warrants group rights? Barry acknowledges that claims made by and on behalf of a group are a different matter than individual claims based merely on a characteristic attributed to group members. His project is limited in scope, however, to considering how to restrict the behavior of groups that violate individual rights. He does not extend his discussion to consider group entitlements. His background assumption is that groups exist and are characterized by self-government, the limits of which with respect to group members he wants to assess. He does not discuss what justifies groups' entitlement to self-government, but the question of entitlement is important if we wish to determine the justifiable limits on their de facto self-government. Some self-governing functions can be ceded without jeopardizing the group, while the revocation of others will change group practices but can still be justified based on the protection of their members' human rights. Still other practices need to be protected if the group is to be preserved. We must determine which ones are which if we are to provide a principled evaluation of group privileges. We therefore need to consider whether the entitlement to self-government is justifiable for a given group and what kind of self-governing powers a group needs based on the nature of the interactions of its members that constitute the group.

Of course, Barry may consider group self-government to be a sociological reality devoid of any corresponding normative entitlement by groups and thus aim simply to sketch out a coping strategy for liberal societies to employ toward illiberal groups. This is so in part because he thinks that although liberals do not have to be committed to promoting autonomy by changing the nature of group membership for minorities, neither do they need to endorse diversity by promoting the flourishing of groups. While Barry does not approve of Michael Walzer's focus on the nation-state as a meaningful group unit, arguing that this focus simply makes national minorities disappear from view,[30] and while he acknowledges that Kymlicka's view is preferable for multinational states, he advocates a third possibility: to consider a multinational state in civic terms as a state of all citizens. This does not solve the problem of groups' entitlements to rights, however, but rather avoids it. To address the entitlement problem, we need to explain what it means to make a state the state of all citizens—even those who think they belong to different national groups or other minorities. Thus, Barry does not consider the large group of cases of group entitlement wherein groups do not violate their members' physical and mental integrity.

We can determine what groups should not be doing to their members from the liberal point of view, but it is also important to ask what non-group members should or should not be doing with respect to a set of individuals who think they are a group. The general entitlements of real-life collectives that constitute the ground for peaceful and productive negotiations among their members remain to be defined.

There are better and worse ways of controlling group behaviors given that they are constituted as individuals-in-relations who mobilize along the lines of group identity. Barry's approach presupposes that the already set boundaries of groups are either acceptable or not meaningful for citizenship in the larger society, because he proposes to control the terms of membership in minority groups only to ensure the basic rights of minority individuals. But not all boundaries are sociologically innocuous and unimportant, as they are characterized in part by groups' relations with non-members and define the meaning of equal inclusion of minority individuals in the larger society. Without rules to determine whether group claims are legitimate and thus whether the state should adopt accommodation strategies that would allow the group to flourish along with those that secure the protection of the members' individual rights, it may be difficult to mediate the relationships between individuals from the group with the rest of the society so as to ensure the equal treatment of all citizens. I agree with Barry that group actions that harm individual members should be controlled or prohibited, and Barry's theory provides valuable guidelines for deciding when a group's actions should be restricted. Barry's identification of eligibility for group rights with the de facto capacity of groups for self-government is well-drawn, but he does not specify more general principles describing what kinds of relations of individuals qualify groups for these entitlements, and thus his theory covers very different ground from mine.

To illustrate my approach to the distinction between individual and group rights, I will start with the example of language rights.[31] The fact that the state language (or languages) prevails in the legal and political institutions even of a state that contains speakers of a number of other minority languages raises the question of linguistic minorities' proper membership in public and political domains and thus their relations to institutions of authority.[32] The use of language in the public sphere is a useful subject for exploring the types of rights that individuals' interactions with their societies generate.

Those language rights recognized in the Canadian Charter of Rights and Freedoms, for example, that are aimed at protecting the official language minorities across the country—Anglophone and Francophone—are group rights, because the protection afforded by the rights maintains the equality of the two majority linguistic cultures in Canada.[33] A different type of right related to linguistic identity is satisfied by providing a courtroom translator to an immigrant who is not capable of understanding English or French. The Supreme Court of Canada considers such translation services to be a formal due process guarantee in order to practice universal justice, not based on the need to respect linguistic minorities. The Canadian legal framework therefore acknowledges individual and group rights as different in their origin and function.

There are other linguistic communities in Canada, however, besides the French- and English-speaking communities. Could the Canadian policy of multiculturalism that promotes immigrants' access to publicly funded media broadcasts in their native tongues, for example, also be considered as being based upon collective language rights? If some but not all Russian-speaking immigrants to Canada want to have access to publicly funded media time in Russian, on what basis do we decide whether their claim is warranted and whether, if it is granted, we are acceding to an individual right to equal treatment or a group right? My answer to this question is based on the consideration of whether a collective agent organized around the preservation of linguistic culture is present. Let us assume that the reason for granting publicly funded media time to Russian-speaking immigrants is the importance to the members of the immigrant group of maintaining the public status of their language. If a group of immigrants exhibits features of collective agency and is not merely classified by outsiders as belonging together on the basis of shared linguistic ability, the corresponding right is a group right.

For an immigrant group to qualify for a group right to language on the basis of identity, the group must have an organizational structure that reflects the identity of individual members who believe that the community exists with the shared goals of practicing and preserving the group's linguistic identity. That the group members all differ from speakers of the official language in sharing a mother tongue is insufficient to qualify them for a group right to language. In other words, the immigrant group needs not only to share a language but also to mobilize in some ways in order to qualify in principle for the possession of the right to language as a group right.

The collective agents that support the group language rights of the French and English linguistic communities in Canada have corresponding loci in Francophone Quebec and the rest of Canada. Under these circumstances, the right of the Francophone Manitobans to be educated in French where numbers warrant falls under the group right to the preservation of the French language for all Francophones in Canada. Perhaps in the case of Manitoba's French-speaking population, the right to language could fall be withdrawn from the aegis of the legal norms of the Canadian Charter that safeguard the existence of the two linguistic communities—and thus it could be justified on a different basis. In such a case, however, we would need first to determine whether there exists, as a group separate from the larger Francophone Canadian cultural community, a collective agency of Francophone Manitobans that is properly mobilized and possesses a distinctive internal constitution of its own. Thus, group as opposed to individual rights are granted to sets of individuals based on the presence of an internal constitution of the type that designates a collective agent.

Now I will consider how collective agents' entitlements differ depending on how they define their characteristic features of membership with respect to other groups.

Identifying the Holders of Primary Versus Derivative Group Rights

We need to determine what kind of benefits (or compensations) groups can justifiably claim vis-à-vis the larger society and what type of entitlement contributes best to their ability to flourish. To illustrate why differentiation between the types of group rights is necessary, consider a few problematic cases. The ability to use the Welsh language is a collective good (a good that serves individuals' interests as members of the group). Not all Welsh are interested in having public education in

Welsh revived. Do only the Welsh who want such education have the corresponding collective interest in it, or are all Welsh the relevant group? If the latter, do the proponents of education in Welsh have a right to such education against both the non-Welsh and the Welsh who oppose it? How should their self-government with respect to language be executed? The justifiable treatment of individuals by the group requires the determination of the nature of the group entitlement. This is so because the right holder and duty bearer vary depending on how a group perceives its constitution in relation to other groups. To determine whether the collective good of speaking French generates a moral right of a similar type for French-speaking immigrants to the United States, Manitoba Francophones,[34] or Quebecers, we need to look at the context in which the right may be claimed.

Identifying the presence of a collective good, moreover, does not on its own allow us to pick out the relevant features that describe the holder of the right to that good. Consider sports, Denise Réaume's example. Playing soccer or hockey is what she calls a "participatory" good for the players (a type of collective good): they have to participate to benefit.[35] However, we can look at playing soccer and its corresponding rights in different ways. My right to join others in playing soccer is as great as your right to play hockey with your team, because as members of our society we ought to be equally allowed to freely pursue legitimate recreational activity, and if one of us is aided in this pursuit by our society, the other has a right to be aided, too. The duty to provide necessary facilities is borne by all citizens, the facilities are sponsored based on an estimate of the average aggregate need of individuals interested in each participatory good, and the collective right to these facilities derives from the interest of players of each game. If there are 15 soccer teams and only 5 fields to play on, however, there is within the local soccer association a clear primary group right of each group claimed against other similar groups to have a fair amount of playing time.[36] The duty falls upon all teams to share the facility equally. Thus, for the purpose of determining the entitlement of a group, we need to distinguish the type of self-government of the group in relation to others.

Or, to take another example, if we look only at the collective good of language, we may divide communities that constitute "us" and "not-us" for the predominantly Anglophone community of Westmount in Montreal, Quebec along numerous lines. First, speaking English is as much of a collective good for the residents of Westmount as it is for all Anglophones in Canada. Second, if we fail to consider the group agents and their relations, candidates for an equal right to the enjoyment of the collective good of language may include any linguistic community: non-Anglophone Quebecers, Francophones of Canada, any of the non-English-speaking immigrant communities in Montreal, and even all Anglophones in Canada (either excluding or including Westmounters; in the latter case, Westmounters appear, as a smaller group, to be in a position to claim the right against themselves counted as members of the larger group). Considering the constitution of group agents in relation to others tells us more about what type of group right they qualify for.

We have established that any agent capable of discursive control in relation to other agents can be a subject of a primary moral right (whether this capacity is realized or not). The possession of discursive control with respect to other agents requires collectives to relate to one another and to resolve problems in accordance with the maintenance of their equal status. It is possible to assess whether this equality is achieved in relevant respects only for those agents that share an aspect of constitution (including self-definition) that makes them comparable to one another. This feature of group constitution essential for discursive control can help us differentiate between groups capable of holding primary rights and the rest: those agents that share an aspect of constitution comparable to other groups are eligible for primary group rights, while the rest are not. Groups' constitutions ought to be perceived as commensurable not only in accordance with a criterion used by an outside observer but also from each participating group's perspective. The groups also ought to be comparable in the eyes of their members, and mutually so. If the Russians think that the Ukrainians are a self-determining group but the Ukrainians think they are not, the belief held by the Russian community does not change the nature of the Ukrainian community. Finally, comparable constitutions matter in the context of group interactions. In a mono-linguistic state, the majority, which is aware of its language and the existence of other linguistic groups, does not have linguistic rights within the state. This majority has a right to self-determination in the international context, and its right to language in this case is not separate from its right to be self-determining.

Group agents do not exist apart from the rules of organization and group aims shared by their members; the mode of being of such agents is a set of interactions among members who are aware of the group's existence. To evaluate whether the standing of the group is equal in relation to other groups with similar collective interests, we must consider whether its members share beliefs both about the existence of other similar groups and about their group's status relative to these other groups. By virtue of their self-definition, the constitutive features identified by the members of the collective agent eligible for primary rights also define the agent's boundaries and its aspired-for or achieved ideal standing in relation to the set of all agents of the relevant type.

Since shared beliefs about members and nonmembers are essential to the existence of collective agents, members of an agent that possesses freedom, defined as discursive control, share beliefs about the group's standing in relation to other such groups. The constitutive features of such an agent include beliefs about the existence of other similar agents and the desired status to be achieved or maintained in relation to them. Because such a collective agent has (or aspires to have) a say about its future, it has (or aspires to have) self-determination, the capacity to be primarily determined by the conditions of its internal life. The limits of self-determining communities are maintained only in relation to those of other similar communities. A collective agent capable of discursive control and hence capable of being the subject of a primary moral right is organized around self-determination. This is the feature of group constitution essential for discursive control.

Why should we not merely define the good or interest that is characteristic of a primary right against the undifferentiated rest of the world that the group sees as "not-us" without specifying the constitution of other agents that are not part of the group? Put simply, the "other" as merely "not-us" can be anything. A set of non-members is itself a non-member, but it has no structure or constitution of its own. Considering the constitution of agency against a non-structured "other as not-us" does not provide for the specific conditions that allow the equal status of the group and "non-group" in discursive control to be assessed, and thus it does not allow us to answer the question whether they have a capacity for holding a primary right. It may or may not be that "not-us" is an agent of the same type as the group. Concentrating only on the internal aspects of group constitution unrelated to the existence, structure, and standing of other groups does not help us determine whether the right in question is primary, because the structure of "not-us" as related to the constitutive characteristics of "us" is important to the outcome of this endeavor.

Réaume argues that groups deserving autonomy are distinguished by the presence of what Hart calls "secondary rules of change and adjudication." These rules, Réaume explains, create internal "bodies or processes with the authority to change preexisting rules and resolve disputes about the rules," and hence they give a group the ability, through "internal decision-making bodies, to interpret its own norms for itself."[37] I agree with Réaume that the correct approach to a group depends upon the constitutional structure of the group. But the presence of such rules is not sufficient in itself to distinguish different types of rights. The presence of secondary rules does not allow us to determine, for example, whether the constitution of a group merely influences the terms of the group's inclusion in the larger society (and hence whether the group's collective goal is merely to maintain its constitution with respect to "not-us") or whether it defines the freedom of the group as it relates to other similar collective agents (and hence whether the group's collective goal is to be determined by the conditions of its internal life so as to maintain its status with respect to other groups of the same kind). Only in the latter case can a group be a subject of a primary collective right, because only then is it capable of being in a potentially equal relationship with other collectives.

Self-Determination

The idea of self-determination as an agent's capacity to be entirely determined by the conditions of its internal life is not confined to the contemporary international framework, but my project in this book is motivated by current international problems concerning group rights. I will explain now how the general idea of self-determination translates into self-determination as the capacity of a group to control its political future. If a group agent perceives self-determination as the good it wants to pursue, it aims to be entirely determined by the conditions of its internal life. This pursuit is relational in a world that contains more than one community, because each group agent can safeguard its autonomous existence only in relation to others. To do so, the agent has to maintain control over its constitution and the elements that sustain it and thus avoid interference by others with its effective agency. Presently, a group agent cannot be entirely determined by the conditions of its internal life in non-political terms, because if the agent does not conceive its self-determination as political, it will be included in the political society of another group and thus be determined by external conditions. Thus, self-determination requires that a group agent have a say about its political future and political organization that places a group agent in control of its membership and the rules of its organization is normally tied to a territory.[38] A group agent that imagines self-determination in non-political and non-territorial terms cannot maintain its status with respect to others as equally free and thus possess a primary moral right to the non-territorial and non-political form of self-determination it envisions. Therefore, the reality of international relations at present requires that self-determination (understood as a group's freedom with respect to a number of other political communities) be conceived in political and territorial terms. In contrast, groups entitlements with respect to language, which I consider in the next section, require external accommodation from a political and territorial unit within which the linguistic group resides, but this accommodation is not characterized by equal freedom. I will discuss the status with respect to self-determination of groups like the Roma that define themselves in non-territorial terms in the next chapter to determine what aspects of a group's constitution place it in the category of self-determining agents.

That self-determination presently requires specific political powers for boundary maintenance is a contingent fact, but this contingency does not make the identification of a moral norm to regulate group relations impossible. I have already explained that contingent properties can acquire a normative dimension if agents have to interact to maintain these properties.

A scheme that identifies the holders of a primary moral right through their constitution in relation to other similar agents works with a very general definition of self-determination that is not couched in the terms of the present international order. If the world changes radically but continues to be composed of a number of communities, the condition of being a holder of a primary right will remain the same: all groups would have to be constituted in a certain way to qualify for the right. Those groups that will not utilize the understanding of self-determination that is contingent upon the world order they belong to simply will not have the capability of holding the right to self-determination because they will not be able to stand in a relation of equal freedom with respect to others. Their aspiration to be a different type of agent will place them outside of the category of holders of the primary right to self-determination.

It also should be noted that in the present international system self-determination is not conceived as the capacity of one worldwide political community to be shaped by the conditions of its internal life (and thus be self-determining, or in control of its future, in a non-relational sense). Such a community could exist. Its members would need to be able to maintain their group identity internally to avoid a split that would make some members outsiders, although they could not engage in self-determination as the exercise of freedom with respect to other similar communities. But if such a community did exist, the problem of moral entitlement to the right to self-determination that now urgently requires resolution would simply disappear. One worldwide political community does not need to relate to others of the same kind or have any status with respect to them and is not a subject of a primary right.[39] It is obviously wrong to think that the self-definition of a political community always presupposes "the other," for in a single world community, this would not be the case. Nevertheless, while a community can be constituted without "the other," it cannot be "free" in the absence of other communities with respect to which it can maintain its status. Primary rights require this capacity for freedom, and my approach assigns primary rights to multiple self-determining communities, though it can nevertheless explain the nature of entitlements of one worldwide community and has resources to accommodate the disappearance and reappearance of multiple self-determining agents or the way self-determination is engendered at a particular historical period.

Presently, any group whose members share a particular kind of political culture—or set of beliefs and attitudes concerning politics—can be the subject of a primary moral right.[40] This political culture includes beliefs about the internal constitution of the group and the group's ideal status in relation to all other agents whose functioning is organized around similar characteristics, as well as the limits of the group's authority meaningful for its members. Thus, unless the constitutive features of membership are shared through such a political culture (and we have reason to believe that the constitutive features of the group have been identified correctly), we cannot conclude that the group is capable of equal freedom with other groups and thus that it qualifies for a primary right.

Group members' notion of the powers and entitlements of the group, which contributes to the meaning of group membership and is shared through the group's political culture, may refer to either the group's achieved status or to the status members believe it deserves. An oppressed national minority, for example, may aspire to exercise self-determination while its real status denies it such power. If the group members perceive themselves as a group similar in kind to groups that possess self-determination and it is reasonably clear that their views are not manipulated but held freely, the group may qualify for the rights possessed by other self-determining groups. Some outside observers may consider the group's demands unjustified, but so long as the group forms intentions and acts upon the set of its constitutive beliefs comparable to the constitutive beliefs of other self-determining agents, it is, as a matter of fact, this kind of agent. Outsiders can try to influence the way the group members perceive themselves, and historically national identities are not set in stone—nations are political communities that can be formed, change, and cease to exist—but a group that is clearly and persistently constituted ought to have its perception of itself accepted at face value.

Basic to the group culture associated with self-determination is the idea that the group is in control of its political future. This implies, first, the belief that membership in the group defines the bounds within which political authority can originate meaningfully for those it governs. That is, political power exercised over the group is authoritative only if it derives from the group as a whole. Second, provided other political communities exist, the members of the group in question share the corresponding collective end of establishing or maintaining effective agency in relation to other groups with similar demands. Self-determination designates an important property of groups that allows them to be compared and to stand in the relation of equality.

Groups that enjoy or aspire to self-determination share an identity that describes a *primary political community* through the ideal correspondence of the identified domain of members to the political power representing them. The entitlement to the right of self-determination is possible only if the group agent is constituted so as to be capable of relating to other similarly constituted communities.

Another feature of the ideal of self-determination as a constitutive collective good for group agents is that the corresponding entitlement is claimed against non-specific others of the same kind and against all of them. A set of other self-determining communities provides a differentiated structure to "not-us." In the corresponding general right, self-determination is claimed equally against all other similar agents, and the right requires the equal standing of the members of the set against one another and constitutes a particular exemplification of their discursive control. Collective agents capable of being in a potentially equal relationship with other collectives are also capable of possessing special primary moral rights based, for example, on treaties among them. The right of Tatarstan to control its natural resources within the Russian Federation is a primary right of a national group based on the division of powers with the rest of the federation. Any primary rights that agents possess—special or general—require the agents' capacity for equal freedom. This capacity is secured within the context of the special rights and obligations toward one another of a number of self-determining agents, as in a federation, by the equal status of groups granted to them by the general right.

Importantly, it is also feasible that equality of status for self-determining groups can be provided in the current international system, although it is not required for the existence of a moral right to self-determination. Self-determining groups do not have to be in possession of their own states; that the satisfaction of self-determination claims does not require the acquisition of independent statehood has been commonly accepted.[41] The equal right to self-determination can be a right to equal status with other self-determining groups within a host multinational state. Group members can develop a double allegiance to the group and the host state (what David Miller calls "nested identity"),[42] but their association with the state is secondary to their group political allegiance and is conditioned upon a proper accommodation of their claim to self-determination.

Thus, the collective good of self-determination allows group agents to claim their entitlement to the enjoyment of the benefits of this good in relation to all other communities of the same kind. The corresponding right can be claimed by any agent of the required type against all non-specific but differentiated "others" of the same kind. The way the collective good of self-determination is constituted makes the corresponding agents capable of discursive control and thus of holding a primary moral right.

Linguistic Rights

As I already discussed, individual rights serve the purpose of ensuring equal individual treatment, while group rights protect individuals as members of groups. The existence of a linguistic community is a participatory collective good.[43] Can a claim by a linguistic minority be construed as a claim against other linguistic groups (including the majority) as equal agents and thus provide grounds for a primary group right? The claim would need to be made against groups similar in constitution—a linguistic minority in Ontario cannot claim the right to language against Canada's right to self-determination or against the right of Catholics to worship. Below, I demonstrate that, in the absence of self-determination claims accompanying linguistic claims, a group linguistic right aiming to preserve a linguistic community exists to grant equal respect to the individual interests of each of the community's members *qua* members of the larger political community and is thus not primary. This is so because the collective good of language, as a constitutive feature of a particular linguistic agent that claims the corresponding right, is defined against a specific other or others that are, moreover, related to the agent in question only by means external to the constitution of the agent.

Language rights can be one of the facets of a more fundamental relationship that qualifies a group for a primary right rather than simply a derivative right. The possession of an official state language (like French in France), for example, is derived from the right to self-determination of the political community represented by the state. Likewise, a linguistic minority that advances a self-determination claim and mobilizes to create a primary political community qualifies for a primary right. In each of these two cases, the group's linguistic relation to other communities is mediated by its self-determining status (or its aspiration to acquire such status), not grounded exclusively in its linguistic identity. Such a community is not purely a linguistic community. A self-determining group agent defines itself against a set of all similar "others," and its right to language (general or special) is primary by virtue of the group's qualification for primary rights. Quebec's linguistic claim, for example, is tied to its claim to self-determination. If this claim changes with time, the constitution of the group will change.

It remains to deal with minority groups that consider the political community they share with the majority to be their primary political community. Under these circumstances, a linguistic community qualifies as a holder of a derivative, and not a primary, right.[44] Identifying who speaks a language does not necessarily define the boundaries of a community that requires the protection of a right to the corresponding language, because the limits of linguistic communities are not imposed by the elements of group constitution associated with the good of language. Elements external to this good (such as rules of political inclusion independent of the good) determine the structure of relationships and the standing of the agent with respect to other agents. There is simply no internal relatedness of linguistic communities to other similar communities imposed solely by the constitutive good of language and regardless of the external political context. Westmounters in Quebec may define their collective good of speaking English against all non-Westmounters, for example, but they clearly do not have the right to language claimed against France, while they can make a convincing case for the right claimed against Quebec or, perhaps, the rest of Canada.[45] The linguistic entitlement of various German-speaking populations in Europe—in Austria and Switzerland, for instance—is "framed" by the political division among and within these territories defined externally to the good of language. The political division makes for specific "others" in each case. Or, the speakers of several very different dialects (as in Croatia) can, but often do not, perceive themselves as having separate claims to language because the structures of the relevant primary political community are shaped by factors external to the good of language. Primary political communities impose the rights structure on language communities, not the other way around. If Anglophone Canadians want to be a separate political community from Anglophones of the United States, it is not the collective good of language that drives their desire to be so constituted. There are so many other features unrelated to the collective good of language that come to play in the formation of primary political communities that it would be gratuitous to claim that language is the constitutive force behind political organization.[46] Linguistic communities are collective agents, but the collective good of language in itself is defined against non-differentiated non-speakers, while, for the purpose of claiming a right to language, membership in the group is defined against others made specific by the political context external to the good. Thus, linguistic rights are not primary.

To further elaborate this claim, let us first consider how claims to linguistic rights can be justified in the case of only two groups, a majority and a minority within one political community. It should be noted that "not-us" for either group is not the rest of the world *simpliciter*. It is not against all of the Francophones of the world that non-Francophone Quebecers would claim the right to language but against Quebec Francophones. "Not-us" is limited for either the majority or the minority to the other *within* the shared political community. What, then, is the constitutive feature of the majority and minority with respect to the other as a group? To make these linguistic communities eligible for primary rights, their constitutive feature needs to be defined with respect only to the good of language in relation to the other.

If a linguistic minority does not advance a self-determination claim, its primary political community is the one it shares with the majority. If the members of the minority were to claim their right to language equal to that of the majority, the claim would be based upon their joint membership in the larger political community. The protection of the good of equal citizenship of the minority and majority members allows the minority to demand the majority's cooperation in the preservation of its minority language. Without the cooperation of the majority, the minority would not have resources to protect its linguistic well-being, and its members demand this cooperation of their fellow-citizens based upon the circumstances of political inclusion in the shared primary political community, such as the ideal of equal citizenship. While the minority's right to language is the minority members' right to the enjoyment of the collective good of language, it is not defined against the majority as a linguistic group but against the majority as an aggregate of individuals with access to a collective good (and a collective interest) similar in kind to that of the minority.

One may object that each of the two groups is a collective agent that qualifies for a group right and that the claims are made by the minority as a group against the majority as a group and vice versa. Since each group is constituted based on the members' shared identity associated with the good of language, in this particular case the linguistic rights appear to be primary. Yet the collective good of language can constitute a community only in some contexts, not regardless of the context. It is only in the particular context of joint membership in the same primary political community that the minority and majority's entitlements to a linguistic right arise. Prior to their inclusion in this political context, they did not have a right. In the case of self-determination, the entitlement to self-determination is prior to the circumstances of the group's inclusion in a particular political arrangement and is claimed against all communities of the same kind. A right to language is claimed only against the group(s) that relate to the group in question in the given political context. Therefore, linguistic communities do not possess features enabling them to be equally free agents based solely on their constitutive feature of shared language regardless of a specific political framework, and they thereby do not qualify for primary group rights. The minority and the majority both have a derivative group right to the preservation of their linguistic communities; their right to language is claimed on the basis of their equal citizenship in the shared primary political community by the members who also share in the collective good of the relevant language.

To find out the entitlements of more than two linguistic communities, we need to determine what group agents are present, how the collective good of language fits with the constitution of each collective agent in relation to others, and what primary political communities provide the framework for their claims. Several agents with the right to language can be compared in terms of how well the larger primary political community satisfies their initial derivative group rights. If one group is given resources for schools, another group comparable in size and circumstances of inclusion may demand similar resources. While a claim is framed in reference to what the other linguistic group received, the right is not asserted based on the relation of mutual limitation of freedom in which these minorities stand to one another. The comparison is rather to the terms another group was able to negotiate with the larger society concerning the status of its individual members both within the group and in relation to the larger society.[47]

Other Minority Rights

Cultural and religious rights are akin to linguistic rights: in the absence of aspirations for its own political community, a minority's claim to the enjoyment of the shared good around which it is organized is based on the relation of its members to non-members within the context of the larger political community it shares with non-members.[48] Given that minority individuals are differentiated from the rest of the citizens by virtue of their participation in the minority group, these rights secure the minority members' equal status in the larger society. A group minority right is claimed against other members of the larger political society on the basis of shared membership in this larger society and not against other collective agents that are similarly situated with respect to the claims the rights in question protect. The collective agent in question does not qualify for a primary moral right, because it does not define itself in terms that allow it to be free equally with other similar agents. The Catholic Church's exemption from anti-sex discrimination legislation, for example, is a group right based on shared ends and rules of acting, but it is a derivative group right that is based on the need for individual Catholics, equal with other members of a state, to have religious freedom and engage in collective actions defined by a shared set of beliefs pertaining to the agency of their religious denomination. Catholics would have this right even if other religious groups claiming special exemptions did not exist in the state.

Not being in a position of equal freedom with other agents does not exempt minority groups from collective responsibility. Collective agents that qualify only for derivative group rights can exhibit free collective action and reasoning and thus can be held responsible for their decisions and actions. If members of a cultural organization decide to have a procession that unintentionally blocks ambulance access to a hospital's emergency room, the ensuing harm to some patients' health is the organization's collective responsibility.

Summing up my position concerning the two types of group rights, the moral status and entitlements of group agents for the purpose of primary rights are defined in relation to those of all other similar agents. Hart's necessary condition for the existence of a moral right is the equal freedom of subjects in a general primary right and, in a special moral right, of subjects and all other agents of the same type. Agents cannot be free if they have no capacity for discursive control. Collective agents can have the capacity for discursive control if and only if their constitution allows them to consider their entitlement in a general relation to all other similar agents, which enables them in principle to be in an equal relationship with these agents. Among themselves, moreover, such groups have the capacity for the mutual recognition of their equal freedom.

All group rights are given to collective agents sharing in the good that the right in question promotes and are claimed against non-members. To determine whether a right is derivative or primary, one must consider how constitutive characteristics of the group in question affect its moral status in relation to other similar agents. Collective agents can have the capacity for discursive control required by primary moral rights if and only if they are in principle capable of acquiring and maintaining an equal relationship to all other similar agents by virtue of their constitution alone and do not require an external authority to shape their membership and relations with non-members.

Groups organized around self-determination define their agency based on the limits of political authority they perceive themselves to be capable of maintaining entirely on the basis of the conditions of the group's internal life, whether the exercise of this authority is realized or only aspired for. The shared good of self-determination around which such a community is organized can be a basis for relationships among such agents based on their equal capacity for freedom, and the corresponding right can be primary. For the right to self-determination to exist, there must be a set of collective agents with similar self-definition and a similar aspiration to control their separate political futures.

Collective goods constitutive of linguistic, religious, and cultural communities do not uniquely designate corresponding collective agents. The boundaries of membership in groups organized around these collective goods are identified by the circumstances of each group's inclusion in its host primary political community. Since this inclusion, external to the corresponding shared good, determines those aspects of the group's constitution that define its status in relation to others, linguistic, religious, and cultural collective agents do not have the capacity for equal freedom required by discursive control. The collective moral rights of these agents are derivative and originate in the moral right of each group's individual members to the protection of a constitutive collective good for the purpose of their equitable inclusion in the larger society. Thus, derivative collective rights mainly serve the purpose of ensuring the equality of citizenship within the same primary political community by supporting the constitution of a minority group for the joint enjoyment of a shared good around which the group is constituted.

We should also remember that introducing group agency into the consideration of collective rights settles the auxiliary question of how to distinguish between derivative moral group rights (linguistic or ethnic rights, for example) and the moral rights individuals possess due to characteristics they share with a set of other individuals (such as the moral right to assistance based on disability): sets of individuals who possess a moral right tied to a shared individual characteristic are not collective agents organized around the characteristic in question, and their corresponding moral rights are neither derivative nor primary collective rights. An individual moral right based on a shared characteristic regardless of the person's inclusion in a group agent (such as a privilege enjoyed by senior citizens) is asserted by the individuals with the characteristic against individuals without the characteristic only on the basis of their equal citizenship in the larger society. It is not claimed based on shared membership in a collective agent (and thus based on a collective good or interest), and it does not generate either a derivative or a primary group right.

Satisfying the exercise of group rights becomes problematic when groups are pitched against their individual members. Should Quebec's Francophones be allowed to send their children to public schools where the school curriculum is taught in English? Such schools are presently designated only for those children whose parents were educated in English in Canada. Or does the right of the Quebecois as a group to preserve French as their language allow them to deny this opportunity to their fellow Francophone citizens? Education in the Welsh language in Wales is a similar case: the native language, dying out due to its prior suppression by the English, is being revived, often against the wishes of English-speaking Welsh families who do not see the value of education in Welsh and prefer to teach their children a foreign language more useful, from the parents' point of view, to the children's future. They see the effort to teach Welsh as a futile nationalist attempt to impose a cultural attribute marginally relevant to their identity.[49] Does the restitution right to correct prior wrongs entitle Welsh nationalists to require that immigrants and native Welsh study the Welsh language in public schools? Moreover, is there a duty on the part of the individual Welsh to preserve their language even if it is beneficial for them to assimilate into the mainstream English linguistic culture?

Let us assume that in a utilitarian calculation the aggregate benefits of linguistic assimilation outweigh the costs of language preservation for individuals; the decision whether the Welsh as a group are to bear the burdens of language preservation or leave it up to individual members to care for their linguistic heritage cannot be justified solely on the basis of this calculation. Any determination about what policy is to be implemented needs to be based on the group preference, which must be determined by means of an appropriate decision procedure. If we consider the Welsh and Quebecois communities as collective agents, we will have a better vantage point for evaluating the claims of linguistic nationalists and considering under what circumstances the Welsh or the Quebecois may decide to abandon education in their language. Individual members will have to bear with the results of collective decision making if it is based on legitimate collective deliberation in accordance with the constitution of the group as a collective agent. If the outcome of this deliberation is that immigrants are to be required to learn Welsh or French, the justification for this decision would be that they have chosen to move to a place where they must live under the constitution of a Welsh or Quebecois collective agent that attaches a great deal of importance to language. The immigrants could, however, have their language rights protected in addition to learning Welsh or French.

The Ontological Status of Group Agents

One may doubt the need to defend the claim that group rights belong to group agents. One may have the same doubt about the claim that self-determination is a primary collective right, that is, a right that belongs to collectives as such. The hesitation to appeal to group agency is usually rooted in a reductionist group ontology. A proponent of this reductionist view argues that groups only have rights because of the individual rights of the members of each group. Even if the reductionist admits that groups have certain interests that are not reducible to the aggregate of individual interests, she would deny that groups actually have an ontological status and existence independent of the individuals that make them up. I agree that group agency supervenes on its individual membership, but this supervenience is more complex than what can be captured by a reductionist view: not just any supervenience generates rights. There are groups that supervene on individual membership but do not possess the capacity for holding moral rights, either independently or in virtue of the rights of individual members.

The refusal to accept realism about the existence of groups may come from a worry that acknowledging the ontological independence of groups assigns to them a moral status equal to that of individuals. On the contrary, attention to group constitution prevents a simplistic treatment of group entitlements and duties as analogous to those of individuals. A realist account works better in explaining different types of group rights; more importantly, it is well-equipped to address the issue of group rights in the transitional and oppressive societies, the political environments that present difficulties for the reductionist. For example, most members of a national group, such as the Chechens, considered the Soviet authority governing them to be illegitimate; most believed that the institutional design of the autonomous republic of Checheno-Ingushetia did not express their group interest in self-determination. Although the Soviet institutions didn't provide the proper environment for the enjoyment of this interest, they emulated a functioning self-determining entity. The rank and file inhabitants of the territory performed many individual and—jointly with other individuals in that territory—group actions that engendered the autonomous unit the existence of which they didn't endorse. These group actions realized the goal of self-determination of the autonomous unit of Checheno-Ingushetia, but not of either Chechnya or Ingushetia. Individuals may have intended to perform the actions that maintained the Soviet institutions to avoid persecution, but they didn't perform them to exercise their group's self-determination. The actions expressed the interest and preferences of the group, but they didn't qualify the group to be entitled to self-determination.

The problem with group interests in oppressive environments is as follows. In group actions prompted by the state, the rank and file members bring about the exercise of self-determination of their political unit, but they do not bring about the enjoyment of the collective good of self-determination that aligns with the shared individual understanding of what constitutes their group interest. Moreover, citizens may believe, as a matter of fact, that participating in the social and political system results in the maintenance of the system as a self-determining entity, but they simply do not endorse this goal.

The reductionist suggests that group interests that generate group entitlements are not reducible to the aggregate of the interests of group members. What interest supports a group's entitlement to the corresponding group right in an oppressive environment? In Checheno-Ingushetia, was it the Chechen people's interest in self-determination or the official interest of Checheno-Ingushetia in self-determination? Both groups supervened on the set of individual members and could have been ascribed group interests independent of the aggregate of their individual members' interests. A reductionist may say that only the group interest in the enjoyment of self-determination that corresponds to the preferences of group members counts. Thus, we should assign the group the capacity for holding the moral right to self-determination only if there exists a shared preference of group members that they enjoy the collective good in question. I agree with the reductionist on this, but her approach is missing an account of how we can identify the state as persisting through time in the *absence* of such a preference, when the majority of citizens do not endorse the enjoyment of self-determination on the terms offered by the state. How does the reductionist account for the continuity of regimes in which a majority or rank and file members do not share in the group interest? If she does so by referring to the continuity of the leaders' plans, or to the continuity of state institutions, would this institutional framework be an ontologically independent entity that expresses group interests and looks after the enjoyment of the corresponding collective goods?

To complicate matters, it could well be the case that the officials themselves act to implement public rules out of fear and not because they believe in their rightness or endorse the institutional group's self-determination. In this case, the day-to-day existence and continuity of an oppressive regime becomes an even greater mystery: no one intends to promote the goals they routinely advance through group actions, but these actions have a corresponding group interest. The group definitely supervenes on its individual members but we cannot give a satisfactory account of how this happens in reductionist terms. Since we need to identify all of a group's interests that supervene over the same set of members in order to consider which ones among them can generate group entitlements, we are committed to some form of realism concerning group ontology. We will be looking at two group interests supervening over the same members engaged in the same actions and holding the same beliefs. We can only avoid confusion if we acknowledge that two group agents exist under these circumstances. This allows us to be careful not to define the group interest associated with the group's entitlement to moral group rights as based exclusively on the manifestation of its elite's views or on the official institutional expression of group identity and the corresponding realization of effective group agency.

Paying attention to shared individual beliefs about group membership and intentions requires us to consider group agency according to the minimal definition of group agency that I put forward. After the existence of group agents and the corresponding group interests in the enjoyment of collective goods constitutive of these group agents is established, we can determine which rights would protect legitimate group interests. Not all interests that are not reducible to individual interests qualify groups for moral rights. According to the mechanism I employ in characterizing group entitlements, group interests belong to ontologically significant entities. However, this mechanism disqualifies those interests that are not supported by properly formed individual attitudes: such interests do not ground moral entitlements for the groups that hold them. Hence, my account can sort out complex cases of supervenience and not make mistakes about group entitlements. It is not more complicated than is necessary for ascribing rights to groups, and thus it may satisfy the reductionist critic.

Practical Issues Associated with Primary Group Moral Rights

This chapter classifies the valid rights claims of various groups by differentiating types of collectives. In this section I consider three issues connected to the application of this classification. First, it needs to be specified by what criteria we are to identify groups that are holders of primary collective rights. Second, we need to clarify how individual and primary collective rights can be reconciled. And, finally, however clear a conceptual distinction between primary and derivative group rights seems to be we need to consider whether there any real differences between the application of primary and derivative collective rights in practice.

The idea of group rights is often criticized due to skepticism that satisfactory criteria can be developed for locating entities entitled to such rights. Julius Grey, for example, claims that collective subjects are not identifiable unless there is a unilateral assertion of membership or some arbitrary process is employed to identify them.[50] But considering the constitution of group agents with respect to their corresponding shared goods not only solves the problem of identifying rights-holders but also makes it possible to differentiate holders of primary collective rights from holders of derivative collective rights.

Looking at the self-definition and goals of a group agent and its relations to outsiders allows us to determine whether the group qualifies for a primary or derivative collective right. Groups that qualify for the right to self-determination can be identified by the kinds of demands they advance and the sets of beliefs that characterize their collective actions.[51] If a group possesses a political culture of self-determination and its members identify with this culture, the group qualifies for holding primary rights. Quebec considers itself a national group with the corresponding moral right to self-determination. Francophone citizens of Manitoba want to receive education in French and do not aspire to be self-determining. The former qualifies for a prima facie moral right to self-determination, while the latter qualifies only for the derivative right of a linguistic minority group. I will deal more with this issue in the next chapter, in which I provide a pragmatic definition of nationhood.

It may be objected that sometimes groups may argue for linguistic or cultural rights but not self-determination because they are too small or scattered to make a claim for the latter, whereas they can pursue the former. In this case, the political calculation of whether to pursue self-determination would seem to influence the philosophical issue of the category of right the group should or does have. I do not argue that those who claim linguistic rights are never self-determining agents; this is simply false. However, group claims important in the context of group rights are relevant only insofar as they *constitute* the corresponding group agents. A group agent constituted as a self-determining group may settle for less than self-determination, but this is not to say that it does not have a moral right to self-determination. If its members define the group as a self-determining group but claim only rights to language or culture, they are constituted as a self-determining agent (for how else would we know that their claim to language rights is not their highest aspiration, but a compromise?).

In all likelihood, the group will pursue self-determination if it can, since it is organized around this idea. If there is no indication that the group defines itself in terms of self-determination, the group qualifies only for a derivative right. Finally, at some point, a group may lose the features that previously qualified it for self-determination, because it simply may not be able to perform the functions required to constitute itself as the right kind of group. A group with very few members may not be able to operate as an agent capable of equal freedom. In this case, a linguistic or cultural claim may truly reflect its constitution. The group may be entitled to some symbolic recognition of its past, but such a group in transition does not qualify for the right to self-determination. If a group has lost its capacity to self-determination due to some prior deprivation by another group, its members need to be compensated, but the group may not be able to regain its capacity for self-determination and may cease being a group that can qualify for a primary right. My approach, by maintaining the distinction between different types of group moral rights, helps to clarify the entitlements of the transitional group.

Voluntarism in defining which group agents qualify for the right to self-determination is avoided, first, because we are looking for relatively stable defining beliefs. Such beliefs are stable in part because they are about relationships with others, often involving long-drawn-out conflicts that require regulation on the basis of group rights. Second, voluntarism is avoided by insisting on a search for the "objectified" beliefs of the corresponding political culture. Although at any given time there has to be a critical mass of individuals who identify with and support the institutions that have grown out of the political culture, continuity is assured, because we are looking for a political culture continuously and jointly practiced by its individual members.[52]

Now let's turn to the second question, regarding how individual and primary collective rights may be reconciled. In the case of derivative rights, individual members of a group are also members of the larger community that offers them some protection against the group (provided the larger society protects individual rights; if not, the problem lies not with group rights but with an oppressive state). On the other hand, the primary moral right to self-determination may appear dangerous, because the protection it gives to groups may enable them to infringe upon the freedom of their individual members to promote the collective good. The objection here is that, at most, human rights can be protected if the right to self-determination is understood as deriving from the rights of the group's members.

We can construe human rights as a fundamental condition for the exercise of collective agency of the kind that qualifies groups for primary moral rights. First, if basic human rights are not respected, it is often hard to even identify a group as a collective agent, owing to the difficulty that the group members face in expressing their beliefs and maintaining everyday group functions. Only after the basic human rights of the members are satisfied and they can function in a minimally normal political and social context can we identify the constitution of the group with sufficient certainty and employ the idea of group rights. Moreover, if group agents are properly constituted around the shared good of self-determination, a territory acquires identifiable structures of authority associated with group membership, which should work to diminish lawlessness, thereby reducing the causes of human rights abuses and providing the conditions for a political environment of the type necessary for the respect of human rights. A territory that encompasses warring factions or is governed by a corrupt government that does not enjoy the support of its citizens does not contain a group agent properly constituted around the shared good of self-determination. (The problem of detecting and identifying group agents in non-democratic or oppressive societies is beyond the scope of this chapter, and I will discuss a cautious approach to the composition of transitional or non-democratic societies to avoid premature judgments about group entitlements in Chapter 4.)

Second, the primary right to self-determination can be demonstrated to be limited by human rights. Should a group that qualifies for the primary right to self-determination possess a state of its own, it is prevented from abusing the rights of its members as much as any other international agent is bound to respect the standard of human rights in accordance with international law. And if the group exercises its self-determination within a federal state, other self-determining groups within the state may assist the international community in assuring the group's compliance with the standard of human rights, both because they would like to improve the state's international standing and also because the group's actions may not be in tune with the norms of behavior agreed upon by all group members of the state. The condition of equal freedom grounds a special right of group members within each state to require from one another equal compliance with the rules of membership in the state, including respect for human rights as the norm derived from international law. Therefore, the primary right to self-determination does not weaken the chances that individual rights will be protected or the means of protecting them.

Moving on to the last question of this section, although differentiating between collective agents with the capacity for primary and derivative collective rights seems to be conceptually important, we need to compare self-determination to other group rights in terms of the type of treatment that satisfies it. Often, the right to self-government is offered in answer to national groups' claims to self-determination. But giving groups a say concerning some governmental policies is also used to satisfy a number of derivative group rights, such as linguistic, religious, cultural, or ethnic rights. For example, one of the recommendations of the Congress of Local and Regional Authorities of Europe to the Council of Ministers,[53] in accordance with the European Charter for Regional or Minority Languages, encourages the preservation of minorities' identity in two ways. First, where minority populations have their own administrative subdivisions, they have to be given adequate competences to protect the minority's identity. Second, where the appropriate administrative divisions are absent, the congress specifies that they ought to be established to afford minorities effective protection. Territorial boundaries should be marked in consultation with the population to prevent the dispersal of minorities. In most cases, however, minorities are required to learn official languages. Article 3 of the Spanish Constitution, for example, states that it is the duty of every Spaniard to know Castilian, the official language of Spain.

If provisions for the protection of minorities afford the minorities the powers of administrative rule ranging as far as local self-government rights, do these provisions answer the claims of those minorities who also demand self-determination? We can determine the justice of offering self-government as a way of satisfying self-determination claims only after we clarify what the right to self-determination means, both for the members of the group and for outsiders. We must consider how the meaning of "self-determination" differs, if at all, from "self-government," and what aspects of individual members' well-being and a group's constitution are attended to by the protection afforded to the group through an autonomy (or self-government) settlement.[54]

Self-determination is the capacity of a group to determine its future political status. Self-government, in contrast to self-determination, requires a group to make and apply laws for itself within the parameters of an already given political status. Self-determination in most cases includes self-governing aspects, but if a group is not in control of its status after having relinquished certain powers and prerogatives, it is not self-determining.

While self-government rights are the most progressive and adequate of all possible rights for the protection of national minorities, national groups' securing of self-government rights does not preclude a situation wherein some national groups are associated with the state while others have self-government rights as a means of relating to the main nation or nations of the state. In such a case, the minorities do not have equal freedom as defined in terms appropriate for discursive control, and it cannot be said that their right to self-determination is satisfied. Self-government, while providing for mutually reduced influence between the state authorities and the minority, is a right *in relation to* the state, to which the power of controlling the group's political status ultimately belongs. Self-determination requires that the group possess a status with respect to its control over its political future equal to that of other national groups with which it shares the state space, including the majority. Self-government that is not accompanied by the recognition of self-determination claims, then, does not give a minority group enough discursive control to maintain its equal freedom and cannot satisfy a primary moral right. Unless minority groups that claim the right to self-determination freely opt for self-government and minority rights as a way of satisfying their claim, these modes of accommodation do not satisfy the right to self-determination.

A self-determining group does not necessarily have to have the highest level of self-government, so long as those powers it does not have are ceded voluntarily and can in principle be taken back. Countries in the European Union, for example, have relinquished many significant functions associated with full self-government, but they still remain self-determining. Canadian provinces, on the other hand, are not self-determining, although they have a very high level of self-government. With the exception of Quebec, none of the provinces wants to be self-determining, at least for the time being. Instead, they locate their self-determining capacity at the level of the federal government, which represents the Canadian nation. Although Quebec has self-governing powers even greater than those of other provinces—for example, it has control over immigration—it does not perceive self-governing powers per se to be a sufficient expression of its self-determination.

Although a substate group that is self-governing is not self-determining unless it also has a say about its political future, it is also not fair to say that a group is self-determining only if it has a constitutional and international right to secede. Determining one's own political status does not straightforwardly imply the right to secession; rather, it requires a group to be able to control its political space in relation to other similar groups. I will argue that there is an essential connection between nationhood and self-determination but not between statehood and either nationhood or self-determination in Chapter 3.

There is a conceptual difference between individual and group rights, but could the measures aimed at preserving an individual human right to nationality approximate the protection that the right to national self-determination can give a group in practice? That is, can a state show equal respect for citizens' national belonging merely by complying with the requirements of the human right to nationality? As they are listed in the Universal Declaration of Human Rights, human rights include equality rights, legal rights, mobility rights, and basic freedoms.[55] Article 15 of the declaration introduces a right to nationality. It states:

(1) Everyone has the right to a nationality.
(2) No one shall be arbitrarily deprived of his nationality nor denied the right to change his nationality.

A set of people who share the same nationality and are protected by the individual right to nationality may not even be a group as defined in terms of collective agency. For example, acknowledging the right of those Anglophones in Quebec who perceive themselves as Canadian not to be discriminated against on the basis of their national identity is not the same as acknowledging that the people of Westmount, a fraction of all Anglophone Quebecers and a group that toyed with the idea of declaring its independence from Quebec, are a national group or that they have a right to self-determination. If the Westmounters are to be granted a group right of any kind, it will not be based on their individual members' rights to nationality. A group right may be given to them based on the members' preferences with respect to what they want for their group, and thus based on a determination of whether the corresponding collective agent exists—a consideration external to the human right to nationality. However, the right to nationality may *seem* to give a group of people who do form a national group the right to self-determination. For example, we may say that recognizing the right of each individual Albanian in Kosovo to nationality amounts to the recognition of the group's political identity as a self-determining people. The protection of group members, however, will have to be translated into the protection of group preferences, which does not fall under the right to nationality.

Finally, I have shown that the shared good of self-determination, unlike the shared goods of culture, language or religion, provides a precondition for the equal freedom of collective agents and can signify a corresponding primary collective moral right. But can the protection of the linguistic, religious and cultural rights of minorities sufficiently address the conditions of their membership in their host states, accommodating them fairly in such a way as to satisfy minorities' claims to self-determination without adjusting their political status? Although the mechanisms of minority rights that are not associated with self-determination can help us to identify and solve the problems of the corresponding minorities, they are not adequate to satisfy the aspirations of minorities to determine their own political status. Groups organized around the shared good of self-determination can be more complex than other minority groups: self-determination can be claimed by a multi-ethnic, multicultural, and multilingual group. Inhabitants of Tatarstan, for example, conceived of themselves as a multicultural nation at the time of their referendum on sovereignty.[56] To comprise its combined linguistic, ethnic, and cultural groups as members of the same community, Tatarstan's identity as a group agent needs to go beyond each group identity: it includes the encompassing political identity that unites all the groups. As a collective agent, such a group is organized around the aspirations and goals that members share for the group as a whole that they do not associate with any other aspect of their identity. Thus, ethnic, linguistic, and cultural minority rights address only fragmented aspects of the shared identity of members of a multiethnic or multilingual group that is also organized around the shared good of self-determination. Supporting the rights of ethnic, linguistic, and cultural minorities in Tatarstan without supporting Tatrstan's self-determination would have failed to adequately address its citizens' membership in the Russian Federation. Groups organized around self-determination can also have similar cultures, like Moldova and Romania, but they are, at least at present, different groups organized around the collective good of self-determination. Linguistic, cultural, and ethnic claims would, therefore, inadequately represent either Moldova's or Romania's interests as a group agent.

The democratic character of the rules governing political life in a multinational state in and of themselves would not allow members to be equal discourse participants in matters concerning their group agency. Membership in the larger state would not satisfy the minority members' individual expectations unless it also provided acceptable terms of inclusion for all of them as members of their national collective agency. Their equal inclusion, then, requires institutional and legal guarantees of the conditions for equal participation in discourse for their group, and thus a chance for equal freedom with other similar groups. Since most nations and states do not match, the idea of a self-determining people is important in the context of belonging to a multinational state. Membership in such a state is, therefore, determined in part by how the state accommodates the self-determination claims of its national groups and thus how it creates conditions for equal status in discourse for all such groups.

Self-Determination as a Moral Right and Its Benefits

Since the benefits brought to groups by substate self-determination are different from those of independent statehood, the challenge associated with my approach to self-determination is to demonstrate that substate self-determination brings tangible benefits to national groups comparable to the benefits of independent statehood. One may argue that there aren't any non-trivial benefits of self-determination—benefits beyond the satisfaction of vanity preferences for one's own flag or Olympic team. Moreover, if groups express their preference for attaining a certain status, this does not mean they deserve to receive it. If self-determination is not a substantial good, it may be morally justifiable to "level down" by taking self-determination from those groups that enjoy it now rather than "leveling up" by institutionalizing a right to self-determination for all groups who desire it. I provide a two-stage explanation of what benefits self-determination can bring to groups and their members. In this section, I consider group aspirations as they relate to the group's constitution and demonstrate that self-determination is a tangible good that deserves promotion through the moral right to self-determination. I explain how such a right can be formulated in Chapter 5. The modified right to self-determination I introduce does not require the acquisition of independent statehood for the exercise of self-determination. This means that minority substate national groups are entitled to self-determination equal to that of other national groups in their host multinational state. In this way, their status is, most likely, "leveled up." For the formerly state-controlling majorities in multinational states, however, this is a form of leveling down. The elevation of the status of other substate national groups will mean that the majority has less power to control them. We need to specify under what circumstances the effects of substate self-determination on the life of the group can be considered comparable to those of independent statehood despite being institutionally different. And if substate self-determination brings significant benefits to groups but these benefits are not as significant as independent statehood, we must explain why this situation is acceptable.

It may be suggested, for example, that presently groups benefit from self-determination only if they either acquire a mononational state with all the privileges of international status or control a multinational state as if it belongs to them and thus disadvantage others. I argue in Chapter 6 that the substantial benefits that self-determination brings can be achieved while respecting the entitlement to self-determination of all groups living in the territory of a political unit. In this section, I only state what these benefits are in relation to the constitutive good of self-determination and what about this good makes these benefits significant even if self-determination is exercised in its modified form.

One may also argue that an approach like mine that values and encourages the preservation of group intentions creates groups where they could have been eliminated. I will leave aside the question whether it is feasible to redesign groups' constitutive features so as to avoid unwanted types of group mobilization. Even if it is feasible, and a group can be eventually redirected to organize around a different type of shared good, in the process of transitioning a group to a different type of collective agency we cannot avoid recognizing what the group was first. We simply must determine this before attempting to redesign its constitution. Once we have recognized and acknowledged the initial form of group members' relationships in their mode of functioning as group members, however, the issue of their moral entitlement immediately comes up. The same issue will arise if we decide that only some groups organized around self-determination are entitled to enjoy the corresponding benefits. Unless a change in group members' shared beliefs takes place, we will still be faced with the residual problem of regulating the relations of those agents who do not relinquish their hope of achieving or maintaining their self-determining status.

Furthermore, if we decide to "level down" and deprive *all* groups of the enjoyment of the right to self-determination (assuming this is feasible), unless this results in the creation of a worldwide political community that is fairly homogenous, we will have to decide who controls the political future of each society and on what grounds, and the problem of regulating relations among sub-units will inevitably arise. Thus, we cannot avoid settling the question whether self-determination is a substantial shared good such that a group's interest in its enjoyment requires a corresponding moral right.

As I established in this chapter, self-determination is a constitutive feature of a particular kind of group agents. Self-determination, as the defining feature of such groups, is the capacity of a group to be entirely determined by the conditions of its internal life, or to have control over its political future. Although this capacity does not need to be realized perfectly (some aspects of group life can be influenced by non-members or ceded by the group), groups of this kind are in a category distinct from others: they are capable of being in relation of equal freedom with similarly constituted group agents. That being organized around self-determination provides group agents with the capacity to hold a primary right is not sufficient, of course, to grant groups the enjoyment of the corresponding right. I maintain that a moral right to self-determination exists based on the corresponding constitution of group agents. First, I will establish eligibility for the right that groups hold in relation to similar agents. Second, I will maintain that the argument for the entitlement to self-determination has effect only if collective agents organized around self-determination are to be preserved. I will defend their right to survival both in relation to other agents and from the point of view of the equal treatment of individual citizens in a multinational state. Finally, since I defend the meaning of national group membership to their members as a question of preference, I argue that individual preference for the preservation of a certain national membership is not arbitrary.

To begin with, then, let us recall why self-determination is a shared good. Self-determination designates the mode of functioning of certain types of groups. It generates a corresponding set of second-order beliefs and aspirations, as well as members' cooperative interdependent actions. Is functioning in this way—being a group whose boundaries demarcate the meaningful limits of authority for the group's members—a moral fact? While the group's relationship to self-determination may be seen in purely descriptive terms—being a self-determining agent implies functioning in a certain way, like being a biped implies moving by walking—there exists a normative connection between agency of particular kind and equality among agents of this kind expressed in the right to self-determination, as in the right of a biped not to be prevented from walking if other bipeds are allowed to walk. The bounds of group agents are historically contingent, but the norms that ought to regulate their relations and prescribe their entitlements are moral. As I discussed in the introduction, sociological and normative realities are not incompatible. Refusing benefits to some groups constituted around self-determination while providing them to other similarly constituted groups amounts to morally unjust treatment. The moral rights of self-determining groups are determined in their mutual relations. Self-determination as a primary right cannot be consistently afforded to some and denied to others. Even if we decide to compensate groups that for pragmatic (or other) reasons cannot be granted the right, this compensation will be based on an acknowledgment of their entitlement.

One may object that even if groups constituted around self-determination are morally entitled to self-determination, to be able to claim it, they must first be morally entitled to survive. Groups are not ontologically prior to individuals, and the moral need for their survival is not immediately obvious. Why should collective agents organized around self-determination be preserved? I advance the pragmatic argument that groups will resist attempts by outsiders to erode their constitutive features in Chapter 5. In this chapter, I am not concerned with pragmatics but with moral entitlements. If it is possible to influence the constitutive beliefs of group members so that they willingly and freely accept the change, this will alter the character of the group agent; if this experience is successfully repeated with a number of groups, it will reduce the number of self-determination claims they advance. (An ideal and presently unattainable solution of constructing one world community devoid of national allegiances would resolve the problem of the right to self-determination, although such a community would still be self-determining in a non-relational sense.) However, if the group members do not accept the change willingly, they will continue to try to exercise their effective agency, and the pressure put on them to alter their constitutive features and to suppress their attempts to mobilize along self-determining lines will have to come from non-members, the members of other group agents. The primary right to self-determination establishes how the relations of agents of a particular kind have to be regulated on a principled basis. It can be formulated as a conditional right: if a set of group agents organized around self-determination is present, they are equally entitled to preserve their constitutive good. Thus, they are allowed to exercise their collective agency within the restrictions imposed on them by the fact of the existence of other similar agents with the same entitlement. An attempt by one or more group agents organized around the shared good of self-determination to influence another group agent similarly constituted in order to prevent this agent from the reasonable enjoyment of self-determination would violate the agents' equality established by the right to self-determination. Preserving some groups constituted around self-determination and not others is not just.

Another angle of approach to the moral right of groups to survival and consequently self-determination is the benefits group members receive from self-determination. One might argue that if members' well-being is protected without self-determination, it is acceptable not to give a group this benefit, even if it is organized around self-determination. That membership in their own group is important to the well-being of members is argued extensively by Kymlicka, Raz, Gans, and other scholars discussed in Chapter 1. Self-determination is a shared good for a particular type of group. Can members of a group organized around self-determination be made to join another group that shares the good of self-determination without imposing an undue burden upon them? Kymlicka shows it is unreasonable to ask an individual to make such a transition, due to the difficulty that normally accompanies it. I think that we can, on the basis of equal respect for individuals, consider the question of surrendering group membership not as one of possibility but as one of preference. If members of one group can become members of another but do not wish to, their preference ought to be respected. The proper maintenance of group agency through the recognition of their preferred mode of mobilization associated with the shared good of their choice creates a basis for individual and group self-respect. This supports the moral right to self-determination only if the members' preference can be accorded weight as a non-arbitrary preference.

Are group members' preferences for self-determination for their particular community as arbitrary as, say, the flavor preference for chocolate over vanilla is? I would argue that they are not, first because arbitrary preferences are preferences regarding access to goods that are equally available (this is what makes these preferences arbitrary), whereas the option of self-determination is not available to most groups aspiring to be self-determining, and thus when it comes to self-determination they are not really allowed to have a preference that might be deemed arbitrary. The flavor analogy here would need to be adjusted: imagine that the chocolate preference of only some chocolate lovers was satisfied, while the rest were given a list of choices that did not include chocolate. The flavors per se have no moral weight; it is the opportunity to choose any of the available flavors that matters. While having a preference is often a matter of taste, the moral aspect of this experience lies in being allowed to have choices and to express preferences concerning taste. Thus, being given an option to assimilate into another self-determining group is not equal to being permitted to remain within a self-determining group, because only some groups are granted the latter option.

The arbitrary preference examples are not analogous to the case of the preference for self-determination also because the options in arbitrary preference examples, such as two flavors of ice cream, satisfy needs of the same kind. If the choice minority members face is between self-determination and other minority rights, such as linguistic rights, these two types of entitlement do not satisfy needs or preferences of the same kind, as I have demonstrated in this chapter. So even assuming self-determination is among the choices groups are offered, which it is not always, the choice between the right to self-determination or other minority rights is not analogous to the choice between two flavors. Then an argument that the refusal to accept the substitution of a similar good, in the event of a "shortage" of the preferred good, is arbitrary does not work for the substitution of minority rights for the enjoyment of self-determination: the option for substitution is different in nature from the denied choice. Therefore, the individual preference for one's own group's self-determination is not an arbitrary preference.

Self-Determination as Beneficial to Group Agents of the Required Kind

My analysis in the chapters to come will clarify the ways in which facilitating the functioning of group agents can limit the destabilizing effects of their claims to self-determination. I suggest that a number of self-determining groups can be accommodated within one state so long as they receive equal recognition of their status. One may object that self-determination in my equality solution will be meaningless, because the "reduced" self-determination I propose makes its attainment less attractive for groups. Thus, while self-determination, if legalized in the way I suggest, may bring some legitimate benefits to national groups, these benefits will not be significant, as my proposal severely limits the ways in which groups can benefit (and presently often do benefit) from their self-determination, such as the full control of the state apparatus—even if this means disadvantaging other groups in the state. However, historically prominent ways of benefiting from self-determination may not be the only way to benefit from self-determination. Groups that benefit from self-determination unjustly do not exercise their freedom properly, in accordance with their moral right.

One may ask what group members will be able to do if granted substate self-determination that they otherwise could not do in a democratic state that respects minority rights. If a democratic state has a principled basis for respecting minority rights, it will include the good of self-determination in the set of shared goods the enjoyment of which qualifies individuals for the enjoyment of the corresponding group rights within the state. This state will include self-determination rights (where self-determination is not considered equivalent to sovereignty) in its list of minority rights and thus will treat national minorities fairly by allowing them to control their political future within the state. Allowing the enjoyment of self-determination to substate national groups makes membership in a multinational state more equitable and just for their members and enhances the legitimacy of such a state. In a state with a national minority, for example, government decisions apply to the minority only if the state's government represents the minority in a just way. A national group's members' well-being in the larger state is diminished by the state's refusal to acknowledge them as a group organized around self-determination. If their right to self-determination is not recognized, they are likely to perceive their membership in the larger state as unequal to that of the majority. Since individuals' beliefs about identity and membership are tied to their group status, failure to recognize their entitlement to self-determination violates the freedom of individual members by disregarding their preferences concerning group membership without providing alternatives.

While a substate option for the exercise of self-determination "downgrades" self-determination from its current association with sovereignty, it is better than the status quo. State institutions will have to be organized so as to treat all national groups on an equal basis, and no group will be able to control the state to privilege its interest over that of other groups. This is a significant benefit for all substate groups. Minorities that were formerly denied self-determination in any form will benefit from the elevation of their status; the majority may perceive its status as being demoted, but this "demotion" allows the members of the majority to exercise their group freedom correctly and increases the stability of multinational states.

Of course, even if norms are formulated and promulgated, this does not guarantee that all group agents will abide by them: they may opt to profit from self-determination by oppressing others. History suggests that it is possible that one group or a few groups will dominate the world landscape. But this is precisely why moral norms regulating self-determination ought to be formulated. Moreover, the constitution of group agency is partly supported through public discourse, and it involves reasoning and justifications. As Buchanan suggests, the mere presence of moral norms supporting legal rules will have a positive effect on the behavior of group agents.

In this chapter, I have considered how to justify the group moral entitlement to self-determination. In Chapters 5 and 6, I discuss the set of advantages allowable under the universal right to self-determination as well as pragmatic benefits of self-determination and how to achieve them legitimately without privileging the interests of one group over those of others within the same territory. I explain why majorities may be motivated to comply if a proposal like mine is implemented in Chapter 5 and consider why "equality within a state" is still self-determination in Chapter 6.

Notes

1. An argument defending the distinction between primary and derivative rights that appears in this chapter was first published in Anna Moltchanova, "Collective agents and group moral rights," *The Journal of Political Philosophy*: 17(1), (2009), 23–46, reprinted by permission of the publisher: Wiley and Sons Ltd.
2. For example, James A. Graff argues that individual human rights alone can justify the creation of ethnoculturally based sovereign states or self-governing entities, while Michael Hartney maintains that the idea of collective rights is not conducive to clear thinking and that the rights of individual members of communities to the preservation or protection of their communities suffice to defend those communities' interests. James A. Graff, "Human Rights, Peoples, and the Right to Self-Determination," in *Group Rights*, ed. J. Baker (Toronto: University Toronto Press, 1994), p. 213; Michael Hartney, "Some Confusions Concerning Collective Rights," in *The Rights of Minority Cultures*, ed. Will Kymlicka (Oxford: Oxford University Press, 1995), p. 221.
3. I do not discuss groups like business corporations, trade unions, parties, or families.
4. Leslie Green, "Two Views of Collective Rights," *Canadian Journal of Law and Jurisprudence* 4, no. 2 (July 1991).
5. Thanks to James Nickel for bringing to my attention the issue of incommensurable types of various collective agents.
6. Leif Wenar offers an extended framework for the classification of rights that goes beyond the dichotomy of the "will" and "interest" conceptions of rights. "The Nature of Rights," in *Philosophy and Public Affairs 33*, no. 3 (Summer 2005). He argues that even the combination of the two accounts is not exhaustive of the incidents that qualify as rights. For the purpose of this paper, I do not need to extend my consideration beyond the incidents covered by the will and interest theories. This paper is about the classification of the moral rights of groups, and the longstanding debate between the will and interest approaches of rights exemplifies a special status of moral rights—it deals with the entitlement warranted by individuals' standing in relation to one another mediated by the system of social rules. Wenar's scope of consideration is broader—he extends his approach to all types of rights (e.g. legal and customary, not only moral) as they are understood in common language use. Since I am dealing with the justifications for moral rights and the two approaches cover the core justifications of rights properly

related to the status ascription, I do not need to go beyond the range of incidents covered by the two approaches.

7. Hartney, "Some Confusions Concerning Collective Rights," p. 210.
8. As Seumas Miller argues, collective (what he calls "social") action, including discourse, is not just any interdependent action: the existence of second-order beliefs about the beliefs of others that also serve as partial reasons for acting can characterize an openly hostile action. Although being based on shared collective ends and governed by a set of public rules are both important conditions for collective action, Miller characterizes social actions more broadly as actions performed in accordance with social forms, such as conventions, social norms, institutions, and social groups. See *Social Action: A Teleological Account* (Cambridge: Cambridge University Press, 2001), p. 6 and Chapter 2.
9. Philip Pettit, *A Theory of Freedom: From the Psychology to the Politics of Agency* (Oxford: Oxford University Press, 2001), p. 116.
10. Christopher McMahon, *Collective Rationality and Collective Reasoning* (Cambridge: Cambridge University Press, 2001), p. 40.
11. To be what he calls an "effective agent," a group ideally has to possess the capacity to formulate its goals, to recognize and follow norms, and to act and evaluate outcomes. On the conception of effective group agency and the relation of identity and agency, see James W. Nickel, ' Group Identity and Group Rights,' in *Ethnicity and Group Rights*, ed. Ian Shapiro and Will Kymlicka, NOMOS 39 (New York: New York University Press, 1997), pp. 235–56.
12. Carol C. Gould "Group rights and social ontology," pp. 43–57, *Groups and Group Rights* eds. Christine Sistare, Larry May, and Leslie Francis; (University Press of Kansas, 2001), pp. 44–45.
13. For a discussion of this phenomenon see Moore, *The Ethics of Nationalism*, p. 106.
14. It can also be the case that in some context speakers of language L have individual rights and in other—group rights; we need to see the context in which we are considering the benefits and the corresponding duties as far as a set of individuals is concerned.
15. I agree with Denise Réaume that the correct approach to a group depends upon the constitutional structure of the group. See "Common-Law Constructions of Group Autonomy: A Case Study," in *Ethnicity and Group Rights*, ed. Ian Shapiro and Will Kymlicka, NOMOS 39 (New York: New York University Press, 1997), pp. 257–89.
16. For example, if we consider the Welsh community as a collective agent, we will have a better vantage point for evaluating the claims of linguistic nationalists and considering under what circumstances the Welsh may decide to abandon their language. Individual members of the community have to bear with the results of collective decision making based on legitimate collective deliberation in accordance with the constitution of the agent.
17. H. L. A. Hart, "Are There Any Natural Rights?" *Philosophical Review* 64, no. 2 (April 1955): pp. 182, 178.
18. Ibid., p. 185.
19. Ibid., p. 190.
20. The tension between the will and interest accounts of rights does not present a problem for collective agents. I will nevertheless briefly consider how a "contractarian" view of rights based on equal freedom applies to individual moral recipients that lack the fully developed or present capacity for agency in order to demonstrate the importance of equality of status within the scope of the right in question. It may be argued that compliance with moral rules required for the treatment of incomplete agents (such as animals) is owed not to them but to other agents, because the members of a society have the right to hold other members who are capable of freedom responsible for breaching moral rules that they have all reasonably accepted as members of the group. In this case, the rights of incomplete agents become merely a figure of speech. A stronger claim, however, is that the rights of incomplete agents can be ascribed in the areas in which their moral status can be compared to that of full agents. Regardless of who executes rights on behalf of incomplete agents, the freedom of full agents can be limited in relevant respects. Animals, for example, do not have a right to go to elementary school,

but they do have a right not to be treated cruelly or killed needlessly. Although the scope their right covers is highly limited, in relevant respects the equality of status of the agents is preserved.

21. It should be noted that in some cases, since collective agents are constituted through the interactions of their members, we may not be able to verify the constitution and intentions of an oppressed group: it is conceivable that when oppression is absent, group members will change them if they are allowed to freely express them.
22. Pettit, *Theory of Freedom*, p. 104.
23. Ibid., p. 67.
24. Ibid., p. 70.
25. Joseph Raz, *Morality of Freedom* (Oxford: Clarendon Press, 1988), p. 208.
26. Leslie Green, "Two Views of Collective Rights," p. 327.
27. Bhikhu Parekh, *Rethinking Multiculturalism: Cultural Diversity and Political Theory* (Cambridge, MA: Harvard University Press, 2000), pp. 213–19; Michael McDonald, "The Personless Paradigm," *University of Toronto Law Journal* 37, no. 2 (Spring 1987): 223.
28. Denise Réaume, "Individuals, Groups, and Rights to Public Goods," *The University of Toronto Law Journal* 38, no. 1 (Winter 1988): 17; Denise Réaume, "The Group Right to Linguistic Security: Whose Right, What Duties?" in *Group Rights*, ed. Judith Baker (Toronto: University of Toronto Press, 1991), p. 120.
29. Brian Barry, *Culture and Equality: An Egalitarian Critique of Multiculturalism* (Cambridge, MA: Harvard University Press, 2001), p. 113.
30. He points out, for example, that Walzer would not be able to account for 20 percent of "Arab Israelis." Ibid., p. 137.
31. Ruth Rubio-Marin distinguishes between instrumental language rights, which are individual in character, and non-instrumental language rights, which are collective. See "Language Rights: Exploring the Competing Rationales," in *Language Rights and Political Theory*, eds. Will Kymlicka and Alan Patten (Oxford: Oxford University Press, 2003), p. 53.
32. On the impossibility of linguistic neutrality, see Will Kymlicka, *Multicultural Citizenship*, p. 111.
33. Ibid., p. 56n.
34. Moreover, does the right to be educated in French in Manitoba belong to individual Francophone Manitobans (although it is a group right to a collective good that cannot be exercised unless there is a sufficient number of Francophone children present in a given area)? See the Canadian Charter of Rights and Freedoms, article 23.
35. Réaume, "Group Right to Linguistic Security," p. 120.
36. I assume here that the allocation of sports facilities is fair across various sports and that the field problem cannot be solved by allocating more funds to the game of soccer.
37. Denise G. Réaume, "Common-Law Constructions of Group Autonomy: A Case Study," in *Ethnicity and Group Rights*, ed. Ian Shapiro and Will Kymlicka, NOMOS 39 (New York: New York University Press, 1997), pp. 257–89: 276.
38. A group can opt for a guarantee from some other group within whose territory it resides that its self-determining status will be respected, but if the group is to remain self-determining, this situation requires a guarantee that its capacity for self-determination can be preserved, such as an agreement that allows the group unilaterally to take back the powers it has relinquished. Even in such an extreme case, the group's understanding of self-determination is political and territorial, because it merely delegates the tasks of maintaining these aspects of its existence to another group, while retaining ultimate control over its political future.
39. I do not entertain the possibility of extraterrestrial intelligent life capable of political organization, and I do not consider human moral obligations to the environment and the animal world in this book.
40. Archie Brown, for example, finds that a useful conception of political culture considers it as that part of culture that bears relevance to politics, while not only laws and formal institutions but also behavior patterns are excluded from the scope of culture. See Archie Brown

"Conclusions," in *Political Culture and Communist Studies*, ed. Archie Brown (London: MacMillan, 1984), p. 155. Stephen White offers a definition of political culture that includes behavior. According to him, political culture is "the attitudinal behavioural matrix within which the political system is located." Quoted in Brown, *Political Culture and Communist Studies*, p. 6. I exclude both behavior and political institutions from the notion of political culture.

41. See Allen Buchanan, *Justice, Legitimacy, and Self-Determination*, p. 69–70; David Miller, "In Defence of Nationality," *Journal of Applied Philosophy* 10, no. 1 (1993): 3–16; and Miller, *On Nationality*.
42. The concept of rival and nested nationalities is developed in Miller's "Nationality in Divided Societies," in *Citizenship and National Identity* (Cambridge: Polity Press, 2000), pp. 114–117.
43. Réaume, "The Group Right to Linguistic Security," p. 127.
44. I discuss minority groups within liberal states here, for the existence of collective agents in nondemocratic societies cannot be confirmed with certainty given the lack of political expression permitted in these societies.
45. Should they legitimately claim the right to self-determination, the context will not matter for the initial determination of whether they have the right. They will be entitled to self-determination (1) by virtue of a particular culture that designates a primary political community (or a warranted aspiration for one) and (2) by virtue of the fact that such communities are present and the right is against them all equally.
46. Perhaps someone like Johann Gottlieb Fichte, who ascribed some primordial force to languages going beyond mere communication and entering the ontological structure of collective agency, might attempt to claim that language is the feature that substantially defines political communities. But by claiming so, he either identifies political communities corresponding to languages or has to prove how the good of shared language defines linguistic communities with respect to one another for their members and not as evaluated by an external observer according to a specially established criterion. (Fichte ranked nations according to the degree to which their languages were "alive" and "connected to the force of nature." A language that ranks highly in both categories, he argued, links the members of the nation to the "whole previous life of the nation.") Fichte, *Addresses to the German Nation* (New York: Harper and Row, 1968), p. 58.
47. If a group wants to separate completely, we may be talking about its claim for self-determination.
48. Even for minority groups that wish to isolate themselves from the larger liberal society in which they are situated, moral and corresponding legal powers over their members have to be reconciled within the framework of the individual rights that are fundamental for membership in the larger society.
49. David Laitin and Rob Reich, "A Liberal Democratic Approach to Language Justice," in *Language Rights and Political Theory*.
50. Quoted in Darlene M. Johnston, "Native Rights as Collective Rights: A Question of Group Self-Preservation," in Kymlicka, *The Rights of Minority Cultures*, p. 182.
51. For an argument of why the group identity/continuity can be explained as the persistence of sets of rules, see Réaume, "The Group Right to Linguistic Security," pp. 124–125.
52. Groups with persistent aspirations for self-determination that exhibit a sufficient number of the features of political culture characteristic of self-determining agents also qualify for the right, even if they do not have institutions of self-government.
53. Recommendation 43, 1998, in Rubio-Marin, "Language Rights," p. 59n.
54. I will provide additional support for the introduction of self-determination as the central notion to consider for the regulation of relations among substate national groups in the next chapter, where I define nationhood and explain its relation to self-determination.
55. Accordingly, political theorists—John Rawls in particular—recognize some human rights as more basic and propose a minimal set of human rights that should be accepted and enforced universally. They do not include the rights of national groups. The fundamental human rights

are limited to basic rights such as the right to life, a right to liberty, a right against religious persecution, and a right to the material conditions of subsistence. See John Rawls, "The Law of Peoples," in *On Human Rights: The Oxford Amnesty Lectures 1993*, ed. Stephen Shute and Susan Hurley (New York: Basic Books, 1993), pp. 43–82.

56. A good argument defending the multiethnic type of national mobilization there can be found in Elise Giuliano, "Who Determines the Self in the Politics of Self-Determination? Identity and Preference Formation in Tatarstan's Nationalist Mobilization," *Comparative Politics* 32, no. 3 (2000):, pp. 295–316.

Chapter 3
A Definition of Nationhood[1]

Actors in conflicts of self-determination employ the notion of nationhood to identify themselves. Yet the fact that they claim national identity does not necessarily place them in the class of nations, nor does it immediately entitle them to self-determination. Judging the legitimacy of granting a particular group the right to self-determination requires determining first whether it qualifies in principle to advance the claim. We need to evaluate the various claims to nationhood and self-determination made by minority groups and to verify the status of various groups presently referred to as "national." Generating a commonly accepted definition of nationhood and clarifying how nationhood relates to self-determination could introduce much-needed conceptual clarity to the assessment of substate groups' entitlements and to the definition of the subjects of the right to self-determination. In the previous chapter, I distinguished between two types of group rights and established that a moral right to self-determination is primary, belonging to group agents constituted so as to be capable of exercising equal freedom with other similarly constituted agents. In this chapter, I define nations as groups organized around the shared collective good of self-determination and defend this definition as providing the conceptual ground to determine the status of and norms for relations between national groups in multinational states.

The notion of national self-determination is widely used now, and by introducing my definition of nationhood I hope to clarify the meaning of national self-determination and clearly distinguish nations from groups that are organized around other types of shared goods. Settling conflicting self-determination claims or designing arrangements for a federal state requires some prescriptive ordering of the notions of self-determination, nationhood, and statehood. I do not yet defend any set of normative principles designed to regulate relations of self-determination among national groups.[2] Rather, I first introduce two criteria that any definition of "nation" has to satisfy to be better at conceptualizing nationhood than the status quo, and I explain how rival conceptions of nationhood fail to satisfy the criteria. Then I put forward and defend my definition of a nation: a collective agent characterized by a political culture of self-determination with which its members self-identify.

Finally, I restate what constitutes the moral foundation of the right to national self-determination and justify my understanding of self-determination as it pertains

A. Moltchanova, *National Self-Determination and Justice in Multinational States*, Studies in Global Justice 5, DOI 10.1007/978-90-481-2691-0_3,

to the definition of nationhood in political and territorial terms. It should be noted that a group can be constituted as a nation (that is, it can be constituted around the shared good of self-determination) and thereby qualify for the right to self-determination in principle but be prevented from being granted the right. This restriction applies, for example, when the form in which the group persistently tries to exercise self-determination is harmful to others.

A General Methodological Approach to Defining Nationhood

The notion of "nation" presently has multiple meanings, including "people," "national minority," "the population of a state," "ethnic group," and "title nation" or "majority." As we have seen, the UN Charter declares the right of all peoples to self-determination, but "people" is not clearly defined and does not in principle exclude substate national groups from the entitlement. In current international practice and law, the terms "nation" and "state" are often used interchangeably. The European Framework Convention, for example, recognizes states as the undersigning parties and emphasizes its signatories' respect for those states' territorial integrity and *national* sovereignty.[3] Although the special nature of national minorities is implicit in the very fact that such a document was adopted, the convention introduces a confusion between statehood and nationhood by both calling state sovereignty "national" and failing to provide an explanation of why states are entitled to national government while minorities are entitled only to cultural, linguistic, and religious rights. International law overall does not define the status or the powers that non-state groups that claim to be nations in multinational states should have in relation to other groups, their citizens, and their own national minorities. The meaning of "national," especially in light of terms like "national sovereignty," needs to be clarified.

The use of the notion of nationhood in the context of formulating norms for the resolution of conflicts of self-determination does not make sense to everyone. Buchanan, for example, suggests regulating secession on the basis of respect for human rights, allowing national groups to secede if the host state is engaged in gross violations of the human rights of the national minority. But the fact that states that do not violate human rights are considered basically legitimate is a point of contention for those groups that demand that their right to national self-determination be respected. Liberal arguments about the neutrality of human rights both acknowledge that state assignment is a result of historical contingencies and presuppose that one can disassociate self-determination and nationhood from statehood by treating individuals equally with respect to their national identity. As I have already pointed out, such arguments are not adequate, because the equal treatment of each individual with respect to his or her nationhood falls short of adequately addressing the claims collective agents advance to control their future political status. Therefore, it is vital to consider rather than skim over the terms of national membership if we are to find norms for conflict resolution, because the notion of nationhood in the context of multinational states describes the mutual definition and self-definition of substate groups that advance self-determination claims in such states.

In this section, I will introduce two criteria that are required for a definition of nationhood to be both principled and effective. Group agents make claims concerning their status and mobilize from an actively maintained "internal" perspective, regardless of whether the identity they construct is perceived as politically valid or historically accurate by outside observers. The vague condition of international law is not helpful when it comes to the problem of the status of substate nationhood in the political landscape of states. For a definition of nationhood to be better than the status quo in dealing with this problem, it needs to be attuned to groups' constitution as they presently relate to one another. The two criteria below, both of which an adequate definition ought to satisfy, reflect this goal.

The Two Criteria

We cannot properly decide whether the differential treatment of national groups is justified on the basis of a definition that presupposes differential treatment. Defining nationhood as having a necessary connection to statehood, for example—what I call the "nation-state approach"—prejudges the outcome of the discussion in favor of the very difference between state-endowed and non-state national groups that is being questioned.[4] Given that it is impossible for every national group to have its own state, when such a definition is used to formulate international legal principles and the domestic policies of multinational states, it disadvantages groups without state institutions that reside within the territory of a multinational state; it cannot be the basis for addressing their claims, as the claims challenge this very contingent distribution of political power associated with statehood. Thus, a definition that gives preference to state-endowed groups based on historically contingent facts is not acceptable.[5]

Criterion 1 (hereafter referred to as "**C1**") grows out of the necessity for a definition of "nation" not to be normative:

C1: A definition should not determine the normative content of the principles designed to regulate relations among national groups with respect to their self-determination claims or any other entitlements. Thus, group rights or entitlements should not be part of the definition.

A definition that pertains to multiple perspectives without privileging any of them captures what is shared by national groups of different kinds and is capable of reflecting their view of their standing in relation to all other national groups they consider appropriate. This allows the definition to account for group agency and avoids identifying national groups based on characteristics perceived as defining only by outside observers. One example of an externally imposed criterion would involve assessing the standing of groups with respect to one another based on the comprehensive idea that language is a major characteristic of nationhood. Romantic thinkers considered relations of national groups with respect to this criterion, not with respect to how the groups perceived themselves in relation to language or to other groups. Johann Gottlieb Fichte ranked nations according to the degree to which their languages were "alive" and "connected to the force of nature."[6] As I argued in the previous chapter, the shared good of language alone does not allow collective agents to relate to others. The nature of a linguistic community's relations with other groups is defined by the political community of which the linguistic group is a part.

Nationhood is a complex phenomenon that includes aspects of personal and group identity, history, culture, and political preferences. All of these features are shared by several kinds of groups, not only by national groups. We need to be able to tell what distinguishes ethnic or administrative units from national groups, what the similarity is between multi- and mono-ethnic national groups, and what differentiates groups with very similar "national" cultures that form different national communities.

Criterion 2 (**C2**) grows out of this need, requiring the construction of a notion of nationhood that maintains the complexity of the phenomenon relative to the context of its use:

C2: A definition should be pragmatic: it should provide sufficient guidance in determining whether a group qualifies as a nation for the purpose of the regulation of relations among the subjects of multinational states and be able to account for changing group identities.

I share Rogers Brubaker's caution concerning the scope and the aims of the idea of "nation."[7] He claims: "Nationalism can and should be understood without invoking 'nations' as substantial entities; 'nation' is a category of practice, not (in the first instance) a category of analysis. We have to understand the practical uses of the category 'nation,' the ways it can come to structure perception, to inform thought and experience, to organize discourse and political action."[8] Like Brubaker, I appreciate the dynamic aspect of nationhood. National allegiances are contingent; identity categories, however—especially translated in the form of group members' beliefs and intentions—do structure the world through collective action. Brubaker states that "Nationness is an event that suddenly crystallizes rather than gradually develops."[9] Yet something constitutes this nationness, for how else can we declare that crystallization has occurred? Identifying its features is the task of a definition of nationhood. If nation-related categories designate something dynamic, this does not mean that they do not designate something real. My theory supports the idea that a national group may be created where no long-lived national group—defined, perhaps, in Romantic and primordial terms—has existed, but it does not diminish the reality of national group agency. National identity is likely to be, as Craig Calhoun argues, a "changeable product of collective action."[10] If a group agent does not have what a metaphysician would call a "strict" identity, however, a national group will still possess a degree of continuity that provides a basis for reference.

We want to know how to regulate the collective actions of groups, even if their identity is changeable. Thus, considering a nation as a special type of collective agent allows us to introduce a category of analysis of practice that accounts for changes while helping to establish a principled basis for the regulation of relations among national groups. A pragmatic, nonessentialist approach should yield a definition that can serve as a situated description:[11] the definition helps us to evaluate the various claims of minority national groups. It should be mentioned, however, that qualifying as a national group is a necessary but not sufficient condition for a group to receive equal entitlement to other similar groups: if a group does not satisfy the definition, it is in principle not capable of entitlement; if the group satisfies the definition, it may be disqualified on other counts.

We could produce a definition by listing the constitutive features of those groups that are now considered nations (namely, state-endowed groups) and asking which among these features are shared by non-state groups claiming a right to self-determination. Or we could start with a broader sample and define what characterizes all those agents that claim to be "peoples" with the right to self-determination. Given that we are looking for a set of constitutive characteristics that allows groups to be compared, we will come up with a similar list of constitutive features regardless of what method we use. If we define as nations a number of stateless groups that share the constitutive features of their state-endowed counterparts, the definition itself has neither "uncovered" a hidden entitlement of substate groups to self-determination nor created such an entitlement.

Say that group A1, which shares state S1 with group B1, claims as one of its constitutive characteristics its superiority to B1, whose members those of A1 regard as essentially non-As. Although this particular feature of A1's self-understanding is important in the context of the regulation of relations between A1 and B1, and although A1 may have something in common with another group A2 in state S2 that similarly defines itself as superior to B2, defining nationhood in terms of superiority to another nation nonetheless would not help to regulate relations among substate groups in the states S1 and S2, because B1 and B2 have to be included in this regulation as well. B1 and B2, moreover, may share a trait in common, such as being victimized by A1 and A2, that is different from what A1 and A2 share; if so, it would provide an alternative—but still not helpful—definition of nationhood.

If in defining what "nationhood" means, moreover, we prioritize A1's and A2's self-understanding and ignore what B1 and B2 think of themselves, we will have failed to create a definition that allows us to regulate relations with respect to self-determination among substate groups in S1 and S2. B1 and B2, assuming they are or aspire to be collective agents with group identity organized around the goal of self-determination and mobilized around plans of action designed to bring their collective goal about, are not going to acquiesce to norms that discriminate against them, because those norms are based on a definition that downgrades the B groups' status. Such a definition would fail at least Criterion 2—that is, it would not be pragmatic, given the likelihood that B1 and B2 would reject it. Now, B1 and B2 may be agents of an entirely different type from those claiming self-determination but may try to advance strategic self-determination claims. In such a case, while they should not be identified as national groups, this exclusion will be due to their failure to satisfy a properly identified set of conditions, not to a definition that generalizes from what is common to A1 and A2. If B1 and B2 do advance self-determination claims in earnest, though, what is relevant to the regulation of relations among the groups in S1 and S2 is that they all advance claims to self-determination: that A1 and A2 do it as well as B1 and B2, and that all of them can obtain self-determination only along with and in relation to the other groups. To evaluate, for example, whether either one of two autonomous groups in the territory of the former Soviet republic of Georgia—Abkhazia, which wants to secede, and Adjaria, which does not want to secede—is treated fairly, we need to establish first whether the Georgians and the Adjarians, the Adjarians and the Abkhazians, and the Abkhazians and the Georgians are different kinds of groups.

Some Definitions

In this section, I will consider current leading types of definitions of nationhood and explain why they do not satisfy either **C1** or **C2**, and thus why they are incapable of providing the foundation for a framework of legal regulations that will be better than the status quo.

The Nation-State Approach

What I call the nation-state approach is formulated in different ways based on how the relation between nationhood and statehood is interpreted. States can simply be defined as nations. Anthony Giddens argues that a nation exists only when "a state has a unified administrative reach over the territory over which its sovereignty is claimed."[12] In this view, units that do not have corresponding states are referred to as nations only mistakenly. To discuss their political situation, Giddens argues, some other category of description should be used.

When states are not defined as nations, the correspondence between the two may nonetheless be presented as either an inevitable or a desirable outcome of political development. A *functionalist account* suggests that the successful functioning of a state leads to the formation of national identity within its borders. Margaret Canovan argues that most democracies are nation-states of one nation. For a state to function properly, she explains, there has to be a sufficient sense of solidarity among its citizens, and nationhood is the best candidate for creating and maintaining such solidarity; in fact, it *is* this solidarity.[13] Other forms of solidarity, like constitutional patriotism or shared political values, are either too weak to keep together a liberal state or are just as particularistic as nationhood and have a tendency to be expressed in national terms.[14]

A *nationalist account* claims that nations ought to have states of their own.[15] According to Ernest Gellner, a state is necessary to maintain a nation's official language, which supports a culture of a homogenized, impersonal, industrialized society with a high level of division of labor. Thus, a nation-building process, if it is successful, results in the formation of a nation that corresponds to a state. In Gellner's view, to resolve an unstable situation in which several national groups reside within the territory of one state, either the state's boundaries have to change or some national groups have to be assimilated. Even if several nations come together to form one state, they will have to create a high culture for this new state, and this culture will correspond to a new nation. Gellner writes that in the "Age of Nationalism," multinationalism was felt to be uncomfortable, and "men then had two options, if they were to diminish such discomfort: they could change their own culture, or they could change the nature of the political unit."[16]

The nation-state approach, therefore, perceives the world as a combination of the real and potential one-to-one correspondence of states and nations. Canovan and Gellner would agree that a regional structure that has several nations within it will either become a new nation-state or will fall apart to form several nation-states, to which it may remain a supranational structure that coordinates interstate matters or takes over some of the functions of each state without significant changes to the state. If a regional structure like the European Union, for example, creates a regional identity, it comes to replace the nation-states that initially composed it. Until this happens, the constitutive states remain nations united by a supranational structure.

The nation-state approaches of Giddens, Canovan, and Gellner provide, first, an accurate account of how collective agency forms when a group is able to control its political space and its boundaries, as well as how it functions. Canovan's and Gellner's positions provide an account of the institutional completion of a collective agent by means of the agent's functioning or mobilizing in pursuit of its identity. Second, the nation-state approach documents how the relations of several communities in one territory have historically led to the crystallization of one overarching national culture, which then became the nation of a nation-state. The approach points to the contingent nature of national identity, which is nevertheless actively created. A third important feature, which in my account of nationhood pertains to groups' entitlements in relation to one another, is introduced by Giddens's emphasis on the relational property of nationhood. Giddens maintains that the plurality of nations is a key to the internal formation of nation-states, for it requires the fixing of borders, and this, in turn, helps to better shape and centralize state domination within these borders. Therefore, nation-states exist only in a complex of other nation-states and are defined as "a set of institutional forms of governance maintaining an administrative monopoly over a territory with demarcated boundaries."[17] In sum, the nation-state approach highlights three important features of nationhood: the coincidence of political and national units, the historical contingency of nationhood, and the relational nature of entitlement to control a political space.

Despite these positive features, however, the nation-state approach associates statehood with both nationhood and self-determination. Since international order is understood as being based on states, and since not all minority groups presently possess or can feasibly obtain a state of their own, this approach explicitly acknowledges the entitlements of only certain groups and thereby violates **C1**. Defining nationhood to imply a necessary connection between nations and states leads to (1) the impossibility of accommodating claims to self-determination made by national minorities or substate national groups, for which international regulation and proper inclusion in the institutional structures of multinational states are especially necessary, and (2) a disregard for conceptions of self-determination that do not fit the mold of nation-state accounts. In this, the nation-state approach mirrors current practices of international politics and law, which acknowledge strong ties between self-determination and statehood. According to these practices and the nation-state approach, nations without states of their own have to belong to some state, and the successful design of a multinational state is possible only at the price of subordinating the national identities of different national groups under the a general national identity of one nation-state. Although the nation-state approach is right to connect the political to the national, its equation of nationhood and self-determination with statehood limits its relevance to the problem of self-determination.

It may perhaps be argued that the nation-state approach is designed only to project what states may become in the future or what they ought to be, not to provide a basis for settling self-determination claims. The nation-state approach concludes that for a multinational state to function, it is necessary to create a political climate and institutions within the state that support an encompassing national identity.[18] Interpreted as an "ideal-world solution" and not a theory of what nations are, however, such an approach would still need to specify the strategies required to achieve or, rather, to approximate the ideal kind of state. In its present form, the nation-state approach does not offer recommendations for successful nation building in a multinational state. Hence, even in its ideal-world version, the nation-state approach is incomplete. When the nation-state account merely predicts (or expresses the desirability of) a multinational state's eventual dismantling or transformation into a one-nation state, moreover, the approach makes itself irrelevant to the relations of national groups in multinational states *before* these changes take place, violating the pragmatic requirement of **C2.**

In fact, even if the nation-state approach is taken as simply an account of how nations have formed historically, it is still incomplete, because it does not address those national groups that have not been completely assimilated and that make self-determination claims to this day.[19] In my account of nationhood, I retain the three important features of the nation-state approach but disassociate statehood from nationhood, on the one hand, and from self-determination, on the other.

David Miller's Definition

One definition that does not introduce normative ranking and hence satisfies **C1** is David Miller's. Miller describes a nation as "a group of people who recognize one another as belonging to the same community, who acknowledge special obligations to one another, and who aspire to political autonomy—this by virtue of characteristics that they believe they share, typically a common history, attachment to a geographical place, and a public culture that differentiates them from their neighbors."[20] The meaning of "public culture" here needs qualification. Federal units of the United States possess a degree of political autonomy; while their citizens perceive them to be political communities with their own governing bodies, most of them think of their states not as nations but as parts of a bigger nation. Members of an ethnic minority also share a public culture, and often they have a degree of autonomy in the formulation and administration of political measures designed to safeguard their culture and language. However, the public culture of an ethnic group is very different from that of a national group. They place different demands on political actors and require different degrees of political autonomy. What is more, states may encompass several separate ethnic identities but only one nationality. Finally, different nations may have similar public cultures: Romania and Moldova share many essential elements of culture, but they certainly have two different public cultures—not as ethnically different groups but as different nations. "Public culture" and "political autonomy" hence can be used as elements in defining not only national groups but other kinds of groups as well. When Miller wants to distinguish between national and ethnic groups, he points out that national groups make a claim to self-determination and create the appropriate organizations and institutions to fulfill the claim.[21] Hence it makes sense to refocus his definition to clarify that the public culture of national groups and their actual or desired political autonomy have to do with self-determination. In the next section, I provide an altered definition that follows Miller's in important ways but focuses it by spelling out the features of nations from the point of view of their constitution as collective agents, which allows us to distinguish them from other kinds of groups.

Subjective Definitions

Several authors use what I characterize as subjective definitions of "nation." Margaret Moore, for example, stresses that there are good reasons to understand "nation" as subjectively defined.[22] She says that "the term 'nation' refers to a group of people who identify themselves as belonging to a particular national group, who are usually enclosed on a particular historical territory, and who have a sense of affinity to people sharing that identity."[23] But if a nation is said to exist when a significant number of people in a community consider themselves to form a nation or behave as if they formed one, then this begs the question, for one has to define what a nation is in order to describe their concept of a nation.[24] One can try to avoid circularity by avoiding using "nation" in describing the group's self-identification. Alfred Cobban, for example, considers that "any territorial community, the members of which are conscious of themselves as members of a community, and wish to maintain the identity of their community, is a nation."[25] In this case, however, the definition does not help us distinguish between nations and populations of cities or ethnic or national minorities, and hence it fails to meet **C2**. The content of self-identification has to be specified.

Walker Connor states that in case of national groups it is not *what is,* but *what people believe is* that has behavioral consequences. The nation is a self-defined rather than an other-defined grouping, he explains, so the facts of origin seldom conform with factual data.[26] While I appreciate that he considers national groups from the "insider" point of view, I disagree with how he fleshes out the content of group members' beliefs. Connor defines a nation as a group of people who feel that they are ancestrally related. A nation, he explains, is the largest group that can command a person's loyalty because of felt kinship ties; it is, from this perspective, the fully extended family. But the definition of nationhood he provides fails to shed light on what precisely in the myth of ancestry distinguishes between ethnic or religious minorities on the one hand and national minorities on the other, thus failing to satisfy **C2**. In this chapter I demonstrate that a particular type of political culture is necessary and sufficient to deal with cases of this sort. One important aspect of Connor's treatment of nationhood is his awareness that conventional scholarly approaches cannot be applied to transitional and non-democratic societies due to the attention the dominant group commands and consequent uncertainty concerning the group identities of non-dominant groups. In the case of Montenegro, he points out, there are Montenegrins as well as Serbs who consider Montenegrins a part of the Serbian nation.[27] Based on this consideration, he argues, we do not know if a nation has emerged there. A definition that pays attention to the political culture of a group is better situated to pronounce on the formation of a nation in cases of this sort. Connor clearly pays attention to the constitution of group agents, but the set of shared beliefs with which he identifies nations is too broad and does not allow him to propose a criterion by which to identify national groups in transitional societies. I share his caution concerning these kinds of societies and deal with them in Chapter 4.

Max Weber suggests the concept of "nation" cannot be stated in terms of empirical qualities common to those who count as members of the nation. Nation, he writes, is a "specific sentiment of solidarity in the face of other groups," and "thus the concept belongs in the sphere of values."[28] Members of a nation share a conviction of "the irreplaceability of the culture values that are to be preserved and developed only through the cultivation of the peculiarity of the group."[29] I support Weber's emphasis on intersubjective awareness, which can account for the active and dynamic aspects of nationhood, but this definition does not allow us to distinguish between national and other contexts in which intersubjective awareness might arise (unless it is circular and takes what a nation is for granted prior to defining it). Therefore, to satisfy **C2**, we need to reveal the constitution of the group in a definition of nationhood.[30]

A New Definition of Nationhood

I use the perspective on collective agency I discussed in the previous chapter to define nations as collective agents organized around self-determination. Nations are groups whose members share and identify with a particular kind of political culture, or a set of beliefs and attitudes concerning politics.[31] A group of people is a national community only if its members believe that they share the end of being a collective agent. Basic to the political culture associated with self-determination, as I explained in Chapter 1, is the belief that membership in a group defines the bounds within which political authority can originate meaningfully for those it governs. That is, political power exercised over the group is authoritative only if it derives from the group as a whole. In addition, the members of the group share the corresponding collective end of establishing or maintaining effective agency. Thus, members perceive their national group as a *primary political community*: there is no larger or smaller political community to which they relate that can represent their agency. Members of a religious community, by contrast, normally consider the larger society to be their primary political community, while citizens of a multinational state consider their national units to be their primary political communities.[32]

The political culture of nationhood defines for co-nationals the conditions under which a political authority is capable of governing them on the basis of dependent reasons—reasons that apply to them.[33] These reasons cannot apply to them only from the perspective of the state power, regardless of the group's position on the issue of membership in the state. National belonging defines for a nation's individual members the appropriate terms of membership in a polity. For example, although the benefits of belonging to a larger state may create obligations on the part of minority groups toward other citizens, such obligations alone do not create the freely endorsed identification of the minority group members with the larger state and thus the appropriate terms of membership in that state. National identity underscores that political power operates meaningfully for those it governs *only if* it originates with the agency on whose behalf the authority operates. Federal authority is meaningful for its national unit only if the primary-level, or unit-level, authority consents to membership in the federation.

One may object that according to this definition, a federation does not count as a nation, whilst its constituent "nations" do, whereas the primary political group for the members of federations like the UK or Switzerland seems to be the whole of the federal state. This concern can be easily resolved based on my definition. If members of a *de facto* federal unit consider the federal state to be their primary political community, the unit constitutes not a national unit but an administrative-territorial unit. (If the members of all federal units feel this way, the federal state and the national group coincide.) My definition avoids rigidly ascribing status to groups based on present geographical divisions and thus satisfies **C1**. I will consider double-level national allegiances in federations when I discuss "nested" national identities below.

Members of a national group not only ought to share the beliefs of a national political culture but also ought to be willing to approve those beliefs as describing what they truly self-identify with. In an oppressive society, people may act in accordance with an official set of beliefs that describes the terms of membership in a national group without acknowledging these official beliefs and the corresponding political culture as truly representing their identity. Such a "vacuous" political culture cannot define a nation. As I discuss in the next chapter, the members of national groups in oppressive societies may have not fully articulated what they identify with, but they do know that they do not identify with the set of official beliefs. Another case when non-identification with the set of officially stated beliefs signals that a set of beliefs does not represent the right kind of political culture to identify a national group occurs when the leadership of a minority group strategically promotes claims to nationhood. If the population to which these claims refer does not endorse them as authentic expressions of its identity, these claims about where the meaningful limits of political authority ought to lie similarly fail to define the national group.

A common objection to theories acknowledging the significance of self-determining communities is that nations are too often "created" artificially, and thus this process should not be encouraged. A definition like mine might be perceived as contributing to the process of creating new national groups—as an elite attempt to encourage nations to form where they would not otherwise have done so. If the elites succeed in creating a national group, however, the nation is created in earnest. The point of my agency-based approach is not to encourage the formation of new nations but rather to reflect the facts of political reality and the life of group agents. If group members all identify with the set of beliefs concerning the bounds and nature of group membership that constitute nationhood—even if they did not identify with the same set of beliefs several years ago—it is unfair to continue evaluating the nature of their group engagement based on the kind of collective agent they used to be. An account of nationhood that satisfies **C2** ought to account for the dynamic nature of group identities, but it also ought to guard against the identification of national groups based on beliefs group members are forced to act upon without accepting them freely; it also should guard against making judgments about group identities based on the unverified statements of elites or outsiders. If neither circumstance that would exclude a group from qualifying for nationhood obtains, however, and if the majority of the group voluntarily accepts the opinion of the elite as their own, then the corresponding group agent is in fact organized as a nation around what was initially the elite-defined or elite-identified set of beliefs. One may argue that the consensus is false (or planted) by tracing the origin of the opinion of the majority to the elite political players who managed to persuade the group members to adhere to the beliefs of membership through some sort of manipulation. But if public consensus in the end was formed so as to reflect the beliefs of what initially was only a narrow segment of public, this cannot be taken as evidence of the non-existence of the corresponding national group. An appeal to this kind of "evidence" may conflate two facts belonging to consecutive stages of belief-acquisition—the fact that public attitudes and opinions originate in the minority opinion and the fact that the majority, after it has acquired these beliefs, holds them "for real" (whatever their origin is).

In what ways can the members of a national group share the end of being a collective agent organized around the good of self-determination? Members give meaning to their idea of nationhood through the notion of the ideal correspondence between the identified domain of members and the political power of a primary political community. Returning to the example of one worldwide political community introduced in Chapter 2, such a community could be considered a nation. Its members would need to be able to maintain their group identity internally to avoid a split that would make some members outsiders, they could not engage in national self-determination as the exercise of freedom with respect to other similar communities. My definition is both able to handle the present conundrums of sub- and inter-state group relationships and to apply to a world without divisions among political communities. Presently, however, members of every national culture are aware of the existence of other groups that share similar beliefs of membership, and they know that each group's actions are in part determined by its respective shared beliefs about what other groups' shared beliefs are. Holding these beliefs implies that they are also likely to have a notion of the ideal mutual standing of groups like them and to share an identity that describes a primary political community. Thus, co-nationals have a notion of the powers and entitlements of their national group with respect to other groups, which they can evaluate by comparing the present status of their group to their notion of the group's ideal standing. Ideally, to relate to other groups, a national group needs to be able to maintain a proper authority and to have control over its membership by achieving proper standing in relation to other collectives. Thus, it needs to have a say over important aspects of the group's relations with other groups, such as the parameters of its inclusion in a multinational state or the degree of interference that other groups can exercise over its internal affairs concerning political governance or even language. In other words, the group's goal is to exercise its ability to have a say about its political future, or a degree of self-determination in relation to other groups that aspire to control their own political futures.

Depending on the group's real situation, its shared end can be either to establish or to maintain effective agency. It needs to be emphasized that the *exercise* of effective agency is not required for a national group to be identified. The presence of a political culture endorsed by the members, who share the end of becoming an effective agent, is sufficient to identify a group as a nation.[34] As I discuss in the next chapter, a nation whose political expression is curtailed has a "potential political culture"—a set of beliefs individuals hold about the community they regard as self-determining and about their government or the dominating nation. If group members' beliefs concerning membership are interdependent but not cooperative, as they would be in a group that discriminates against a set of its members, however, we would need to be cautious about treating the group as a collective agent and assigning it rights based on its constitution.

In short, then, *nationhood can be defined as a political culture based upon the shared end of acquiring or maintaining effective agency having to do with self-determination*. Nations, then, are the corresponding collective agents organized around self-determination. "Self-determination," as I defined it in Chapter 2, is the capacity of a group to control its own political future. The current—relational—meaning of self-determination is closely associated with the acquisition of a state of one's own, but in principle it does not have to be. Sharing a state with others does not necessarily preclude a group from being self-determining as long as it has a say about the terms of inclusion and a chance freely to agree to belong by, for example, choosing not to exercise a constitutional right of exit.[35]

Although nations require some form of self-determination in order to exercise effective agency, my definition does not immediately translate into the right of national groups to self-determination. Whether to grant the right to a national group requires separate consideration. A group qualifying as a national group may perceive its self-determination as trumping that of another group or groups. In this case, the group would not have the right to self-determination, although it would satisfy at least one necessary condition to qualify for the right—that of being a national group. My new definition of a nation, therefore, does not promise the enjoyment of self-determination to national groups, nor—because the realization of self-determination need not be associated with the acquisition of independent statehood—does it entitle national groups to statehood.

If we define nations on the basis of their possession of a political culture that defines the limits of meaningful authority for their members, we rule out as not being nations those linguistic, religious, cultural, or ethnic minorities that make claims to accommodation within existing limits of power. A cultural community that thinks its claims can be satisfied within the larger political community does not aspire to be self-determining; a cultural community that believes its culture can be protected only if it has its own primary political community does. Thus, if a group's shared beliefs about membership are about defining the terms of membership *within* a given political community and not about belonging to this or to some other political community, the community we are looking at is not a nation.

One might object that this criterion fails to exclude groups that are obviously not nations, such as self-governing municipalities or groups that possess other institutional arrangements associated with the middle level of democracy. But the political culture associated with the middle level of democracy defines itself as limited by its inclusion in the larger body of members of a political community (usually a state). A city government that aspires to city-state status, that is prepared to be fully self-determining with all ensuing responsibilities, and that is supported by its population *can* potentially represent a national group; however, if its citizens acknowledge that their power is limited and applies only to the areas delegated to them by the state or federal government, they perceive the larger community to be the primary locus of legislative and executive power over them and cannot be a nation. A national group aspires to operate over the domain of members in its relation to nonmembers, with the shared goal of safeguarding all the powers, rights, and immunities its members have in relation to other communities of a similar sort. The powers of a city government are not defined in relation to other city governments but by the division of competences within the state. Or, a Parent-Teacher Association can decide upon certain rules guiding citizens' behavior and use political means to implement them, like raising taxes to fund school programs enacted through a municipal referendum. But the Parent-Teacher Association influences the lives of other citizens only in a very limited way: it determines educational policies, but it does not decide how to relate to other political communities and it does not normally question the limits of the larger political community. (If it does, this may signal that there is more than one national group present within the territory of the state.) Although educational decisions made in Buffalo, New York, may take into consideration what is being taught in Toronto, Ontario, this thinking is framed by and operates within an already present political culture of self-determination within the United States. The association can pass decisions concerning some national ideals and symbols,[36] but parents and teachers do not determine the basic outlines of the national political culture and its ideals, they only have a degree of discretion concerning how to implement them. A change in the national political culture can be initiated from the middle level of a democracy—for example, parents' and teachers' attitudes and actions with respect to the Pledge of Allegiance can influence the national culture in the long run—but any such change can only be enacted by the government associated with the national group at large. Besides, such a change is likely to be about the terms of membership, not its bounds. A self-determining group (usually called "a people") has the capacity to be entirely determined by the conditions of its internal life and thus to be a self-sufficient political community.

Political elements of nationhood (such as claims to political autonomy or self-determination) are recognized by many authors,[37] but their notions of nationhood also include other elements that go beyond this particular type of political culture. Thus, it could be objected that although it may be necessary to establish the presence of a political culture of self-determination in order to be able to distinguish between national and ethnic groups, my definition is too narrow in its focus on political culture alone. Below, I consider why the presence of such a culture, together with self-identification, is sufficient to define nationhood.

Why Political Culture and Not Culture?

There are two interconnected characteristics of culture that are commonly identified as relevant to its being used in concepts of nationhood. The first is that culture is shared by the members of a nation.[38] The second is that members of nations recognize one another through their common culture.[39] Culture also allows others—nonmembers—to recognize members of a nation. By considering the process of naturalization, however, I will establish that it is sufficient for individuals to recognize one another as belonging to the same or different *political* cultures associated with self-determination in order to determine their corresponding joint or separate national membership. Although not all national groups are willing to accept immigrants as citizens, I will use this example to highlight what kind of culture is important for characterizing "open" nations and will then explain why the same kind of culture suffices for "closed" ones as well.

Foreigners living either abroad or within the territory of a nation cannot claim membership in the nation merely by virtue of their desire to belong, even if they share many traits of what is referred to as "national character." For a national of Z to become a member of X, Xians have to recognize the Zian as a co-national. A private recognition and acceptance of the Zian by each Xian is not enough, even if the Zian is a very famous person whom everyone wants to have as a co-national. Xians realize that their approval has to be publicly communicated. There is also an understanding among co-nationals that they have the power to accept a foreigner because, as a national group, they are in charge of regulating their membership. The recognition of a foreigner as a new member is achieved in big, impersonal communities through the mediation of the institutions that symbolize the power of the people of X, and it is a political expression of their national identity.

The transition from being an outsider to being a member does not signify that the culture of the Zian has changed, although some naturalized citizens are willing to undergo, and are successful at achieving, difficult cultural assimilation. Compare a visitor to X who shows many traits of the national character, such as language, pronunciation, culture (as both a set of habits and common cultural images), knowledge of literature, and so on, to an immigrant citizen of X who has not yet culturally assimilated. What kind of culture will allow co-nationals to recognize the latter but not the former as one of them? It is status as a member in relation to the national political culture—a set of shared beliefs about the limits and membership of the political community—that makes the latter into a co-national. A person living in a suburban area of southern Ontario, for example, is not much different culturally from a suburban dweller in the bordering area of the United States. Their respective beliefs about belonging to two different political cultures, however, make them members of two different national groups.

Whether shared beliefs constitute part of a national group's political culture depends on the context of their use. The belief that French should be the language of Quebec, when expressed by a member of the Francophone community who is concerned with the survival of this community's culture, is a cultural belief. This same belief is a part of Quebec's political culture, however, if it addresses the corresponding right Quebec's citizens claim to have: the right to choose, as a self-determining community, which direction Quebec's culture is going to take and which aspects of its government are to be promoted. To cite another example, citizens of Ontario and Michigan may not have the same attitudes toward state-sponsored health care. Their attitudes are a part of culture to the extent to which they relate to co-nationals' shared way of life, characterized by such features of national character as self-reliance or generosity. But their attitudes belong to political culture insofar as they are a part of a general disposition toward the items that ought to be controlled in order to maintain the political identity of the Canadian or American peoples.

This is not to say that all the beliefs of a particular political culture need to be agreed upon or shared by all members of a political community. Co-nationals may disagree about many issues, such as which party should be in power, or about moral values, and they may also have very different cultural and ethnic backgrounds. People in the same political culture, however, disagree about issues other than those that relate to belonging to the culture. They agree that they belong to the same collective agent and that they ideally ought to share a political community. Even in the extreme form of national disagreement, a civil war, the contested issue is normally not whether national membership is to continue to be shared but rather a particular version of nation building. It has to be clear, however, that there is a limit to the kinds of arguments, controversies, and disputes that can coexist within the same political culture. A disagreement about the status of a secessionist group in a state whose other citizens think that the group should remain within the state's borders transcends the limits of one political culture and presents a conflict of self-determination between two different political cultures, because the secessionist group does not want to belong to the state. The Georgian and Abkhazian or Russian and Chechen conflicts, for example, are not civil wars or fights against terrorists, but rather conflicts between two nations.

I do not mean to suggest that language or the customary beliefs, social forms, and material traits of a racial, religious, or social group beyond the political realm are not important. What I suggest is that concentrating on political culture is sufficient for determining what a nation is for the purposes of regulating relations among national groups.

It could be objected that political culture may be sufficient to define nationhood in an open society because, first, this political culture is the shared societal culture and, second, because the group members—normally—accept people from other cultural groups, but that political culture is not sufficient to define a national group that is very exclusive in defining its characteristic features. I would argue that it is fair to define through political culture not only open but also ethnically, culturally, or otherwise exclusive nations. An exclusive cultural nation, Y, may identify a set of features necessary for membership and consider those who do not possess them to be nonmembers. If Y seeks protections and exemptions within a broader political culture, it is not a nation but an exclusive ethnic or cultural group. But why is Y's relation to a particular kind of political culture sufficient to identify it as a nation? The exclusive national group uses special characteristics to identify and control the set of members of its political community. Thus, it possesses or aspires to possess the capacity to determine the limits of meaningful political authority. If eventually Y relaxes or changes its exclusive criteria of membership, it will still remain a nation: it is not the particular criteria but what it wants and can do with them that defines what kind of group it is. So if we determine that Y possesses a political culture with the shared goal of becoming a collective agent and pursuing self-determination, we have sufficient information to identify Y as a national group. It would also be possible on this basis to define the division of powers with the neighbors in the region, within a multinational state, or both in order to assure Y's capability to control its exclusive membership (provided it does not interfere with the self-determination of others).

Defining nationhood may appear more difficult when we consider complex (or "nested") national identities. A nested nation is a group with a "split-level," or double, identity and a double allegiance to its (usually federal) state and its national group proper, such as the Scots in Britain or the Catalans in Spain.[40] Such groups' members consider themselves to be members of both their national group and the larger state—that is, to be both Scottish and British, or Catalan and Spanish. In contrast, rival nationalities do not associate with their host states, and they advance their claims to self-determination as secessionist claims. Miller, who introduces the distinction between nested and rival national identities, emphasizes that national groups normally aim at political autonomy as an independent unit.[41] Thus, a precondition for a group's successful existence as a nested nationality is that the recognition of its aspiration to self-determination *within* the larger state be acceptable to its members. It is precisely when a group perceives that the satisfaction of its self-determination claim is possible within the state in which it is included that its double identity is formed; otherwise, nested national identities may very easily become rival national identities. Thus, my definition of nationhood provides an appropriate background for the explanation of nested national identities. The concept of nationhood as limited to political culture, moreover, correctly registers the change of group identity from non-national to national. It also correctly indicates the continuous existence of a nation, even if its ethnic and cultural makeup changes.[42] It is the emergence or the continuous presence of a political culture expressing a group's will to be self-determining that allows us to identify it as a national group.

History, attachment to a territory, and culture are often considered as separate and independent variables in formulations of the concept of nation. For the purposes of defining what a nation is, however, history and attachment to territory should be regarded as features of political culture. Specifically, elements of political history—historical events in some way relevant to self-determination, such as battles for independence, first meetings of the nation's parliament, the dates of the different decrees and declarations announcing the main principles of the political system and nation's Constitution, the rights and responsibilities of its citizens, and parables about founding historical figures—are part of political culture.[43] Geographical facts about a nation can be closely connected with historical ones, but their relevance to political culture lies in the description of the nation's borders, of its minority nations or its diaspora abroad, of the geographical locations of friendly and hostile nations, and so on.

Those events that are considered to be a part of national history are taught in schools and discussed by the media. These events are selected and interpreted by the group, and the choice of nationally significant historical events may be different at different moments of the nation's existence. Some historical events are forgotten and others overemphasized, mythologized, or both.[44] Eric Hobsbawm points out that sometimes even historical continuity has to be invented. He also notes that ancient materials can be used to construct invented traditions of a novel type for quite novel purposes, while some old ways are deliberately not used or adapted.[45] Thus, the means of what Gellner calls "high culture" serve the purpose of mobilizing agency by furnishing political culture with a record of historical events that can be shared by members to make their membership meaningful in terms of historic continuity.

Like history, attachment to territory becomes part of the mobilization of a national collective agency. It designates a relational property national groups possess even when based on the same historic and geographical facts. Kosovo Albanians and Serbs share a common history, for example, and are attached to the same territory. But the common facts of history and geography become parts of very different narratives, because these narratives are constructed from each group's shared perceptions of the limits of its membership and authority in relation to the other group. It is the sense of history as it is included in political culture that is relevant to the concept of the nation.

The same nation, moreover, may have more than one version of its national history. Disagreements about history within the same nation may be "points of common concern"[46] perceived as different versions of the same history. But if there are several radically incompatible versions of national history in circulation, this may signal that the political unit is in a state of crisis and that it may be composed of more than one national unit. In the case of two nations, even those events upon the interpretation of which the nations agree are perceived as belonging separately to "their history" and to "our history," and thus are made meaningful only when included in the respective contexts of political cultures. Therefore, history can be only looked at in relation to nationhood as part of political culture: the same historical events belonging to two different sets of beliefs about membership (which constitute the corresponding collective agents) are two different histories for the purpose of the characterization of national groups. When I speak about the political culture of a nation, I include elements of history and territory in the notion instead of considering territory, history, and culture as three independent national characteristics. Only those elements of history and territory that belong to political culture should be considered to identify national groups. Thus, the concept of nationhood as limited to political culture associated with effective group agency can correctly register the change of group identity from non-national to national. It also correctly indicates the continuous existence of a nation, even if its ethnic and cultural makeup changes.[47] Thus, my definition satisfies **C2**.

Definitions that use culture instead of political culture in the notion of a nation pass **C1** but fail **C2**, because the idea of culture, when not qualified as political, is too inclusive to distinguish between national and ethnic groups and too exclusive to unequivocally recognize multicultural nations.[48] A typical culturalist definition that exhibits this weaknesses is Joseph Stalin's. He defined a nation as "a historically evolved, stable community of language, territory, economic life, and psychological make-up manifested in a community of culture."[49] He clearly would not have recognized a multilingual or multicultural nation as a valid one. Moreover, transitional societies whose identities are in flux require us to concentrate on the aspects of collective agency highlighted by my definition to determine whether, in the dynamics of change, any transition in national allegiance has taken place and whether it is over. The culture of a group may remain the same at the same time that it splits into two national groups with two different political cultures, or changes in culture may occur in the context of stable national identity. Looking specifically at political culture in its connection to collective agents' political aspirations allows us to register these changes.

To identify a collective agent that satisfies a necessary condition for holding a primary moral group right to self-determination, we need to look at the set of second-order beliefs constitutive of membership in it and determine whether they relate to self-determination as the group's shared good. In this section, I demonstrated that we can identify national groups through the presence of a particular type of political culture characterized by sets of particular beliefs, but not necessarily corresponding institutional structures. To determine whether a national agent is present, we need to look for the expression of the group's constitutive beliefs and for the members' self-identification with these beliefs. If our search indicates that a political culture of the required kind is present, the group is a nation. If these beliefs are not expressed in non-democratic contexts, however, we cannot be sure what nations are present in a given territory. In the next section, I will briefly consider how potential political cultures can be expressed. I will provide a more detailed consideration of potential political cultures in the next chapter.

The Expression of Potential Political Cultures

I have already explained why the requirement that the political culture that characterizes a nation must be endorsed by co-nationals excludes official cultures in an oppressive society from being considered as nations. But what exactly constitutes national political cultures in the partial or complete absence of corresponding public spheres, and how can the beliefs and attitudes that constitute such cultures, which I call "potential political cultures," be expressed?

The structures of self-government and the corresponding political cultures of the national republics in the former USSR could not be considered to be expressions of these nations' political cultures. They were official government structures with corresponding expressed sets of officially endorsed beliefs about and attitudes toward politics, controlled by the center and incorporated into the overall communist political culture, which, moreover, was based on the Russian language. Hence, official political cultures were "vacuous" to the extent that people did not identify with them.[50] A vacuous political culture is usually accompanied by one or more potential political cultures, which are to a great extent imagined by co-nationals, since they do not have outlets for systematic expression. For the members of potential political cultures, however, these cultures represent shared sets of beliefs about the meaningful limits of political authority and about membership.

Different ways of expressing these beliefs exist. When national groups have institutions of self-government, the limits of membership defined in vacuous and potential political cultures largely coincide, but co-nationals do not self-identify with the official forms of their group representation. Rather, they share beliefs negative in relation to the vacuous culture in the form of "an official belief that X is not true." In the absence of proper political expression, they do not necessarily articulate the content of their national political culture, although they can transmit cultural identity traits and do not disagree with the limits of membership. Circumstances permitting, a vacuous culture may be accompanied by a real political culture with limited expression as well. (Take, for example, the existence of *Solidarnost* in Poland.) A good example of a positively expressed potential political culture was that of the Kosovo Albanians under the Yugoslav regime after their autonomy was abolished.

Although co-nationals cannot be sure about the beliefs others hold due to the lack of communication in the public sphere, their sense of national belonging and their conviction that this belief of membership is shared by others can nevertheless be verified. The beliefs of the potential political culture can be shared in a variety of contexts, such as church, some nongovernmental organizations, and political parties, if they are permitted,[51] and they can be different in different areas populated by the national group. The whole of the national political culture exists as a set of incomplete and overlapping spheres of expression maintained by pockets of horizontal ties among citizens. The sets of beliefs representing a potential political culture may be different in different areas populated by the national group and may be expressed in various ways. A potential political culture is, therefore, public, and it is commonly recognized through a set of shared beliefs that are not as elaborate and complete as those of a nation with a fully expressed political culture but are often discernible nonetheless.[52]

One can base pronouncements about which national minorities may be present in the territory of an oppressive state and evaluations of their treatment by the state to some extent on analysis of the dominant political culture and its institutions. When a national group, usually a minority, is severely discriminated against and lacks the means of expressing its political culture, its identity is inadvertently confirmed and publicly expressed in a negative form by the hostile attitudes of the political culture of the oppressing nation. Exclusionary treatment by the authorities aimed at the suppression of the minority identity, such as an explicit prohibition of any political institutions for the group or a targeted violation of its members' human rights, can indicate the group's existence. A potential political culture of the minority nation is provided, as its public expression, an "exoskeleton" of the set of beliefs of the vacuous political culture. The reaction of the dominant culture does not allow us to determine with certainty what type of group a suppressed minority is, although we may be able to guess by the kind of things the group is prohibited from engaging in.

Nevertheless, the presence of a potential political culture, especially in its "negative" expression, is not a fully reliable indicator of the presence of national groups. Sometimes, the suppression of a group may lead to the group's losing its constitutive features: its agency can be destroyed. Nevertheless, if a potential political culture survives, minority co-nationals recognize one another, first, through what they consider to be their shared traits (which may vary across the group due to the lack of communication). Some of these shared traits might be recognized by the larger society for the purposes of exclusion. The minority members also share identification as being "not-them"—not the majority. For example, Crimean Tatars who were deported from their territory in 1944 were able to fully express their political culture when they were repatriated after the fall of the Soviet Union. It is wrong to think that their political culture was always there in a complete form, just waiting to be expressed. It has undergone significant changes over the last two decades, evolving from claims to cultural protection to full-fledged claims to self-determination. The political culture of Crimean Tatars nevertheless always had a "negative" expression in the official Soviet political culture that attempted to eliminate Tatar national identity.[53] My definition of nationhood identifies potential candidates for nationhood in such cases, which is the best that can be done when political expression is controlled.

Since membership in a potential political culture is sometimes not entirely defined even for its members, their beliefs may change when their culture acquires full expression and their collective agency has a chance to actualize. For example, it would have been a mistake to consider Moldovans a part of the Romanian nation based on the beliefs about the limits of their political community expressed by the potential political culture they identified with under the USSR. But a judgment about their desire to be an independent nation would have been both wrong and premature if it had been made during the Soviet era: it was simply not clear what Moldovans' national identity would be until they had a chance to express their effective agency properly.[54] It should be noted that the full expression of a political culture does not prevent its future changes: the Moldovan identity may revert in the future to pan-Romanian, but the issue of the detection of a potential political culture will not arise, because the change will be accompanied by a freely expressed and verifiable identity.

The uncertainty of potential political cultures calls for what I will call the "cautious approach" to claims to nationhood in oppressive or transitional societies. The presence of a vacuous culture tells us that we should pay attention to changing or not clearly expressed national identities and suspend our judgment concerning the national composition of the society in question. This does not mean, however, that the formulation of principles for the regulation of relations among national groups should be withheld until the final composition of a transitional multinational state is determined. On the contrary, defining in advance the terms of interaction among any national groups that might emerge within the territory of the state facilitates peaceful political changes during the transition to democracy.

This forward-looking component notwithstanding, it is worth asking whether the seemingly agnostic stance of the "cautious" approach impairs the capacity of the international community both to pass judgments about the makeup of oppressive multinational states and to act to aid oppressed non-state groups in such states, especially national groups without any self-government structures. For although having a set of general norms is important for the regulation of relations concerning self-determination, they cannot be applied properly if we do not know what kind of group we are dealing with and whether the minority in question requires the protection of only minority (linguistic, cultural, or ethnic) or also national (self-determination) interests. I consider how to approach these problems in Chapter 4, which deals with potential political cultures in greater detail. Here I would like to merely point out that the effort of the international community to improve oppressive states' human rights records increases the chances that we can learn about their national makeup with more precision.

There are also some other benefits of applying the cautious approach to evaluating the expressed national makeup of an oppressive country. Such an approach would have called into question the officially promoted national structure of the former Soviet Union due to its lack of freedom of speech and expression, which prevented all voices from being heard. The cautious approach would have required a skeptical attitude toward the officially expressed national identities until it could be shown that the official division into national groups and their hierarchy was accepted and maintained voluntarily in a political climate free of coercion. The vacuous character of this hierarchical structure could have been determined by looking at the self-identification of the members of the groups in question.

Why Self-Identification is Not Enough to Define a Nation

The existence of potential and vacuous political cultures points to the importance, in defining national groups, of individual identification with a set of beliefs about national belonging. The self-identification of group members alone is not enough to define a nation, however. A group of people in a given territory cannot be defined as a nation on the basis of simple summation of the majority individual preferences, for several reasons: If the majority in a given territory thinks it constitutes a nation and a 30% minority in the same territory thinks it is a different nation, 50% plus one may override the minority's national identity. Majority rule is not capable of recognizing permanent minorities.[55] Using census data regarding individual identification will not do because of the familiar problem of distinguishing between ethnic and national minorities, which threatens the violation of **C2** unless some collective forms of identification are considered. Recording which individuals consider themselves Russian or Ojibwa in Minnesota, for example, does not explain whether these individuals are organized as group agents around some shared goods and, if so, what type of group they constitute.

As I mentioned earlier in the chapter, if it is suggested that at each particular moment a nation exists when a significant number of people in a community consider themselves to form a nation or behave as if they have formed one, then, lest we beg the question, we need to explain what the ground for their behavior is and what this behavior involves—to define the content of their belief of national belonging. An important feature of national belonging is that national identity requires some public endorsement through a shared political culture. Although individual self-identification is very important for determining what groups form a nation—and not only for potential political cultures—when the populations of two or more nations are thoroughly mixed, only identifying political cultures of self-determination makes it possible to determine which nations are present within the territory of a state.

To identify with a belief of national belonging, an individual has to believe that others do so as well. This requires a public framework that generates and reaffirms second-order beliefs of belonging, including the notion of shared group ends. In a historical perspective, this system of beliefs needs to be passed along to future generations. Even if it is not the case that every individual has a reflective wish for self-determination, individuals identify with the political culture that is shared and endorsed by their co-nationals. Even for potential political cultures, self-identification cannot be the only characteristic that defines nationhood, for the endorsement of a political culture characterizing a nation cannot be exclusively private.

Finally, defining nationhood on the basis of the summation of individual identity claims does not guarantee that we can distinguish between rival nation-building strategies of the same national group or between those of rival nations in the same territory. Two or more competing conceptions about the political future of a group of people living in a particular territory represent rival nation-building strategies if the same belief about the limits of membership in a political culture is shared by all competing ideas. Rival nationalities normally perceive themselves to be separate political communities, whether in the presence of rival claims to the same territory or in their absence. By looking for a political culture defining membership in a primary political community, one can detect whether a conflict is over the control of the same political sphere or whether it is about acquiring another, independent one, and therefore whether there is more than one political culture present. Based on this criterion, in the transitional period after the fall of the Soviet Union, for example, Moldova was not only faced with two competing nation-building efforts within the Moldovan nation but also with a rival Russian-speaking nation formed in the Transdniester region.

What happens when there is no unanimity among the members of a group concerning what political culture to identify with? Is the decision about what nations are present in a given territory still based on majority endorsement and corresponding participation in a collective agency? The summation of majority preferences correctly indicates what nations are present in a given territory only if we take into consideration all the political cultures within this territory. The majority of Canadians include Quebec as a part of the Canadian nation. To determine whether it is indeed so, however, we also need to look at the majority preferences within Quebec, since the province exhibits a political culture of nationhood. Within Quebec and other provinces, moreover, there are First Nations (the indigenous populations of Canada), whose majority vote within their groups has to be considered in order to determine the true national makeup of Canada. Finally, if there are Anglophone groups in Quebec claiming self-determination, we need to determine their status based on which political culture they relate to. It matters whether they want to be independent of Quebec on the ground of being Canadian, not Quebecois, or on the ground of being an independent collective agent with a separate political culture.

Finally, how does my notion of nationhood work when some individuals aspire to self-determination, others oppose it, and yet others are indifferent? How many members of a group have to identify with the political culture of the group as a self-determining group for us to think of the group as a nation? In this case, we still need to consider what political cultures associated with self-determination are present in the territory in question, for the individuals who oppose the group's mobilization in terms of the shared good of self-determination still associate their political membership with some primary political community. Determining what self-determining communities exist within a given territory avoids the conundrum that Margalit and Raz's approach to self-determination faced in assigning a nation to the majority on a given territory regardless of the presence of minority nations. It is also possible that one or more of the political cultures associated with self-determination will not be stable, creating disagreement about the type of group mobilization present in a territory. In this case, to assist a peaceful mobilization, whatever shape it may assume, legal frameworks should be available to accommodate several possible scenarios in a transitional area. I discuss the issues associated with formulating a constitution for a transitional area in the next chapter.

A subjective definition stating that any group that claims it is a self-determining national community should be considered such satisfies **C1** but not necessarily **C2**, for such a definition may fail to render a clear verdict on the national make-up of a territory with mixed national groups or to distinguish competing nation-building efforts and rival nations, and thus it is not sufficiently pragmatic. Moore points out that self-identification can help in defining jurisdictional units in a case of several self-determining groups.[56] A group's claims can be identified in such a case only by reference to a political culture, however, and thus only if they belong to a properly constituted collective agent. Hence, not only culturalist but also subjective definitions, when clarified to satisfy **C2,** converge on the elements by which I identify nationhood.

Summing up, a nation is a collective agent characterized by a political culture organized around the idea of self-determination and with which members of the nation identify. This definition does not settle the question of the entitlement of national groups in advance, and therefore it satisfies **C1**. The definition satisfies **C2** because it provides distinctions among various groups based on their self-definition as collective agents and accounts for dynamic changes in national identities.

Nationhood and Self-Determination

Having defined national groups, I can now restate what constitutes the moral foundation of the right to national self-determination. In Chapter 2, I argued that the right to self-determination is a primary moral right of a certain type of group. The entitlement to the right to self-determination results from the very nature of collective agents organized around the constitutive shared good of self-determination and the relations of equality among them. National groups are defined by their ability to be determined by the conditions of their internal life, and they inherently need to exercise self-determination to maintain their constitution. Thus, they possess a moral right to self-determination.

It would be wrong either to allow the enjoyment of the benefits of self-determination only to some national groups or to deprive all of national groups of the right to exercise this capacity. Even if there were a way to level down the allocation of the benefits of self-determination by reorganizing the world community into a few oppressive states that inhibit attempts by any national groups to mobilize, it would be the wrong thing to do, since self-determination promotes important moral values. Given the dynamic aspects of nationhood, it is important to provide a framework that helps group agents to form and actualize correctly rather than in a way that is detrimental to their members and individuals outside of the group.

As I discussed in Chapter 2, certain views on self-determination held by members of a group divest the group of the capacity to be equally free with other groups. This happens when the group's conception of self-determination does not correspond to a form practicable in the international world in which the group exists. Presently, this can happen if self-determination is not understood in political (and, by extension, territorial) terms. Nations, very generally, can be defined as units of self-determination, but my definition of a nation as an agent organized around a *political* culture of self-determination is rendered in terms of the contemporary understanding of self-determination. In this world, groups with a non-political idea of self-determination are placed in a category other than "nations." Does this aspect of qualification for nationhood and the right to self-determination tie my approach to political contingencies, thereby making my approach so narrow that it runs contrary to the meaning of moral entitlement?

"Practicable" does not mean "currently practiced by the majority." It refers to the broadest possible and conceptually coherent application of the general idea of self-determination in the present international system, as constrained by the requirements of moral acceptability. I create a comprehensive classification of different types of group agents to ensure that their existence is protected through a principled determination of their entitlements based on their constitution. Group agents can move from one category to another if their internal constitution changes.

A group that has the intention of being determined by the conditions of its internal life needs to protect its freedom and acquire the form of control for doing so required by present circumstances. The group members have to formulate their intentions accordingly. This is why it is imperative to define a morally acceptable form of self-determination that is also practically possible and thus capable of becoming an international norm.

If a group agent does not intend to organize so as to be capable of being equally free with others, the group agent is not a nation. If a group agent declares that it is self-determining but is content with non-political forms of group organization, the life of this group is inevitably shaped and controlled in significant ways by the political society within which the group is included, whose constitution is external to the group. This turns a group into an agent that qualifies for a derivative right, because the group in the end only wishes to be better accommodated within the larger society. A group can delegate the maintenance of some important functions of its self-determining status to a larger group within whose territory it resides, but such a group can be said to preserve its capacity for equal freedom only if it is able to unilaterally take back the powers it has relinquished. Even in such a case, the group's understanding of self-determination is political and territorial, because it merely delegates certain tasks of maintaining these aspects of its existence to another group while ultimately retaining control over its political future. Before the group opts to enjoy self-determination in a "reduced" form, it first conceives of itself in terms of being self-determining in the "right" way.

Let us consider how this analysis applies to a group like the Roma who claim to be a non-territorial national group. To determine whether the Roma are a nation entitled to self-determination or an ethnic group that deserves only polyethnic rights we need to consider if they are organized around the *political* culture of self-determination and consider the group's intentions. If they conceive of their nationhood in terms of political self-determination, they need to be accommodated properly. Since agents that are capable of equal freedom need territory for their political pursuits it should be then considered how to provide them with territory or how to assure that the powers they delegate to other, territorial groups still safeguard significant control over their group constitution. I discuss possible accommodation for territorially dispersed groups in Chapter 6. If the Roma do not conceive of their nationhood beyond certain self-governing powers within the political and economic structures of their host states, they function as an ethnic group. This does not, of course, exclude the possibility that they may eventually transform into a national group.

My concept of nationhood is clear enough to specify the potential holders of the right to self-determination, and it does this better than the existing international system. The present legal right to self-determination belongs to occupied or colonized national groups, but this definition of its subjects is unhelpful in a multinational setting. In an occupied territory with several national groups, does each of them deserve the right to self-determination (and in the present system, a state of its own), or do they have to exercise the right jointly and hence share a state? We still need to define those groups that qualify to enjoy the right—even a very exclusive right—to self-determination. But it is much easier to do this with a comprehensive conception nationhood at our disposal. The common acceptance of my definition of nationhood could help with the assessment of substate groups' entitlements and the definition of the subjects of the right to self-determination.

My concept of nationhood is open and inclusive, because it can characterize nations universally, while a great number of features beyond the political culture of self-determination characterize national groups only disjunctively. I do not consider political culture organized around the shared good of self-determination to be the only important characteristic of nationhood. There may be other features that some or all national groups share. I only argue that the presence of this type of political culture is necessary and sufficient to characterize nations, especially in the context of the right to self-determination. The notion of political culture associated with self-determination also captures the dynamic aspects of nationhood, such as changes in or the emergence of new national allegiances, which are an important feature of contemporary political landscapes.

Being a description of a universal property of national groups, presently in relation to other such groups, my definition sets the ground for looking at the self-determination of every group as limited by the exercise of self-determination by other groups, and it therefore provides for restrictions on the right. Whether the communities' mobilization is undesirable depends on the norms guiding a nation's relations with others, but it is not the definition that determines the outcome.

In the next chapter, I consider how to treat group agents in transitional societies. I establish an applicable norm regulating the right to self-determination in Chapter 5, and in Chapter 6 I show how it can be enforced.

Notes

1. Parts of this chapter are an extended version of the argument in Anna Moltchanova, "Nationhood and Political Culture," Journal of Social Philosophy, 38(2), Summer 2007, 255–273, publisher: Wiley and Sons Ltd.
2. One such set of norms, for example, would recognize the universal right of such groups to self-determination but disassociate self-determination from the acquisition of statehood as I demonstrate in Chapter 5.
3. Council of Europe, European Treaties, ETS No. 157 (Framework Convention for the Protection of National Minorities, Strasbourg, 1.II.1995), http://www.coe.fr/eng/legaltxt/157e.htm.
4. Different versions of the nation-state definition are supported in Margaret Canovan, *Nationhood and Political Theory* (Cheltenham, UK: Edward Elgar, 1996), pp. 69, 119; Ernest Gellner, *Nations and Nationalism* (Oxford: Basil Blackwell, 1983), pp. 1, 43; and Anthony Giddens, *The Nation-State and Violence*, volume 2 of *A Contemporary Critique of Historical Materialism* (Cambridge: Polity Press, 1985), p. 119. I consider these three definitions on the next section.
5. Many contemporary conceptions of "nation" are informed by the historically contingent dichotomy between state-endowed and substate national groups. Michel Seymour, for example, defines a nation as a national majority alongside national minorities and ethnic groups and formulates his idea of a national culture on the basis of the majority culture. See *On Redefining the Nation*, Cahier No. 97–01 (Montreal: Universite de Montreal, Faculte des arts et des sciences, 1997).
6. Such a language, he argued, links the members of the nation to the "whole previous life of the nation." Fichte, *Addresses to the German Nation*, p. 58.
7. Rogers Brubaker, Nationalism Reframed.
8. Ibid., p. 7
9. Ibid., p. 19.
10. Craig Calhoun, "The Problem of Identity in Collective Action," in *Macro-Micro Linkages in Sociology*, ed. Joan Huber (Newbury Park, CA: Sage, 1991), p. 59, quoted in Brubaker, *Nationalism Reframed*, p. 20.
11. It is impossible to achieve a "detached," unconditional definition of nationhood using the methods vividly described by Ernest Renan in his "Qu'est-ce qu'une nation?": "Ce que nous allons faire est délicat; c'est presque de la vivisection; nous allons traiter les vivants comme d'ordinaire on traite les morts. Nous y mettrons la froideur, l'impartialité la plus absolue" [What we are going to do is delicate; it is almost like a vivisection; we are going to treat the living as normally we treat the dead. We will use cool reason, and absolute impartiality.] In *Œuvres complètes de Ernest Renan* (Paris: Calmann-Lévy, n.d.) tome 1, p. 888.
12. Giddens, *Nation-State and Violence*, p. 119.
13. Canovan defines nationhood as follows: "A nation is a polity that feels like a community, or conversely a cultural or ethnic community politically mobilized; it cannot exist without subjective identification, and therefore is to some extent dependent on free individual choice, but that choice is nevertheless experienced as a destiny transcending individuality; it turns political institutions into a kind of extended family inheritance, although the kinship ties in question are highly metaphorical; it is a contingent historical product that feels like a part of the order of nature; it links individual and community, past and present; it gives to cold institutional structures an aura of warm, intimate togetherness." *Nationhood and Political Theory*, p. 69.
14. Ibid., p. 97.
15. Gellner, *Nations and Nationalism*, p. 1.
16. Gellner, *Conditions of Liberty: Civil Society and Its Rivals* (London: Viking Adult, 1994), p. 108.
17. Ibid., p. 121.
18. Yael Tamir, for example, argues for the weakening of the structure of the nation-state as one of the options for the accommodation of national minorities. See *Liberal Nationalism* (Princeton: Princeton University Press, 1993), p. 72.

19. Gellner's theory is a good reflection of a particular type of nationalism—the nationalism of the minority nations in the time of industrialization and the fall of the great empires. As Roman Szporluk points out, however, Gellner missed that the former imperial centers were also undergoing the process of nation building, that there were different national responses to modernity within the same nations, and that there were often other ideas about national identity besides the official line. Gellner "was less ready to recognize that modernization profoundly affected also the so-called 'old continuous nations'—that *they* too were undergoing a crisis during transition to modernity, as they faced the task of creating *their* nation-states on the ruins of their respective imperial 'Megalomanias.'" He "paid little attention to intranational and international relations, including situations, common in Eastern Europe, when one and the same ethnic group was an object of rival nation-building efforts at the same time—invoking different ethnic, historic and political arguments for its cause and proposing *different* national responses to modernity." And "He did not consider the possibility that the...[people]... themselves might have other ideas, besides the official one, about their national identity: he refused to concede that national identity is a subject of intranational contestation and the ideological sphere is a battlefield in the struggle for hegemony within the nation." See Roman Szporluk, "Thoughts about Change: Ernest Gellner and the History of Nationalism," in *The State of the Nation: Ernest Gellner and the Theory of Nationalism*, ed. John Hall (Cambridge: Cambridge University Press, 1998), pp. 35–36.
20. David Miller, "Secession and the Principle of Nationality," p. 266.
21. David Miller, *On Nationality*, p. 113.
22. Margaret Moore, "On National Self-Determination," pp. 900–913 in *Political Studies* 45(5), p. 905.
23. Moore, "On National Self-Determination," p. 905. A similar emphasis on the subjective factor is present in the works of Seton-Watson (H. Seton-Watson, *Nations and States* (London: Methuen, 1997), p. 7); Cobban (A. Cobban, *The Nation State and National Self-Determination* (London: Collins, 1969), p. 107); Philpott (D. Philpott, "In Defense of Self-Determination," 352–85 *in Ethics*, 105/2 (1995), p. 365), Norman (Wayne Norman, "Theorizing Nationalism (Normatively): The First Steps," pp. 51–66 in Ronald Beiner, (ed.), *Theorizing Nationalism* (Albany: State University of New York Press, 1999).
24. Lea Brilmayer provides a similar criticism of the subjective approach in the context of the decisions made by a group concerning their status and self-determination in "Secession and Self-Determination: A Territorial Interpretation,"177–202 in *Yale Journal of International Law* 16(177), 1991, p. 177).
25. Alfred Cobban, *The Nation State and National Self-Determination*, (New York: Crowell, 1969), p. 65.
26. Walker Connor *Ethnonationalism* (Princeton: Princeton University Press, 1994), p. 202.
27. Ibid., p. 213.
28. Max Weber, *Economy and Society: An Outline of Interpretive Sociology*, ed. Guenther Roth and Claus Wittich, 2 vols. (New York: Bedminster, 1968) 2: 2, p. 922.
29. Ibid., 2, p. 925.
30. Michael Hechter's approach to nationhood also emphasizes subjective features of the phenomenon.: He associates any type of nationalism enacted in the name of a politically self-conscious nation to engender a demand for national sovereignty and thus places nationhood in the right context Hechter bases his understanding of national identity in cultural distinctions, however; I will discuss how this kind of approach fails to satisfy C2 when I explain why political culture is enough to characterize nations. Michael Hechter, *Containing Nationalism* (Oxford: Oxford University Press, 2000), p. 96.
31. Archie Brown, defines political culture as that part of culture which bears relevance to politics; he excludes formal institutions and behavior patterns from the scope of culture. Brown, A. "Conclusions," in A. Brown (ed.) *Political Culture and Communist Studies* (London, The MacMillan Press Ltd., 1984), p. 155. According to Stephen White, political culture is "the attitudinal behavioural matrix within which the political system is located." (Brown, *Political Culture and Communist Studies*, p. 6) I exclude both political institutions and an unqualified idea of behavior from the notion of political culture.

32. Although my definition of a nation follows David Miller's in important ways, it is different in that it concentrates on political culture and not on culture. Miller describes a nation as "a group of people who recognize one another as belonging to the same community, who acknowledge special obligations to one another, and who aspire to political autonomy—this by virtue of characteristics that they believe they share, typically a common history, attachment to a geographical place, and a public culture that differentiates them from their neighbors." See "Secession and the Principle of Nationality," p. 266. When Miller wants to distinguish between national and ethnic groups, he points out that national groups make a claim to self-determination and create the appropriate organizations and institutions to fulfill the claim. See *On Nationality*, p. 113. Hence, it makes sense to refocus the definition to clearly identify that the public culture of national groups and the actual or desired political autonomy have to do with a special type of political culture.
33. The idea of legitimate authority as being based on dependent reasons can be found in Joseph Raz "Authority, Law and Morality," in Raz, J. *Ethics in the Public Domain* (Oxford: Clarendon Press, 1996), pp. 210–237.
34. I will consider incomplete ways of maintaining a political culture associated with nationhood in the section on potential political cultures.
35. It is enough for my project to assume the truth of a point widely accepted in the scholarship on nationhood, namely, that it is not necessary that statehood and nationhood be firmly associated. For example, see David Miller (1996) "Secession and the Principle of Nationality," p. 261–282; Buchanan, A. "Recognitional Legitimacy and the State System."
36. If we consider Ernest Gellner's position, all education run by a nation-state is thoroughly nationalistic. See *Nations and Nationalism*.
37. David Miller and Margaret Moore emphasize the importance of political self-consciousness for nations as opposed to ethnic groups. See David Miller, *On Nationality*, p. 113, and Moore, *The Ethics of Nationalism*, p. 6. Robert Ware offers a concept of a nation as a political group in a given territory sharing common projects and common will. See "Nations and Social Complexity," in *Rethinking Nationalism*, ed. J. Couture, K. Nielsen, and M. Seymour (Calgary, Alberta: University of Calgary Press, 1996), pp. 135, 157.
38. Thomas W. Pogge, for example, defines a nation as "a potentially self-sustaining community of people bound together by a shared history and culture." See "The Bounds of Nationalism," in *Rethinking Nationalism*, ed. J. Couture, K. Nielsen, and M. Seymour (Calgary, Alberta: University of Calgary Press, 1996), p. 463.
39. Miller, "Secession," p. 266.
40. Miller, "Nationality in Divided Societies," in *Citizenship and National Identity*, pp. 125–141.
41. Ibid., p. 127.
42. Like "societal culture," an idea used by Will Kymlicka in his theory, a political culture can stand some changes but remain in existence. See *Multicultural Citizenship*, p. 87.
43. The interpretation of the same historical events can be different at different times, under different systems of government, or in different parts of the nation. The reunification of Ukraine and Russia in 1654 by Bogdan Khmel'nitsky, for example, was considered under the socialist government to be a landmark event in the development of the nation, and Khmel'nitsky was regarded as a hero, while another historical figure, Getman Masepa, was considered a traitor for signing a treaty with Sweden some 50 years after the reunification. He was defeated by Peter the Great, and the defeat was considered another landmark of Ukrainian history. Masepa was considered a hero by nationalists, however, while Khmel'nitsky was regarded by them as an unwise politician who made the wrong ally. Nowadays, in the official Ukrainian history, Masepa is not a traitor anymore, and Khmel'nitsky is not a hero. There is a new, more balanced attitude to the history of Ukraine. It is acknowledged that the way Ukrainian history was written under the Soviets was a result of the policy of Russification waged by the center, and that Ukrainian history was considered from the Russian point of view. For a comprehensive analysis of Ukrainian history, see Orest Subtelny, *Ukraine: A History* (Toronto: University of Toronto Press in association with the Canadian Institute of Ukrainian Studies, 1993).

44. Ernest Renan defines a nation as emphasizing commonalities and the forgetting of historical events, which leads to divisions: "L'essence d'une nation est que tous les individus aient beaucoup de choses en commun, et aussi que tous aient oublié bien des choses...tout citoyen français doit avoir oublié la Saint-Barthélemy, les massacres du Midi au XIIIe siècle" [The essence of a nation is not only that all members have many things in common, but also that all of them have forgotten many things. . .all French citizens had to have forgotten Saint-Bartholomew, the massacres of the Middle of the 18th century.] See "Qu'est-ce que'une nation," p. 892.
45. Eric Hobsbawm, "Introduction: Inventing Traditions," in *The Invention of Tradition*, ed. Eric Hobsbawm and Terence Ranger (Cambridge: Cambridge University Press, 1983), pp. 6–8.
46. David Laitin, "Political Culture and Political Preferences," *American Political Science Review* 82, no. 2 (1988): p. 589.
47. Like the societal culture, an idea used by Kymlicka in his theory, a political culture can stand some changes but remain in existence. (Kymlicka, Multicultural Citizenship, p. 87). He defends the distinction between immigrant and national minorities. (Ibid., Chapter 5)
48. Another "political culture" concept of a nation is offered by Robert Ware, who says that a nation is a political group on a given territory sharing common projects, common will; a nation is different from nationality, which is understood as a people with the shared language, culture, ethical beliefs. He points out that there can be identical nations but not nationalities. (Robert X. Ware, "Nations and Social Complexity," pp.133–160 in *Rethinking Nationalism*, at pp. 135, 157) In his concept of a nation, it is not clear what the difference between national and ethnic minorities is.
49. Joseph Stalin, *Marxism and the National Question: Selected Writings and Speeches* (New York: International Publishers, 1942), p. 12.
50. Archie Brown characterizes an "official political culture," which I call a "vacuous political culture," as follows: "Official political culture represents official norms, desiderata and political goals rather than societal values and beliefs, attitudes towards authority to be fostered in the mass of the population; the type of political participation which is encouraged; the interpretation of the country's history which is favored; the attitude adopted towards political organizations other than official; the view taken of religion; the nature and extent of political information deemed appropriate to possess for citizens; and the goal, or goals, in terms of which present labours and sacrifices are justified or legitimized." See *Political Culture and Communist Studies*, p. 180.
51. The Greek Catholic Church, for example, was prohibited from functioning in the former USSR in the regions of the Western Ukraine incorporated into the USSR in 1940. However, there was an underground network of Greek Catholic priests who would perform some basic rites, such as baptism. For the people who lived in areas where such networks existed, the networks symbolized their distinct status and continuity with the past. Not all the territory had such networks, however, and many did not know about their existence. For this part of the population, self-identification with their nation was expressed in other ways. They would put their children in one of the Ukrainian schools that were allowed in the Western Ukraine, for example, as an expression of their belief in their national belonging. Still others would turn to the writings of the intellectual nationalist dissidents to find an expression and confirmation of their national beliefs. Though the people of the Western and Eastern Ukraine have had different religions, political beliefs, and ideas about nation building—even their languages have been somewhat different—they perceived themselves as one people, and when they could build their own state after the fall of the USSR, they did, often disagreeing about methods and ideology but not about membership and their right to self-determination. I would like to thank Natalka Patsiurko for her information on the Western Ukraine.
52. Potential political cultures can also have a corresponding set of beliefs and attitudes expressed by co-nationals abroad. This expression does not always correspond to and cannot immediately stand in for a potential political culture of the nation in the homeland. It first needs to be verified whether this set of beliefs is indeed how the nation in the homeland perceives its own status.

53. For the history of the Crimean Tatar nation in the USSR and for some recent developments, see Belitser, N., Orlyk, P. *The Constitutional Process in the Autonomous Republic of Crimea in the Context of Interethnic Relations and Conflict Settlement* (Kyiv, Ukraine, Institute for Democracy, 2000); Pohl, J. O. "The Deportation and Fate of the Crimean Tatars," presented at the 5th Annual World Convention of the Association for the Study of Nationalities, 13–15 April 2000, Columbia University, New York.
54. This is not to say that basic beliefs of potential political cultures always change when they are "actualized." The Lithuanian national political culture, for example, did not undergo radical changes after its proper actualization.
55. Making a higher than 50% threshold necessary for decision-making can lead to the problem of supermajority, when a minority of citizens decides the fate of the country (for example, if 70% is required to make a decision, 31% against it could thwart what is clearly (69%) a majority preference (for a discussion of supermajorities see Robert A. Dahl, *Democracy and Its Critics* (New Haven and London: Yale University Press, 1989), Chapter 11).
56. Moore, "On National Self-Determination," p. 905.

Chapter 4
Potential Political Cultures

In the previous chapter, I defined a nation as a group of people whose members self-identify with a political culture of a certain kind. This political culture is related to the group's shared goal of maintaining or acquiring collective agency that would enable it to control its political future. I also established that nations have the capacity of being free in relation to other similar agents and thus of holding a primary moral right. The self-identification component in my definition of nationhood is designed to exclude vacuous political cultures in transitional or oppressive societies, but it is these societies that most need claims to self-determination on their territory to be regulated.

Political culture is a set of beliefs about and attitudes toward politics shared by group members. The beliefs concern the locus, origin, and character of political authority. Political culture has different features in a democracy than it does in an oppressive political regime. Its scope ranges from political cultures that have corresponding public spheres and institutionalized structures to express them to political cultures that have neither. At one end of this continuum is a perfect democracy that provides ideal conditions for a collective agent's deliberations, goal setting, and the realization of what John Rawls would call "the ideal of public reason." A government conforms to this ideal when it governs a group on the basis of reasons that apply to the group members' situation and when the set of beliefs that motivates individuals' actions as members of the collective agent is the set of beliefs expressed in the public sphere. On the other end of the continuum is the political culture of a people living in a totalitarian society. Whether the people is a national minority without the structures of self-government or a majority with formal access to the institutions of self-government, they cannot call the government their own if they do not identify with the set of beliefs expressed in public sphere. They possess what I called a "potential political culture."

The introduction of the notion of potential political culture raises several points of concern. In an environment in which a group cannot express its beliefs and attitudes, the detection of both the group and its political culture can be problematic. What attests to the existence of the kind of political culture that characterizes a nation in an oppressive society? The problem of detecting national groups in oppressive societies is in fact a problem for all accounts of nationhood except those that ignore substate national groups altogether. In response, we might either limit the range of

A. Moltchanova, *National Self-Determination and Justice in Multinational States*, Studies in Global Justice 5, DOI 10.1007/978-90-481-2691-0_4,

situations to which our account of nationhood applies or treat vacuous cultures as expressing national identities, but neither option is satisfactory. Applying the notion of nationhood to only a limited group of agents does not help to address the self-determination claims of groups in transitional societies, and considering vacuous cultures to characterize national groups undermines a principled application of the right to self-determination and ignores the "real" national make-up of states. Estimating the degree of "reality" of various expressions of nationhood in oppressive societies helps specify the subjects of the right to self-determination with more precision. Thus, we need to take a closer look at national identities in oppressive societies.

In Chapter 3, I indicated how an oppressed group's political culture might be expressed. This chapter considers three problems related to the notion of potential political culture that need to be resolved to bolster my argument. The first problem concerns the determination of the entitlements of substate groups when they cannot properly express their political cultures. We can often detect the existence of a group that is being oppressed, but the changeability of identities and the limitations on expression may hinder the application of normative principles regulating the group's status even if such principles are formulated, because we may not be able to determine with sufficient certainty what the group is entitled to—whether it is a cultural group, a national group, or something else. The second problem has to do with the application of the cautious approach to nondemocratic societies with only one nation on their territory. By asserting that vacuous political cultures do not characterize national identities, the "cautious approach," which I introduced in the previous chapter, may hold back the application of the normative framework even for relatively obvious cases of national identity (for example, nondemocratic states with one national group where state boundaries are the same for vacuous and for potential cultures). The seemingly excessive strictness of the approach requires us to clarify the distinctions between vacuous and potential political cultures in cases where a set of beliefs exists that appears to belong to both vacuous and potential cultures. The third problem is the seeming unreality of nationhood for all but democratic societies implied by the idea of potential political culture. The idea of potential political culture may seem to suggest that only democratic countries can be treated as real nations, while all other communities are faced with some degree of potentiality, because only in democratic societies can the beliefs of the political culture associated with nationhood be fully expressed and acted upon by the members of the nation. This, too, may seem to make the notion of political culture too restrictive.

I begin by elaborating on the meaning of political culture in general in order to explain which of its elements are associated with nationhood and how they are expressed. I then offer solutions to the three problems that constitute the central focus of this chapter.

Political Culture: Overview of the Continuum

With respect to the scope of political culture, the most minimalist notion characterizes it as a set of attitudes, beliefs, and values that together establish a general orientation toward political action. A more inclusive notion adds social practices to attitudes and beliefs, and the most encompassing idea of political culture includes political structures, as well.[1]

Should we consider social practices to be part of political culture?[2] Estonians who participated in elections for the USSR Supreme Council did not, for the most part, perceive these elections as a social practice that embodied their group identity. If this social practice was made meaningful by them, it was not in a way that was at all straightforward: their shared motivation for voting was perhaps based not on the belief that by doing so they expressed the will of the people but rather on the belief that refusing to vote would have undesirable consequences. It is clear that the motivation behind the performance of an action matters in identifying what political culture is present and whether there is more than one. The action of voting cannot be understood to characterize a political culture unless it is placed in the context of individuals' attitudes toward this practice. Behavior can therefore be included in the notion of political culture only with some reservations, and if we are to include it we first need to determine what moves individuals to act. To uncover individual dispositions to behave, we will have to pay attention to what normative beliefs about practices individuals endorse, and because patterns of behavior in oppressive societies are not directly related to these normative beliefs, I do not include social practices in my notion of political culture: we can learn all we need to know to identify a political culture with which individuals self-identify by considering their beliefs and attitudes.

Should the notion of political culture include political structures? Political structures do not have direct relation to political culture, as evidenced by the formation of Polish national identity, which Stephen Welch describes as a negative response to the political structures imposed on the Poles at the time when their national identity was emerging. Since the Polish nation was characterized in opposition to existing political structures, these structures could hardly be considered a part of the Polish nation's political culture, although they helped it emerge. Nor do all already formed political cultures have a clear set of corresponding political structures. I define political culture, then, solely as a set of beliefs about and attitudes toward politics.[3]

Individual beliefs about politics can be presented as descriptive beliefs, while their attitudes toward politics can be presented as a set of normative beliefs. For example, "I believe that Quebec is a nation" is a descriptive statement, whereas "I believe it is wrong that Quebec is not given national status" is a normative statement. Hence, we can impose a more uniform description on what constitutes a political culture: a political culture is a set of descriptive and normative beliefs about politics. Below, when it is not important for my presentation to separate beliefs and attitudes, I will use "beliefs" to refer to both descriptive and normative beliefs. For a political culture to characterize a nation, individuals need to self-identify with the set of beliefs characterizing the corresponding political culture. To self-identify with a set of beliefs, individuals have to both be capable of forming dispositions to behave based directly on these beliefs and to approve the beliefs' propositional content. I will deal more with the notion of self-identification in the next section. When an individual is motivated to act directly in relation to a certain belief, this individual develops a disposition to behave.

In different contexts, different beliefs and attitudes have to be shared to characterize a political culture. If we try to identify what political culture is shared by individuals in relation to a democratic process, the beliefs under consideration do not necessarily have to reflect particular national allegiances. But if political culture is employed as a category for the purpose of defining nationhood, the relevant beliefs are different from those considered with respect to the democratic process. Citizens of a multinational federal state share the culture of democratic participation but have different national cultures. Differences in democracy or values, for example, do not adequately describe the relationships of different national groups, because the same nation can encompass different sets of values, while different nations can have similar value systems and cultures. Norwegians and Swedes have similar attitudes toward and beliefs about the principles of social and political justice, the relationship of citizens to the state, and so forth. The political cultures their individual citizens share are similar in many respects, but the beliefs of members concerning the bounds of membership in their political communities and the corresponding collective agents differ.

The elements of political culture relevant to defining nationhood, then, are not connected to just any type of political practice that a collective agent is involved in, but only to the elements of the group's internal constitution that allow it to relate to other similar groups. Moreover, these elements are not selected merely to compare political systems of different nations (for example, limited monarchy versus presidency). Their purpose, in other words, is not to explain how the political cultures of different nations are different or similar, but rather to provide a meaningful description of the fact that there are different nations. The beliefs found in a political culture characterizing a nation are of a kind that both can be universally found across national cultures and can account for the plurality of national groups. The political culture of nationhood includes, therefore, a set of constitutive beliefs that also allow all national groups to relate to one another. Such a set is relatively narrow and includes the beliefs shared by the members of a national group about the essential elements of their group's organization, about the ideal status that the members envision for the group's authority (presently always in the context of its relation to other groups and thus about the standing and the limits of collective agency in its relation to other similar agents), and about the outreach of this authority—about which people are considered fellow nationals. Thus, a political culture of nationhood is limited to the beliefs individuals hold about themselves as members of a collective agent that include (1) criteria for membership and (2) the shared goals of the national group tied to the realization of its self-determination.[4] The political culture associated with nationhood is enhanced by the proper actualization of group agency, which includes the expression and regeneration of the beliefs shared by the members of the political culture.

Defining nationhood in terms of political culture captures the properties of nationhood that are most important for the corresponding collective agents' mutual relations. Political culture of this kind, however, permeates different areas of culture and is reflected in other kinds of beliefs about nationhood, such as attitudes toward immigration and immigrants and toward the protection of the national culture.

Allowing foreigners to join or refusing them the privilege are decisions related to the regulation of group membership. The key cultural protection issue relevant to the political culture of nationhood is the belief shared by co-nationals that as self-determining people they have the power to protect their national culture. In Quebec, for example, the issue of cultural protection is considered to be crucial partly because it is presently one of the most important—and politically available—ways of expressing nationhood, which designates the self-determining power of the Quebecois. The issue of the survival of the French language may become less important if Quebec is recognized as a nation within Canada.

I do not consider a national political culture to be equivalent to the political aspects of culture. The notions of culture and political culture designate different, although often overlapping and mutually reinforcing, domains. Generally speaking, there can be several cultures and one national political culture, as in a state with several ethnic groups. It would be wrong to think of a political culture as tied to a culture and inevitably tracking cultural changes. There is no strict correlation between cultural change and changes in political culture. Will Kymlicka uses the example of Quebec in his description of what he characterizes as "societal culture." He points out that the "culture" of Quebec changed significantly after the Quiet Revolution but that the "societal culture" remained the same.[5] I would prefer to describe this change as a change in the *culture* that was not accompanied by a corresponding change in the *political culture* of self-determination. There is no direct correlation in the other direction, either: a culture may at first have no accompanying political culture of self-determination, as in the case of ethnic minorities, but with time, if the group identity develops into a national identity, a political culture of self-determination can appear while the culture remains basically the same. Political culture, in other words, is relatively autonomous from the culture of a society.

Potential Political Cultures

"Potential" in "potential political culture" is not equivalent to "unexpressed" or "partially expressed." Some potential political cultures *are* unexpressed political cultures. This is often the case for occupied nations whose political cultures have been suppressed. There are many other situations, however, where potentiality is not characterized exclusively by lack of expression. I already mentioned the possibility that after a potential political culture is allowed proper expression, it may either turn into an ethnic culture or split into the political cultures of several nations. Thus, potential cultures can be expressed without being "actualized."

In the previous chapter, I sketched a number of ways in which a potential political culture can be partially expressed. Some are expressed negatively: a set of beliefs constitutive of the minority group agency is not expressed in public sphere, but beliefs and actions of the majority culture are mobilized against what they perceive as the collective agency of the minority. It is usually the case that a "negative potential political culture" is driven by negative attitudes toward a vacuous political culture, either the group's own or the majority's or both, shared by the members of the minority culture.

A potential political culture can be negative "from within" with respect to its vacuous counterpart in several ways. In a majority nation, co-nationals may share a belief that they do not self-identify with the existing official expression of their national identity without having a clear idea of what their national identity should be. In such a case, the system of connections that allows the belief to be a verifiably shared second-order belief is not elaborate and lacks proper expression. Many group members can be sure only of what they collectively do not want or deem false or ridiculous: the system of officially propagated beliefs. If a proper positive expression of the potential political culture is hindered, how are the constitutive beliefs shared? This general question must be clarified for all kinds of potential political cultures.

In the case of the negative expression of a minority's potential political culture, the minority can mobilize around its rejection of those policies that the majority has aimed against it, even if the policies are aimed at the very elimination of structures of communication among minority citizens. The minority may also try to preserve the group practices that maintain its identity.

Minorities with officially established structures of government may have a negative potential political culture of a mixed type. In the former USSR, national and autonomous republics and districts had officially sanctioned political cultures that were supposed to express their peoples' attitudes toward and beliefs about their nationhood. They had local vacuous political cultures that expressed the official national identity. Their potential political cultures were expressed negatively with regard to their own vacuous political culture and with respect to the political culture of the USSR.

Often the expression is of a potential political culture is fragmented. The same idea of group membership may be expressed in various spheres of interaction among group members, but the group members may not communicate across these disparate spheres of expression and may not know about the existence of other venues in which their shared second-order beliefs of membership could be affirmed. Such a culture carries "positive" elements of expression that go beyond the denial of the vacuous culture's beliefs, but only through a set of isolated or overlapping pockets of horizontal ties among citizens. Although the beliefs of membership shared by individuals in each of these pockets roughly converge upon the same set of members and the basic constitutive features of the group, it is the fact that they are not explicitly shared by all members that gives the political culture its potential status: the whole of the national potential political culture can be described as an imagined framework, because it exists without its members knowingly sharing the beliefs of membership across all of the disparate spheres of expression. A group of citizens may consider another group of citizens with whom they cannot communicate to be co-nationals, but they can only behave within their "pocket" in accordance with beliefs about membership that they cannot verify. In a real political culture that is actualized properly, members can verify their second-order beliefs of membership in everyday public discourse with all other individuals whom they designate as members, because the expression of these beliefs is available publicly within the domain populated by the group.

Potential political cultures are often supported or expressed, and thus partially turned into political cultures, by co-nationals abroad. The existence of a political culture in exile gives a boost to the internal potential political culture. It is better, however, to treat the "political culture of exile" as a potential political culture for the nation in the homeland, for if the political culture is not expressed in the homeland, it is not clear how the nation in the homeland perceives its own status.

A potential political culture may be expressed but not actualized. Within the spheres in which beliefs about membership can be communicated, the members may be reassured that others share their beliefs, but the culture will still be potential if they are prevented from acting to exercise their group agency. They can act upon their beliefs, that is, but not in ways that would directly correspond to the proper actualization of their beliefs of membership, and thus they cannot function as an effective agent in accordance with the group's desired entitlements. The group members are more likely to act publicly upon the set of beliefs promoted by the vacuous culture. I will discuss this in detail when I deal with the second problem with the notion of potential political culture. The group members of course can attempt to change the circumstances of their political life, but in doing so they would act upon beliefs about what ought to be done to elevate or restore their group status based on the discrepancy between their real situation and the ideal of group agency they share.

I will now move on to consider the solutions to the three problems I need to address. First, I consider how the introduction of the notion of potential political culture influences the formulation of an approach to nationhood in nondemocratic and transitional societies and the corresponding solution to the problem of minorities' entitlements in such societies. Then I explore the relations between vacuous and potential political cultures, concentrating especially on the sets of beliefs that appear to belong to both cultures. I conclude that simply because the same beliefs may be attributed to both cultures does not mean the potential and vacuous cultures overlap, because the propositional attitudes individuals hold toward the sets of beliefs clearly demarcate the potential political culture from the vacuous political culture. This conclusion completes my defense of the cautious approach to nationhood and of the dichotomy between vacuous and potential political cultures that I propose. Finally, I show that the idea of potential political cultures does not result in defining only democracies as capable of nationhood, which would result in a drastic reduction of the numbers of groups that qualify as "real" national groups. Although there is a threshold for the degree of expression required to determine whether a group is a nation, groups in non-democratic societies can be considered national groups for the purpose of regulating their relations with respect to self-determination provided the terms of the regulation of claims to self-determination can accommodate changes in the national makeup of a transitional multinational state, which are often inevitable.

Three Problems

Entitlements of Substate Groups

Let us assume for a moment that new rules for the protection of national minorities are in place, and the international community is ready to act. A national minority oppressed to such an extent that it has only a potential political culture may not benefit from the creation of new arrangements if its entitlement to self-determination cannot be determined with certainty. An oppressed group may have political identity (mostly negative) based upon the belief that it does not identify with the oppressing state and that its identity is not expressed in the political culture and structures of this state. To the outside observer, the presence of this political identity, or psychological identification with membership in the group, indicates that the group exists. It is not clear, however, what type of political culture is properly the group's own, as its inability to function in the public sphere means that its identity cannot be communicated on a wide scale or thereby actualized. In the absence of expressed and recognized communication among citizens about the group's identity and its shared nature, it is hard to tell whether the group possesses the political culture required for nationhood. In the process of transitioning from a negative potential political culture to an actualized political culture, the group could develop into a linguistic, ethnic, or cultural community with a corresponding political culture. Or the group identity could transform into that of a national group—or more than one.[6]

The problem for international regulation in the case of potential political cultures, then, is that we cannot decide about a group's proper entitlements before the group is sufficiently actualized. It is not clear if a claim to self-determination made, say, by a national leader in exile truly reflects the existence of a nation. The Kurds in Iraq under Saddam Hussein were clearly severely discriminated against. There was no doubt that they existed as a group and that their human rights were violated. But beyond the demand that their human rights be respected, it was not immediately clear what kind of entitlement the Kurds deserved—whether they were a minority nation or an ethnic group. It could not be determined, moreover, whether only the Kurds in the territory of Iraq were a nation or whether these Kurds formed a nation together with Kurds outside of Iraq. Although we can make a provisional pronouncement about the character of a group based on the known content of its members' beliefs, the verification that comes from the proper functioning of a group in the political sphere is not available in cases of oppressed groups. It may appear, then, that the notion of potential political culture is not particularly useful for determining the entitlements of minority groups in oppressive or transitional societies because it does not help to identify the type of the minority group in question. The benefits of formulating norms for the regulation of self-determination claims and corresponding entitlements are not clear if the nature of the entitlements of substate groups cannot be determined. Below, I explain the ways in which the notion of potential political culture *can* assist in the formulation of basic principles for the arrangements of multinational states and international norms guiding such arrangements.

Potential cultures can be expressed in some ways, listed above, and thus can give some idea of the presence of national groups within the territory of an oppressive state. More significantly, the idea of potential political culture also allows us to formulate general principles for the regulation of substate relations in transitional societies, provides a warning against unjustifiable assumptions concerning the national makeup of such societies, and helps us to formulate norms that both limit unwanted behaviors and prescribe acceptable behaviors for a variety of provisional scenarios in the development of substate groups' relations.

In order to formulate the principles of an international arrangement that will take national minorities into consideration along with nations, it is not necessary to be able to determine with absolute precision which groups are nations and which are not in all societies. The practical significance of the notion of potential political culture is that it clarifies what ought *not* to be assumed and accepted as true about the relationship between political culture and the nationhood of substate groups in oppressive and transitional societies. It points out that a vacuous culture cannot be considered a national culture; even if no expression of potential political culture is detected, the notion of potential political culture retains its warning function and suggests that it is necessary to look beyond the official expressions of political culture. If sometimes it is not possible to determine the entitlement of a particular group with certainty, even if a potential political culture is detected, adopting the notion of potential political culture nonetheless directs our attention to some possible changes (namely, changes in national allegiances) and to the fact that there may be several nations emerging within the territory of a former oppressive state. Potential political culture also indicates that the mode of actualization of group agency may not directly correspond to the type of agent it seemed to correspond to, as what was tentatively a national group may mobilize to become a group with ethnic culture but no political culture of self-determination, or vice versa. Moreover, the strategy for approaching nationhood in transitional and oppressive societies can establish a set of conditional entitlements to be realized depending upon which circumstances apply to a given group at a given time. (In a way, it could provide an algorithm for solving the issue of future entitlement.)

Such a strategy for approaching nationhood in transitional societies consists of the following four basic steps.

1. It ought to be accepted that if there is a group with an actualized political culture of self-determination, and if the people of the group identify with this political culture, this group is a nation. If such a group makes a claim to self-determination, the international community needs to address the claim.[7]
2. We then need to formulate the norms regulating relationships between stateless and state-endowed groups with respect to self-determination. I formulate and defend the modified right to self-determination, which applies to both state-endowed and stateless groups, in Chapter 5. The right asserts that self-determination is a right to equal treatment within a multinational state. It specifies that only states that respect the equal status of different national groups within their territory, along with human rights, are just states.

3. We must take a cautious approach to treating oppressive states and their substate groups as nations. Judgment about nationhood in such societies should be suspended until national minorities (and the majority) are able to express and actualize their potential political culture (even minimally), offering the international community a better chance of verifying their claims to self-determination. To facilitate the process, the international community should insist that human, cultural, and linguistic rights in the oppressive states be respected,[8] including such basic freedoms as freedom of speech and association.

   Without considering the demands of the actualized agency of the Kurds in the Iraqi political arena, for example, we will not know within which boundaries they perceive their membership to lie. The notion of potential political culture leads to an approach that determines what ought *not* to be assumed before a collective agent can express its preferences. In the case of the Kurds, it could not be assumed either that the Kurds in Iraq's territory are a part of the larger Kurdish nation divided among several countries *or* that the Kurds in Iraq are a separate nation until it was clear that Kurdish collective agency was operating freely enough to allow us to see what kind of agent the Kurds are and what beliefs about membership they share. It is a different question whether, if they perceive their national group's boundaries as crossing over the state borders of Iraq, they ought to be considered as having a right to secede. My approach to irredentas, which I will discuss in the next two chapters, requires that the Kurds have a right to equal self-determination within Iraq, not secession.

   There is no doubt that factors of political life influence how a group's actions and self-perception develop. Given the political options the Kurds in Iraq now face, they might be more inclined to mobilize along the lines of self-determination within Iraq, especially given international support and the U.S. presence, if they are satisfied with the terms of their inclusion. The contingency of mobilization confirms the insight that it is hard to determine a group's nature precisely until it has actualized its collective agency to a certain extent.
4. Rather than wait to formulate general principles for the arrangement and regulation of national relations for multinational states until the final crystallization of the nations in a given territory takes place, it is possible to formulate a set of normative guidelines for the treatment of substate national groups. These guidelines could include a general statement of principles upholding the equality of status of all national groups in the territory of a multinational state regardless of whether national allegiances change. Such a statement would conform to the general norm of equality of self-determination for state-endowed and substate groups and would assert that whatever nations there are or will be, they should be provided with opportunity equal to that of other substate groups to satisfy their aspirations for their political futures within the state. These norms will inform the general strategy for transition.

This strategy would need to explain how to approach the claims that minorities advance. It could require that no claims advanced by substate groups should be ignored and prescribe what claims (and what ways of advancing them) are legitimate. To determine the legitimacy of claims, we would need a list of entitlements organized by type of group (cultural, national, ethnic, religious, and so forth) and of criteria for determining a group's type. To adjudicate a claim to self-determination, for example, such a strategy would need to specify the meaning of the right to self-determination within a multinational state and determine what groups (and at what stage of actualization) qualify as national and under what circumstances they do or do not deserve to have their claims fulfilled.

Even when it is not clear what type of political culture is present and a group is not being considered a nation for the purpose of the immediate regulation of its relations with others on the basis of nationhood, the cautious approach requires that a set of hypothetical options be made clear regarding the satisfaction of the groups' different possible claims. Therefore, when it cannot be decided whether a group possesses a political culture of self-determination, the group will not be completely excluded from the regulation of relations among national groups and the reach of the international legal system, but instead will be included provisionally. If the group claims that it is a nation in the future and this can be verified, it will have the right to be afforded proper accommodation, the general conditions for which will have been specified in advance.

International principles for the regulation of relations among national groups that have been accepted and promulgated ahead of the finalization of the national makeup of transitional multinational societies should assist in the more peaceful formation of nations within these territories. National minorities will know that their basic moral entitlements will be acknowledged and supported during a time of transition. Those minorities that are in a position to mobilize in various ways will be able to decide what they wish to attain and will be assured that whatever route they choose, their entitlements will be protected. They will therefore be less inclined to make extremist claims of the kind such groups often make in the present international system in order to receive attention in a world order that favors the entitlements of states. Thus, while mechanisms for the protection of human, linguistic, and cultural rights are already being applied, the basic international norms guiding relations among national groups in multinational states should also be available. The cautious approach to nationhood in transitional and oppressive societies would not preclude but rather would encourage the inclusion of such societies in the realm of the international regulation of relations among national groups.

The process of formulating the constitution of a transitional state may seem to present a problem for the cautious approach. The overall approach to nationhood and self-determination I propose addresses the question of what type of guidance international law ought to provide regarding norms and principles for conflict resolution; general principles, however, have an important but limited role when it comes to the formulation of domestic constitutions like the constitution for Iraq. The norm of equality for all national groups that exist or will emerge on the territory of a state is important, for example, to the formulation of the state's constitution, but when we are not sure about the nature of the entitlements of the agents involved in the process, the approach might seem to do little more than provide guidelines for the group's treatment that depend on what the group in question turns out to be. In other words, while it matters a great deal for the constitution that is being drafted what its subjects are entitled to, when the cautious approach is taken they are not really entitled to any permanent rights until they prove to be a national group or a group entitled to some other type of right. Does my theory presuppose that international law ought to mandate that constitutions be malleable and open-ended? Such a requirement seems highly unrealistic and would require the international community to interfere with the domestic affairs of states to a degree that simply cannot be sustained. But though international law has imperfect influence when it comes to the domestic affairs of states, I will argue in Chapter 6 that just norms have a certain self-maintaining force that might assure their overall maintenance. As a general guideline, international law might require that the constitutions of multinational states (1) refer to or include a list of the entitlements for different types of minority groups and make sure it is clear that a group can be considered as a candidate for the enjoyment of a particular right only when it can prove with reasonable certainty that it is indeed of a qualifying type; (2) specify the steps involved in the amendment of status (how substate groups can apply, what has to be verified for them to change their status, the norms for negotiating and power sharing, and so forth), and (3) not deny outright the possibility of including substate groups.

The international community would, in the case of the Kurds, have to ensure that their needs were taken into consideration (in the form in which they are currently expressed) in the formulation of the new Iraqi constitution. What is more, the cautious approach warns us that the negotiation of political relationships among substate groups does not end with the signing of any constitution and that international monitoring may be required to assure that minorities' demands are met. Overall, no basic principles are immune from amendment even in a democratic state, and the issue of the constitution for a transitional state might be reformulated so as to require a mechanism that does not prevent possible future amendments from being included in a constitution that is being created.

One concern connected to the application of the norms I propose is that a nondemocratic government might decide to suppress the actualization of a national group by refusing to accommodate its institutions and in this way prohibit altering the basic principles of its domestic arrangement after the text of the constitution is adopted by the country's legislature. If the persistent and sufficiently expressed demands of a national group for a certain constitutional status and other types of accommodation are repeatedly ignored, however, the cautious approach requires that the international community interfere to aid agents that qualify as nations in having their self-determination claims accommodated within their host states. If the state is democratic and it succeeds in persuading the collective agent in question to settle for a set of cultural rights, there is nothing wrong with such an outcome, provided it is reached by means of acceptable political methods.

From the point of view of international agencies, although nationhood in oppressive societies should be approached with caution, the notion of potential political culture keeps options open for the application of rules regulating relations among national groups in the future. Identifying a potential political culture is by no means a definitive judgment about whether its members qualify as a nation, but instead describes adequately the situation of uncertainty in which the cautious approach ought to be adopted. This approach also warns against taking at face value the national makeup of nondemocratic states. Although the presence of potential political cultures does not signal the presence of national groups within the territory of a state with any certainty, it is definitive enough to indicate to the international community that it should attempt to influence oppressive states in order to make them improve their treatment of minorities and allow them more freedom of expression. The cautious approach, when combined with a set of general international rules for the regulation of substate self-determination claims, urges international agencies to remain alert to changes in national identities until the presence or absence of national groups can be established. It also provides general principles according to which national groups' entitlements can be specified and proposes guidelines to follow in the transitional period, and it demands flexibility in the formulation of internal laws so that they include provisions for changes in the national makeup of states.

Distinguishing Between Vacuous and Potential Cultures

In an oppressive society, there are often some institutions for the realization of the collective agency of the people (like the Supreme Council of the former USSR), and the collective agent is often able to act politically (as in participation in elections or May Day demonstrations and various forms of discourse surrounding "workers' solidarity" in the former USSR). I have labeled the set of beliefs and attitudes associated with these institutions and activities "vacuous political cultures."

The cautious approach seems to apply in a straightforward fashion to cases of extreme subjugation of incorporated national minorities, where such minorities do not possess any self-governing structures, formal or informal, and expressions of their nationhood are banned from the public sphere. There are some cases, however, in which the approach might appear unnecessary. In a mononational nondemocratic environment, beliefs about nationhood will seem to overlap in the vacuous and potential political cultures. Potential and vacuous political cultures converged, for example, in Ukraine under the Soviet regime upon beliefs concerning the membership and the territory of the corresponding national group. In such a case, the set of beliefs of the vacuous political culture might seem to characterize a nation. Thus, treating some oppressive states as representing nations may seem to be warranted. Differences between the potential and vacuous cultures, it appears, could be explained as disagreements among co-nationals about competing paths of national development: one may say that the cultures share basic beliefs but differ in some extras, like sets of beliefs about the values of democracy or one-party rule.

Therefore, when it comes to the claims to national self-determination advanced by the official (vacuous) political culture of a mononational nondemocratic state or of a mononational substate group with its own territory and self-government structures in a nondemocratic environment, it is not immediately clear why one ought to treat these claims within the framework of the cautious approach rather than consider the vacuous political culture as characterizing a nation.[9] These cases uncover a broader issue: it needs to be explained why under conditions of uncertainty it is preferable to consider none of the vacuous political cultures in oppressive or transitional societies as representing nations, rather than most or all of them. After all, it would make the design of international legal rules easier if we considered vacuous political cultures in oppressive states to represent nations until this assumption was proven false. Below, I demonstrate that vacuous and potential political cultures do not in fact share the same basic beliefs in the sense required to make them identical with respect to their participation in the construction of a collective agent. The vacuous cultures cannot constitute group agents based on the sets of beliefs they promote because most individuals do not act directly based on these beliefs.

It is important to distinguish between two questions: whether in a mononational oppressive state the vacuous culture characterizes the nation and whether mononational oppressive states ought to be considered nations with respect to the international legal order. I have answered the first question negatively and proposed the cautious approach as a response to the second question. This approach ties the answer to the second question to the answer to the first; in other words, it requires that issues of internal self-determination (democratic self-rule by the people) be taken into consideration when dealing with external self-determination (the absence of external rule over a national group). Given that formal acknowledgment of nondemocratic states in international politics is a matter of fact, it is also important, therefore, to clarify what exactly is being acknowledged: the sovereignty of the state over its territory or the nationhood of the people of such a state. The cautious approach does not preclude the regulation of relations among existing international agents, but it requires that judgment about nationhood and its corresponding moral entitlements be suspended and attention be paid to changing and emerging national allegiances.

Cases that are problematic for the cautious approach appear to blur the distinction between potential and vacuous cultures because some basic beliefs that characterize nationhood, such as beliefs about membership and boundaries, appear to be shared by vacuous and potential political cultures. In Chapters 2 and 3, I established that group members must self-identify with a set of beliefs in order for those beliefs to characterize the group agent. To self-identify with beliefs, group members must be capable of developing a disposition to behave directly based on the beliefs and must form a normative attitude of approval toward their content. Closer consideration of beliefs that allegedly overlap between vacuous and potential political cultures shows that even if individuals know and approve of the propositional content of certain beliefs that are shared between the vacuous and potential political cultures, they do not behave based directly on these beliefs, and thus there is no true overlap between the cultures. To support this point, below I will discuss three types of beliefs in a vacuous political culture: those whose propositional content the members of a national group consider to be false, those whose propositional content they may perceive as true as a matter of fact but not approve of, and thus which do not have corresponding normative beliefs; and those that the members believe to be true and may want to endorse but on the basis of which they do not directly form a disposition to behave due to the oppressive context of their society. (In the first two cases, by extension, members do not form a disposition to behave directly based on the beliefs). The problematic beliefs this section addresses belong to the third category. I will start with the third type of beliefs and state my hypothesis concerning why individuals do not behave based directly on the content of these beliefs. Then I will consider the other types of beliefs to support my hypothesis and conclude that only the beliefs and corresponding attitudes of a potential political culture properly characterize nationhood.

True Beliefs that Individuals May Have Reasons to Endorse—The Hypothesis

The following beliefs appear to be shared by vacuous and potential political cultures in the two cases that present problems: Everyone would appear to agree to some general statements about membership, such as "N is a nation," and about territorial boundaries, such as "T is N's territory." Thus, within the contexts of both the vacuous and the potential political culture, a person may assent to both propositions, affirming "I believe that N is a nation" and "I believe that T is N's territory." Moreover, individuals may even normatively believe these propositions, that is, they may want to endorse the truth of both statements and believe that "It is good that, as a matter of fact, N is a nation, and T is its territory." Still, it is my hypothesis that for most citizens of oppressive states, it is not the beliefs of the vacuous culture that motivate them to act but fear of the consequences if their actions do not follow a pattern that conforms to those vacuous beliefs. Even if groups can act as collective agents within a vacuous culture, their members' reasons for action—even if they act seemingly in accordance with the beliefs of the vacuous culture—are not based directly on the vacuous culture. Suppose a citizen of N believes that "N is a nation" is true and endorses this belief. It is likely that if N is an oppressive society, when the citizen engages in actions accepted by the vacuous culture to exhibit her approval of the belief that "N is a nation," the citizen is doing so from fear of the consequences that might ensue if she fails so to act. This is likely to be the case because the citizen's actions would have to conform to a conjunction of beliefs, the content of some of which she would deem false or would not approve. For example, most citizens of the former USSR who might have carried a slogan reading "Long live the Soviet Socialist Federal Republic of Russia" would have done so in order to conform to the expectations of the party and of Soviet officials that they behave in accordance with the official complex of beliefs. Their action would not have been directly motivated by their approval of the idea that "Russia is a nation," even if they would have independently endorsed it. Furthermore, the content of the belief "Russia is a nation" is not the same as the content of the belief "Russia is a socialist nation." I will consider this difference in more detail below. Only the beliefs of the potential culture directly characterize the citizens' disposition to behave and thus constitute their reasons for collective action. I will return to a discussion of the official national identities in the former USSR after I discuss other types of beliefs in the vacuous culture.

Other Types of True Propositions

Individuals clearly do not believe what they deem false. Thus, they would not be motivated to act upon or approve of beliefs based on statements the official culture tried to promote that they believed to be untrue. There are some propositions, however, that are believed to be true as a matter of fact whose corresponding descriptive beliefs belong to both vacuous and potential cultures. Yet the corresponding normative beliefs concerning attitudes that ought to be taken toward the descriptive beliefs and connected to motivations for acting are not necessarily shared by the two cultures. A person may believe a proposition as a matter of fact ("P is true") or normatively ("I endorse that P is true"), but sharing a descriptive belief is not enough to create the meaningful agreement concerning its content required to directly motivate individual or collective action. An unqualified statement about the beliefs shared between vacuous and potential political cultures disregards this distinction between descriptive and normative beliefs.

In order to illuminate the distinction between normative and descriptive beliefs and corresponding types of agreement, consider the example of the former USSR. One of the propositions to which the population of the former USSR was supposed to develop an attitude of moral approval was "The Party is the core, and the Soviets are the basis of our society" [*Partia–eto jadro and Soveti-eto osnova nashego obschestva*]. This belief was a focal point for the system's existence and was deeply connected to the membership and self-determination of the people expressed by the vacuous political culture. All citizens were supposed to memorize this sentence, and it was also in the Constitution. Yet different attitudes toward the belief existed at the levels of vacuous and potential political cultures. In the vacuous political culture, the belief was a fundamental guiding tool, with moral overtones. That the party was the core of society was perceived to be good, because the party represented the forces of historical progress and by virtue of this possessed a superior kind of knowledge about the needs of the citizens and all other peoples of the world. The descriptive belief that the party was the core of society belonged to the potential political culture, too, but the normative belief that corresponded to the proposition in the potential political culture was different from that of the vacuous culture. The proposition designated a reality against which most people were afraid to speak out, because the party was the core of everything, and party members, who were supposed to observe and guide others, were present at all levels of society. Members of the potential political culture believed that there was nothing good or historically progressive about the party—an attitude quite different from the official attitude. Thus, the potential political culture presented a different normative framework of interpretation and generated, subsequently, a different agreement regarding what attitude to take to the content of the official beliefs. Acting as if one acknowledged the sanctity assigned to the statement in the vacuous political culture was a necessary move Soviet citizens had to make when asked about the subject. Many of them did so not as a matter of faith, however, but as a matter of strategic survival, even if most people were not willing to actively recognize or publicly acknowledge the strategic self-deception involved. Within the contexts of both the vacuous and the potential political culture, it made sense to say, "I believe that the Party is the core of our society," but a different attitude toward the expressed proposition and a different disposition to behave was presupposed by the belief in the two cultures. Normatively, then, the belief in question was a different belief in each of the two different contexts.

Archie Brown says that potential and vacuous political cultures (he calls them "dominant" and "official" political cultures, respectively) in Russia were more closely connected than in other republics of the former USSR[10] and that official and dominant cultures throughout the USSR had three elements in common: fear of chaos, patriotism, and heroes. But characterizing political cultures by listing sets of beliefs to which people assent ignores the crucial variable of members' self-identification. The same proposition, when looked at in different contexts of understanding and interpretation, is associated with different normative beliefs and different shared meanings. That the propositional content of the two sets of beliefs describing the group is the same in a mononational group does not say much, then, about the meaningful differences between the vacuous and potential political cultures. The normative aspects of these beliefs are likely to belong to different schemes of interpretation and different behavioral dispositions.

Of course, individuals often hold a mixture of beliefs made up of different combinations of propositions associated with vacuous and potential political cultures, especially when different members of a society have different levels of assimilation into the official culture and different levels of loyalty to it. Moreover, individuals switch between systems of interpretation at different times. Even if individuals have mixed beliefs, however, vacuous and potential political cultures' different systems of interpretation help to sort them out. This is another reason to look at the context and particularly at behavioral motivation, not at mere sets of propositions, when we determine what political cultures are present in a territory. Doing so allows different sets of beliefs to be more effectively distinguished in terms of where they stand with respect to the composition of a group agent. It should be emphasized that often we can only determine where individual allegiances lie if we consider individual self-identification with the whole complex, or with most of the beliefs that a political culture comprises.

To return to Brown's assertion, at the level of the potential political culture, the fear of chaos in the former USSR was a fear that chaos would result in even more brutal oppression, while at the level of the vacuous political culture the government perceived chaos as a threat to its power, which was allegedly the power of the people. Approximately the same list of national heroes existed in both the potential and the vacuous political culture. Nonetheless, the images of these heroes were used in different contexts and for different purposes. Brown reports that Lenin was a hero and that huge numbers of people lined up to see his body in the Mausoleum. The question that needs to be investigated is *why* they did so. Imagine a person from a small town going to Moscow and then coming home to be asked, "Did you go to the Mausoleum?" Answering "No" to such a question would have been dangerous. What is more, one might have visited Lenin's body out of mere curiosity to see a man who remained omnipresent even after death, and one might have done so without feeling the awe required by the vacuous culture. Lenin had an impact on people's lives, but the vacuous and potential political cultures nevertheless disagreed in how they evaluated that impact. The state used various techniques to connect the name of Lenin to different contexts that were more or less meaningful for the people. The Communist Party widely used the epithet "holy" with Lenin's name: his name was supposed to be a holy name to every Russian heart. This use of language connected his name to the pantheon of other, less political Russian heroes, like Pushkin and Glinka. In order to make Lenin closer to the people, the vacuous political culture characterized him as "the most humanistic human" (*samii chelovechnii chelovek*) and, to appeal to children, as "Grandpa Lenin" (*dedushka Lenin*). Even if Lenin retained his significance to some, it was often perceived in the potential political culture that what he had wanted and fought for had been distorted and forgotten by the communists and that they made a mockery of his name and used it to cover their own mistakes.[11] Thus, the fact that Lenin was regarded as a hero in both the vacuous and the potential political cultures of the USSR does not mean that there was a single attitude toward him in these different contexts.

Hence, the beliefs that characterize vacuous and potential political cultures may be characterized by the same propositional content, but group members' differing attitudes toward these beliefs, revealed within the normative frameworks of interpretation and disposition to behave, make the two cultures different, even if the propositions to which these attitudes are directed are the same.

The Web of Beliefs and the Motivation to Act

Communist ideology declared that the people of the land had been transformed by socialism into a new type of people, the "Soviet people," striving toward communism and having their will expressed and guided by the party. This idea of socialist membership identified the primary characteristic of belonging to the USSR as the territory bounded by socialism. The ideas of national belonging and self-determination thus were inextricably bound with the communist ideology. "Russia is a nation" would not stand alone in the vacuous culture apart from "Russia is a socialist land." Russia as a self-determining entity was understood in both Russia's vacuous and potential political cultures as lying within the same borders and having the same members. The potential political culture, however, had a different understanding of the very mode of existence and expression of a Russian national identity. For example, the potential political culture perceived it to be a mistake that Russia did not have its own parliament and TV station, but instead utilized those of the USSR. This expression of national identity was considered right in the official ideology—that the Union Parliament reflected Russian identity was perceived in the vacuous culture as a reflection of the fact that the Soviet Union was built around Russia.

Although vacuous and political culture converged upon the content of the descriptive belief concerning boundaries of and membership in a number of national republics, regions, and districts, the modes of expression of national identity inextricably linked to the descriptive statement diverged in the potential and vacuous cultures so as to prevent meaningful agreement in the corresponding normative beliefs. National republics had officially maintained folk cultures that were to a great extent artificial—not because they did not include elements of national dancing or singing, but because they were constructed and imposed with a particular ideological purpose and were practiced within the overall context of the socialist culture: they were vacuous cultures developed by the center. Another area of identity-maintenance where beliefs from vacuous and potential political cultures diverged was a set of formal institutional arrangements for national groups based upon a complex hierarchy (including national republics, national regions, and national districts) associated with the degrees of access to institutional expression political power. While the two cultures for each national group recognized in the hierarchy would generally agree on membership, they would disagree on how it was expressed.

Individual dispositions to behave cannot be reduced to mere assent to isolated propositions. Meaningful agreement about the beliefs of a political culture that motivate people to act derives from different frameworks of interpretation in vacuous and potential political cultures; the context of the vacuous culture does not generate a normative agreement that motivates individuals to act directly based on this web of beliefs. Earlier in this chapter, I mentioned that I do not include behavior among the characteristics of political culture, and one of the central reasons I exclude it is that individuals' actions may conform to the official beliefs of a vacuous culture while being motivated not by these beliefs but by fear of the consequences of failing to behave in the prescribed way. As I just discussed, their lack of motivation derives from three factors: some of the official beliefs are false, others fail to engender normative attitude of approval, and finally, the web of beliefs of the vacuous culture "tints" the beliefs to which individuals assent by mixing them with other beliefs that individuals do not endorse.

The beliefs of the vacuous political culture do not motivate individuals to act directly; rather, they tell them how to act so that they will appear to be motivated by the vacuous culture. Thus, individuals do not self-identify with the vacuous political culture, and the existence of an overlap in the propositional content of beliefs between vacuous and potential cultures does not mean that the cultures themselves overlap.[12]

Differences in the relationship of individuals to beliefs in the two political cultures are substantial enough to validate the use of the dichotomy between vacuous and potential political culture and to justify the cautious approach to nationhood in oppressive societies. The cautious approach, based on the idea of potential political cultures, helps us to formulate principles regulating the relations of national groups in transitional and oppressive states by taking into consideration the possible existence or emergence of nations and by ruling out vacuous cultures as representing the true national makeup of a multinational state. If one were to restrict oneself to the consideration of fully expressed political cultures, one would miss an important area of international relations that needs regulation: the formation of national identities in transitional societies. This process is largely about defining relations among national groups within the territory of a multinational state by defining power divisions, demarcating spheres of influence, and negotiating privileges, powers, and exemptions, among other things. It is important to formulate principles to regulate these relations, because their development has a profound effect on the future makeup and stability of multinational states. The cautious approach warns us not to take identities at face value or to identify world actors as what they are not. It anticipates possible changes of identity and, together with the principles of arrangement for multinational states that should be formulated and promulgated by the international legal system, provides support for developing national groups, although this support may not be as full as that given to actualized political cultures.[13] The coexistence and opposition of vacuous and potential political cultures highlights that the international community needs to take a certain kind of attitude toward national minorities—an attitude that is attentive to their potential political cultures—to maximize the chances of creating a balanced arrangement in a multinational state once it enters a transition from being an oppressive to a democratic state.

Democracy and Nationhood

Since one of the elements potential political cultures lack in order to be actualized is proper expression, it may appear that democracy, which allows the greatest degree of expression in the public sphere, stands on the opposite end of the continuum from oppressive states and properly represents the type of collective agent that qualifies as a national group, while different degrees of potentiality are deviations from this epitome of nationhood. This understanding of the continuum of political culture is incorrect, however. Connection to democracy is good for the actualization of agency represented by nationhood but not necessary for the set of beliefs associated with nationhood to exist, and a country's commitment to democratic governance cannot on its own produce proper accommodation for national identities without the "admixture" of the idea of nationhood.

Concentrating on the democratic end of the continuum excludes from consideration or portrays as imperfect many groups whose relations need to be regulated. This complicates the formulation and enforcement of norms for the regulation of relations among national groups. Focusing solely on democratic states would be like defining the term "government" as referring to democratic regimes only and then evaluating all other types of government in relation to this perfect type. This would require to label as "not a government at all" or "somewhat a government" a great number of political actors that democratic countries have to deal with. While we can evaluate a government as good or bad from a liberal point of view, we cannot conclude that it is not a government simply because we have developed a very limited idea of what qualifies as one. Moreover, a notion of nationhood based exclusively on democratic political culture would fail to satisfy C2, the constraint on the definition of nationhood that requires that it provide sufficient guidance in determining whether a group qualifies as a nation for the purpose of regulating relations among the subjects of multinational states. The merit of the notion of political culture lies not in its providing the theory of nationhood with a precise tool for determining what qualifies as a nation or for evaluating how well a group approximates the national ideal; rather, it lies in its ability to render a picture of nationhood that does not treat substate groups in nondemocratic societies as unequal but rather includes them, even if only provisionally, in the international community.

Part of the population may consider itself a separate nation even in a perfect democracy. Although such a group's claims can be freely expressed in the public sphere, this does not automatically guarantee that its interests will be reflected in political decisions and implemented in the design of institutions of power. Even if a national minority is proportionally represented, it may be outvoted on important decisions concerning its future. In order for a national group to be represented as a group in the legislative body of a country, the democracy principle should be supplemented by the idea of nationality, the latter being the basis for justifying changes to the design of the institutions of power and redrawing the boundaries of administrative units.[14] A national group may want its self-determination claims to be reflected in a form separate from the existing system of institutions, moreover.[15] A model of "nationality-friendly" democracy that accommodates national minorities through a particular process, like deliberation based on the power of rational argument, might be proposed, but such a model presupposes that an initial step has been undertaken before the deliberation begins to determine which groups are to be included in the deliberation and what their mutual status in the process should be. Such a step would not be taken on the basis of democratic principles alone. The nationality principle, which requires the acknowledgment of the existence of substate groups and the importance of recognizing their identities, is thereby entered into such a model as an independent variable. If a nationality-friendly democracy is shown to be capable of accommodating national minorities, this does not mean there is a theoretical connection between nationhood and democracy. The conditions of deliberation were modified by the principles of nationhood and equality, with democratic background principles being sufficiently neutral to be receptive of group identities of this particular kind. In reality, representation and voting are based on group interests and preferences, and if the interests of the minority run against some interests of the majority, the minority usually loses. This is a grave situation if the minority is a permanent one. The case is made worse if a permanent minority is a national minority, for it will want a separate set of institutions expressing its self-determination. Thus, the ideas of nationhood and democracy are conceptually compatible but not dependent upon each other. Democracy does not lead directly to the realization of national self-determination claims, although such claims can be more easily expressed in a democracy.

Robert A. Dahl points to the existence of the problem presented for majority rule by the justification of the boundaries of a democratic unit. The problem arises from the fact that the democratic process—and majority rule in particular—assumes "the existence of a political unit, within which a body of citizens must arrive at collective decisions," while "nothing in the idea of majority rule provides a rational justification of the boundaries around any specific unit."[16] The question of what constitutes the best unit for democratic rule is beyond the democratic process and the majority principle itself.[17] If a permanent minority is a national minority as well, the rules of the democratic process alone would not allow for the expression of its self-determination and nationhood. Democratic rule can also belong to local or supranational levels of government and have nothing to do with nationhood. Thus, for distinguishing the levels of democratic self-rule and drawing the boundaries of the units of democratic self-rule, it is necessary to look beyond democratic principles. If we wish to describe adequately what is meant by "the people" apart from a set of individuals involved in democratic participation, we must supplement democratic principles with an explanation of the boundaries of the field of power (why "we" is such that it is held together through, for example, interpretations of history, traditions, and so forth in the political culture of a national group). It is necessary, in other words, to see why a particular collection of individuals considers itself a people and to explain this perception of the limits of the group as a collective agent. This aspect of self-understanding and motivation to act could be missed by definitions of nationhood that are based solely on the measure of democracy. [18] Frans De Wachter, for example, states that "the only attribute that the group must share in order to be a nation is the will to cluster around the universal reasonableness of democratic principles."[19] But if this approach is taken, it must be explained whether there are any features of the group that identify it prior to or in relation to the political identity of the group associated with the will of the people to be a democratic society.

Even if ideas concerning national belonging can be expressed in a democracy, it may be impossible to legitimately act upon them because these ideas are about the limits of political communities. Hence, in the case of minorities, following the rules of democratic participation alone will not guarantee the actualization of their political cultures unless the notion of entitlements associated with national identity is incorporated in the process of designing the basic norms for the organization of a multinational state and is made into either a procedural or a constitutional constraint on the democratic process. Citizens of various national groups in a territory of a multinational state may share a will to be governed democratically but consider the democratic process to be localized primarily within the political boundaries of their respective national units while nevertheless being committed to the statewide democratic process as well (via the federal parliament and other institutions of the federal authority, for example).

The notion of nationhood I propose calls for concentrating attention on the internal constitution of a group, on its self-perception and motivation to act to fulfill its goals in relation to other national groups that also make claims to self-determination, as well as in relation to existing governments, many of which represent the nationhood of a select number of national groups. I highlight the relational and relative nature of nationhood rather than its particular relation to a democratic, authoritarian, or other kind of political organization. The mechanism required for the institutionalization of self-determination claims does not rely on democracy, but rather on the equal recognition of different national groups by granting them equal status with respect to self-determination and thus a chance to actualize their collective agency.[20] This does not, of course, prevent the international community from failing to recognize a group as a national group if the political regime that governs it is too oppressive for its claims to nationhood to be verified.

Implications and Advantages of the Nations Approach

In this and in the previous chapters, I have proposed that a nation has a political culture with which people self-identify and that this political culture is associated with the goal of maintaining or acquiring collective agency having to do with self-determination. I have also suggested that such political cultures do not have to be democratic to be identified as national cultures: it is sufficient that political cultures have access to the proper actualization and expression of their collective agency. Otherwise, they are potential political cultures. It needs to be emphasized that the human rights of group members need to be respected for such a pronouncement to be made, in part because we want to make sure that we have correctly identified nations. Once a group is identified as national, its enjoyment of the right to self-determination, to which the group is in principle entitled, can be made conditional upon its human rights record. I will talk about how to reconcile the universal right to self-determination with demands of respect for human rights in Chapter 5.

The notion of potential political culture is theoretically useful because it supports the internal consistency of the notion of political culture. It is useful practically because its inclusion when thinking about nationhood helps us to formulate a coherent approach to oppressive and transitional societies that provides guidance for dealing with change in these societies. Countries that do not allow expression to political cultures should be treated with caution with respect to national identity. Their official (vacuous) political cultures should not be considered as defining a nation, and careful attention should be paid to signs suggesting that potential political cultures exist in their territory. Once efforts at improving opportunities for political cultures to be expressed are made in such nations and prove at least partially successful, it may become easier to determine the national makeup of these countries.

A group can only be identified as a nation if it expresses its political culture sufficiently to reach the level at which it can be determined that members of a group share the required kind of beliefs and can identify with them. The idea of potentiality is used to indicate that the level of expression is not fixed and that the idea of nationhood should be considered dynamically. We may conclude that the group is a national group, even if its members still need to meet certain conditions in order to be able to act upon their beliefs. However, with many groups that have potential political cultures, we simply cannot tell with certainly whether they are nations or will ever become nations. What we can tell is that a certain degree of actualization is required for a potential political culture to become a candidate for nationhood, for only when a group expresses its beliefs can we know whether its members identify with them. This fact implies that in cases of totalitarian and transitional societies, it is possible that new nations will emerge apart from those officially presented, and this possibility has to be reflected in the norms guiding the arrangements of multinational states. What is more, it would be good if all state arrangements, even those of democratic states, were made with the dynamic nature of nationhood in mind. Thus, the idea of potential political culture provides a perspective on nationhood that gives useful guidance for formulating the principles that regulate relations among nations.

The merit of the notion of political culture lies not in its providing the nations approach with a more precise tool for determining what qualifies as a nation but rather in the formulation of a dynamic approach to the treatment of nations in international relations. While it creates a clear criterion for the recognition of national groups and the assessment of claims to self-determination made by them for most societies, it also provides a basis for dealing with changing national identities and national identities that are not yet clearly expressed in transitional and oppressive societies. Although the presence of a vacuous political culture indicates that judgment about nationhood should be suspended, the concept of potential political culture makes it possible to set up the basic arrangement of a multinational state even before it has become fully democratic and its national composition finalized. My approach calls for the determination of the entitlements of different types of minorities and the requirement that they be accommodated depending on the type of their agency; this implies that if the type of a group's agency changes, its accommodation has to change as well. The principles regulating relations of self-determination can be introduced while nations are still being formed in transitional or formerly oppressive societies, thus permitting, in time, a more equitable distribution of power in a given territory. In the next two chapters, I will demonstrate that having such principles in advance and steering transitions in terms of them can help regulate the conflicts that often result from uncontrolled transition.

The proper actualization of potential political cultures requires that the problem of the entitlements of various national and minority groups be resolved. The problem for the present set of norms of international law, even in cases where national groups are unequivocally recognized, is that national groups' entitlements are construed in a way that does not satisfy their members. The modes of actualization allowed to substate national groups are limited in advance, and their desire to transcend the limits of the legally acceptable creates a problem for the territorial and political stability of their host states. A group may be given a second-best option of self-government when it demands self-determination. Such an option is acceptable if the group's right to self-determination is recognized and it voluntarily agrees to self-government or if all similar groups are provided with the same arrangement, "leveling down" their entitlements. Both options presuppose that the group is considered equal to other groups of the same type. The absence of equal status and the presence of grievances related to the status and equality of a group with respect to self-determination should bring our attention back to the mode of recognition those national groups that are clearly nations deserve. My definition of nationhood, which includes the idea of potential political cultures, creates a conceptual basis for formulating principles of reform for the international legal system, which I propose in the next two chapters, because it does not introduce inequality among state-endowed nations and substate national minorities, can handle changes in national identities, and allows us to include nondemocratic societies in the regulation of relations among national group agents.

Notes

1. Archie Brown, for example, finds that a useful conception of political culture considers it as that part of culture that bears relevance to politics, while not only laws and formal institutions but also behavior patterns are excluded from the scope of culture. See *Political Culture and Communist Studies*, p. 155. Stephen White offers a definition of political culture that includes behavior. According to him, political culture is "the attitudinal behavioural matrix within which the political system is located." In ibid., p. 6. And Stephen Welch points out the necessity of transcending the dichotomy between culture and social structure and includes social structures in his definition. of political culture. See The concept of Political Culture (London: Macmillan, 1993), p. 79.
2. Joseph Schull, for example, states that social practices embody the self-definition of a people and are also made meaningful by them. See *Russian Political Culture and the Stateless Intelligentsia* (Montreal: McGill, 1986), p. 18.
3. If I were to include social structures, I would concentrate only on those related to self-determination, and then only on those with which people self-identify, which is redundant with respect to my definition.
4. The way beliefs are considered depends on the general approach to culture taken. There may be different views on what a culture is and, consequently, on what a political culture is. The positivist view of culture suggests that the existence of a particular culture inheres in the lives of its membership and that the culture's value is derived from this embodiment. The essentialist model of culture presupposes the existence and particular emblematic features of a given culture regardless of its membership. The critical view of culture presupposes that cultures do not designate stable realities and are, rather, a medium and consequence of social relations. On models of culture, see *A Critical View of Cultural Essentialism: The Native Women's Association of Canada, Problems of Inequality and Aborignal Self-Government* (Montreal: McGill University Press, 1995), pp. 31–32. I agree with the critical view and consider political culture neither as a set of beliefs that is expressed, for example, in a particular ideology, nor as a sum of individual beliefs about politics. Beliefs describing political culture cannot be depicted without reference to individual attitudes toward them and to the relations that shape individual beliefs. It would be hard otherwise to use the notion of political culture to describe a situation in which several political cultures—or a vacuous and a potential political culture—coexist within the same state.
5. Will Kymlicka, *Multicultural Citizenship*, pp. 87–88.
6. This point is connected to the objection that an approach like mine may stimulate creating nations where otherwise another type of group agent would emerge. It is true that a group with an unknown constitution can develop in several ways, but if the norms regulating any

type of group relations are in place, there is no harm done with any type of actualization, even if it could have been turned into a different group. In the case of particularly severe oppression or genocide, the will of the group to exist as a collective agent may be destroyed, and the remaining members of the group may want to opt only for a set of linguistic or cultural rights.

7. In Chapter 6, I will consider why it is better to accept the general rule of supporting groups that make self-determination claims even if there is a chance that such claims might become a tool of political bargaining. I already pointed out that this is why political culture is important: a claim to self-determination made by the leaders of an ethnic group would not qualify this group as a nation unless it is supported by the type of political culture characteristic of a nation, although in principle it can change into this kind of claim over time.
8. A document similar to the European Framework Convention for the Protection of National Minorities could be introduced and implemented.
9. There are two reasons to keep the cautious approach in the case of oppressed minorities. First, although the boundaries of a national minority's territory might be appropriate, the minority does not identify with the vacuous political culture of self-government because it is oppressive, like the central government, and because for the most part it represents this central government. The other reason is the random nature of the assignment of self-government structures in "national minority—friendly" totalitarian states. In the former USSR, for example, many national minorities were ranked and given autonomous or Soviet republic status. There were, however, many other national minorities that did not benefit from such status or that were in the sorts of arrangements that did not suit their national identity.
10. Brown, "Conclusions," p. 188.
11. The maniacal insistence on Lenin's inclusion in every context—children and teenagers wearing badges with his face on their chests from the age of seven to the end of high school, for example—or the insistence that he was always right would often plant a suspicion in an individual's mind, prompting this person to resort to coping strategies such as self-deception.
12. It would be interesting to see a study of the motivations of those who have enforced official norms in repressive states. It is likely that such people are not motivated by their belief in the truth of the state's pronouncements but rather by the goals of a system that required for its stability that they oppress the rest of citizens or set an example of proper behavior for them.
13. This support would, nonetheless, assure minorities that they are going to be assisted in the implementation of their rights, while also providing a useful framework for the consideration of national dynamics.
14. It is possible that a minority could be represented not as a result of a special policy but by chance, especially if it is territorially concentrated and the representatives of the national minority win in all electoral districts of its territory. This, however, does not constitute a systematic connection of nationhood to democracy. Besides, even if the minority group's representatives are always elected, the group can still remain an underrepresented permanent minority if voting in the legislative body is not designed in such a way that permanent minorities have a say in its decisions.
15. John Stuart Mill, for example, thought that different nationalities, granted that they are democratic and geographically concentrated, should have different states: "It is in general a necessary condition of free institutions that the boundaries of governments should coincide in the main with those of nationalities." See "Considerations on Representative Government" in *Utilitarianinsm, On Liberty, and Considerations on Representative Government* (London: J. M. Dent and Sons, 1991), p. 394. Nationality was an idea suitable for the justification of the boundaries for Mill, because he considered aspiration for self-rule to be a characteristic of a nation. Ibid., p. 391.
16. Robert A. Dahl *Democracy and Its Critics* (New Haven: Yale University Press, 1989), p. 147.
17. Ibid., p. 148.
18. Given the historical coincidence of the rise of democracies and nationalism, a democratic definition may appear quite natural. Other historical coincidences have been pointed to as significant: the development of industrialized societies and nations has been mentioned by

Gellner, while the rise of print and widespread literacy is important to Benedict Anderson's theory of nationalism. Theorists opposed to the democratic conception of nationhood, Yael Tamir among them, point out that the historical coincidence of the emergence of nationhood and democracy does not mean there was influence or inherent connections between the two.

19. Frans De Wachter "In Search of a Post-National Identity: Who Are My People?" in *Rethinking Nationalism,* ed. Jocelyne Couture, Kai Nielsen, and Michel Seymour (Calgary, Alberta: University of Calgary Press, 1996), p. 201. He also stresses that "the people" appeared on the political scene only in the eighteenth century, when a bond based on common belonging to a nation or a people came into existence. Political forms of organization tended toward the homogeneity of "a people" after peoples democratically freed themselves from monarchs (Ibid., p. 200).
20. Not all problems of sharing power are national problems. A federation, for example, can consist of territorial as well as national units. My task in this chapter, however, is not to provide an account of how institutionally to promote equality among all sorts of political units, but only of how to provide an equal recognition of national groups in a multinational state. Such a state may need basic principles for accommodating mixed federal units (territorial and national), which I discuss in Chapter 6.

Chapter 5
The Modified Right to Self-Determination[1]

Most individuals never choose the political communities they belong to. Their accidental endowment with membership at birth develops over years of social conditioning into a full-fledged national identity. That individuals are habituated into being a part of some group or collective agent does not diminish the importance of their membership to the individuals, however. As I discussed in Chapter 2, membership in national groups can be considered a matter of non-arbitrary individual preference. Such a preference ought to be considered regardless of whether changing membership from one political community to another is difficult enough to make it unreasonable to require it under normal circumstances. An individual preference for membership in a certain group would retain its importance even if individuals were perfectly capable of switching membership but perceived such a change to be undesirable. What if minority members want to retain their national identity, which they perceive as shaping their lives in meaningful ways, but do not want to be included in the larger political community of the host state? Under what circumstances is it justifiable to respect their preference? Can we limit their freedom by rejecting their choice not to associate with the larger community and demanding that they remain within its borders?

It is customary to think that the governments of legitimate states are entitled to act in certain ways. These governments are understood as representing certain collective agents and treated as if they were acting on behalf of such agents. This attitude is justified on the basis of the ideal of legitimacy, which suggests that states ought to derive their power from the people whom they protect and govern. The idea of global justice within a world order based on states requires us to formulate some guidelines for appropriate relationships between governments and minorities in their territory. In this and the next chapter, I provide a set of guidelines for the regulation of self-determination claims in multinational states that allow us to determine under what circumstances the international community can reasonably place a demand on substate groups to remain within the borders of their host multinational states and to adhere to rules of behavior consistent with the terms of their inclusion in these states.

In Chapter 2, I established that self-determination is an important good for a particular type of group agent that warrants, in a world with more than one community of this kind, the assignment of a primary moral right to groups organized around this good. In Chapter 3, I defined nationhood as political culture with

A. Moltchanova, *National Self-Determination and Justice in Multinational States*, Studies in Global Justice 5, DOI 10.1007/978-90-481-2691-0_5,

which individual members self-identify and which is related to the limits of primary political communities and their relations to other such communities. Thus, a nation can be considered to be a group agent constructed through the engagement of a set of individuals with a political culture of self-determination. When a group qualifies as a nation, it satisfies a necessary condition for the possession of the moral right to self-determination, but this does not mean that the national group ought to enjoy the right. As Jeremy Waldron points out, rights imply limits on the harms and losses individuals and groups can reasonably be expected to put up with.[2] In this chapter, I argue that the violation of a group's right to self-determination is an unjustifiable loss for the group that should not be imposed on it, provided that (1) the ideal of self-determination is not understood as the unconditional acquisition of independent statehood and (2) the formulation of the right includes safeguards against enjoying the benefits of self-determination in a way that harms other groups or non-member or member individuals. The right can be granted to a group if its aspirations (and corresponding sets of constitutive beliefs) are satisfied in a way that is consistent with the realization of self-determination as a universal moral right equal for all national groups. It remains to formulate the moral right to self-determination in a form acceptable for this purpose; that is aim of this chapter, in which I introduce a modified right to self-determination.

First, I provide additional arguments that justify granting national groups their entitlement to self-determination in several contexts. I then present the modified right to self-determination, which grants all groups—state-endowed and non-state alike—equal moral status with respect to self-determination. Finally, I show that the introduction of the modified right to self-determination would preserve the territorial integrity of multinational states better than alternative proposals that ground the criterion of legitimacy for multinational states only in respect for human rights, and, second, that the modified right provides for an acceptable theory of international relations.

National Groups' Entitlement to Self-Determination

I discussed the entitlement of national groups to self-determination from the point of view of collective agency in Chapter 2. The moral right to self-determination at the group level is based on collective agents' interest in full personhood and freedom; it provides conditions for discursive control that define limitations that groups can impose on the freedom of one another as equals. If a group is prevented from controlling its membership and the limits of its political space, it is harmed, because it cannot properly actualize its agency. Moral rights protect important goods; in the case of collective agents organized around self-determination, the enjoyment of their constitutive shared good satisfies their basic interest in sustaining themselves through equal freedom with other similar agents.[3]

In the first part of this section, I argue that the failure to accommodate national groups' self-determination claims violates minority individuals' autonomy and the equality of their citizenship in the larger state as compared with the members of the majority. I also provide an argument based on Rawls's original position to defend that equal treatment of substate national self-determination is just. The second part of the section looks at pragmatic arguments.

Moral Arguments

It is generally understood that a moral right implies a good, interest, or some other aspect of the well-being of its holders that justifies imposing a duty on others to protect this aspect of well-being.[4] I demonstrated in Chapter 2 that the right to self-determination is a primary, not a derivative, group right. This means not only that it is a right to a shared (collective) good but also that the right is not derived from the individual members' enjoyment of the shared good: it exists at the level of the group agent. Here, I am going place the ideal of self-determination in the context of citizenship in multinational states. I will justify the right of national groups to self-determination by approaching self-determination as a good from the perspective of a group member who is also a citizen of a larger multinational state. Before I begin with arguments based upon the individual interest in equal treatment by a multinational state, it should be noted that in Chapter 2 I also ranked the exercise of human rights over the primary moral group right to self-determination, so that non-compliance with the standard of human rights results in the limitation of the enjoyment (or the denial) of the collective right.

Equal citizenship presupposes that all persons ought to have the same fundamental status as equal participants in the most important political decisions made in their societies—what Buchanan calls "a right to democracy."[5] However, what constitutes *their* political societies? Government power raises moral issues of legitimacy and requires us to explain under what conditions the members of a group of people would treat the government as *their own* political authority—as the authority they consider morally justified to rule them.

National membership, by defining limits of membership in primary political communities, determines the conditions under which the individual interest to be governed on the basis of dependent reasons can be satisfied. National identity offers a vantage point for evaluating and forming attitudes toward any political power exercised over a group. Thus, national membership is an important good for individuals.[6] The existence of this good depends on the ability of a group to maintain its identity internally and in relation to outside individuals and groups.

Choices Regarding Which Minority Rights to Protect

As I discussed in earlier chapters, the European Framework Convention for the Protection of National Minorities lays a foundation for the protection of the individual members of national minorities against discrimination and for the maintenance of their national identity via a set of cultural, linguistic, and religious rights. I also argued that co-nationals who control the religious, linguistic, and cultural aspects of their lives still may not control their national identity.[7] When a choice is made concerning what minority rights to protect, one may argue for preference to be given to cultural, linguistic, and religious rights over self-determination because language and culture may appear to be primary, while political culture is more of a matter of choice: it may seem to be much easier for an individual to become a member of another primary political community than to adopt the culture of another group.[8] Hence, this line of argument goes, it is much less justified to deny individuals equal recognition as members of a linguistic, religious, or cultural community than as members of a political one. But members of a minority may prefer the culture, religion, and language of the larger nation to their own as simply more convenient: the members of the minority may wish, for example, for their children to be educated in the dominant culture's schools because they are readily accessible and foster socially valuable linguistic skills. In a sense, their children are "born into" the culture and language of the majority because of the availability of the majority's cultural goods. Minority rights to culture, religion, and language are nonetheless considered fundamental, because it is recognized that existing alongside a majority community puts pressure on smaller groups and dominates the minority individual's choices. To ensure the freedom of choice for all citizens, the minority must viably be able to choose to exist in their own language and culture. Provided this is accomplished, should a minority citizen decide to switch to the majority language or culture, her choice would not be forced. The ease with which an individual can immerse herself in a different milieu and the convenience of this transfer does not truly determine the value of the individual identity the milieu can provide. If the self-determining status of a national group is not recognized, all group members will be pressured to pursue assimilation into the larger state's political community, a forced choice that violates their members' autonomy. In this case, even though a minority member may be capable of joining the majority's political culture or immigrating, what is important is that she would not perceive either of these outcomes to have been the result of her free choice, since the choice she wished to make was interfered with. As I discussed in Chapter 2, individual preferences concerning national membership are not arbitrary.

One may object that limiting individuals' options concerning what political communities to belong to does not *unjustifiably* restrict their autonomy. Any requirement to obey the law, after all, restricts individuals' autonomy: being legally required to drive on the designated side of the street limits our options and forces us to be in a particular relation to drivers going in the opposite direction. If a person prefers to drive on the side opposite the one required by the law, the elimination of this option restricts her autonomy, but not in the same way as would the demand that she change her national allegiance, because the latter prioritizes and ranks some group memberships over others. As I demonstrate below, this violates individuals' equal status as citizens. Moreover, if it is possible to organize multinational states so as to satisfy their substate groups' aspirations for self-determination—and the goal of this book is to demonstrate that it is possible—then limiting individual autonomy so as to give state-endowed collective national agents precedence over those without states is not justifiable.

If such minority rights as language and religion are considered fundamental, then membership in a national political culture should be given the same importance. For individuals, having a say in determining the fate of the communities that they and their fellow nationals believe they share is as important as speaking their language or maintaining their religious practices or cultural habits, and it is unjustifiable to protect the latter but not the former.

As I explained in Chapter 2, it is often considered sufficiently fair treatment to grant national minorities varying degrees of self-government within their host states. Self-government allows a group to make laws for itself only within the parameters of a given political status. Rights to self-government, then, do not allow group members to determine their relations within the larger society to the extent necessary to protect their equal say in the most important political decisions in the state. If, to begin with, the members of a group do not have a say about their membership in the state, they are governed, on the balance, by the members of the larger community. To maintain their group membership and to have effective agency over time, they need to control the parameters of their inclusion in the multinational state and be granted input regarding the boundaries of their community and its relation to others. Thus, to have control over its membership in a multinational state, a national group needs to have a say in *whether* and *on what terms* to belong to the state and in *who* can belong to the community. For example, Quebec has control over immigration into the province, for example, but not over the terms of its membership in Canada as a national group rather than a province. Quebec's citizens do not have a say in whether they should belong to Canada, for there are no legal norms to regulate the political outcome of a referendum on belonging that could ensure that a negative outcome would be complied with. Chechnya, whose future is determined by the Russian Federation as a part of Russia's political future, would become self-determining within the federation's territory if the following conditions for the inclusion of its political community obtained: (1) it is in Russia voluntarily (that is, it can be determined by reasonable means that the people of Chechnya prefer to remain part of Russia, even if this preference is contingent upon the fulfillment of some claims put forward by them to the federal state), and (2) there is a guarantee that Chechnya's people will have a say in issues vital to the existence of their political community. Thus, it is important for the members of a national group to see that the political institutions connected to the determination of their future political status express the group's perception of its collective agency as a type of political community endowed with the power to control its membership in the state. Since national membership is an important preference of individuals and is tied to the self-definition of individuals as group members, supporting the effective agency of their group supports the individual good of national belonging. Substate self-determination affords the required type of control over co-nationals' political future that self-government does not.

Equal Citizenship in Multinational States

Even if we need to respect citizens equally concerning their national belonging, however, it may be that we can deprive each citizen of some but not all features pertaining to their group membership while still treating them equally. Why not politically assimilate national minorities by denying them substate self-determination but also change the political culture of the majority by making the majority learn minority languages or incorporating some minority cultural practices in the majority culture, for instance? The demand of assimilation not only unjustifiably reduces a minority individual's choices and thus her autonomy, as I discussed above, it also treats the individuals from minorities unjustly in relation to majority individuals. Although everyone's national identity is a descriptive fact when it is considered as one among other characteristics of an individual in isolation, national identity acquires a moral dimension when it characterizes *relations* among persons (both individual and collective). The members of the minority and the majority would have to give up preferences that are not equivalent. The minority individual would relinquish a preference to be governed by what she perceives as her own political community in order to join another such community. This would prevent her from politically associating with other citizens in the way she prefers to. The majority citizen would spend time learning another culture's language or acquaint herself with the culture or even give up some income to support the corresponding government policies. This would not prevent her, however, from politically associating with the citizens of her choice. Even if this assimilation created equal conditions for the minority individual's inclusion in the larger state, it would do so at the price of unjust treatment. In addition, if an individual cannot remain a member of her own national community but instead is forced to assimilate into another, she must also by extension redefine the terms of her membership in the larger state, which would otherwise be mediated by her membership in her own political culture. A minority member would have to undergo a change of membership and forge a new allegiance to another community; members of the majority would not need to do the same. Finally, there is a strong chance that the minority member will not be fully accepted after her change in membership, while she will have lost the protection of her political community. Her incomplete assimilation will prevent the intended equality of citizenship it was introduced to achieve. Thus, a state respects the rights of its citizens only if it creates conditions of equal political membership for all of them. Individuals do not want to be governed by a political culture that is not their own—a culture that originates from beyond what they define as their political community. If a person's national community must give up the self-determination that the majority is allowed to exercise, and if she is forced to seek her primary political community within the larger state, she has not received respect equal to that granted to other citizens, because her interest in leading her life within the political community of her choice has not been respected equally to the equivalent interest of majority individuals.[9] Unless minority members choose to assimilate, equal respect for the national belonging of all citizens requires at a minimum the maintenance of the national minority's control over its political future within the state.

At the group level, the right to self-determination of the majority is advanced (and the corresponding preference of its members is satisfied), while that of the minority is sacrificed (and a similar preference of the minority members is ignored). One may say that this sacrifice is a small price to pay for peace among national groups. Not allowing national groups to effectively exercise collective agency, however, causes the deterioration of this agency and makes it more likely that self-determination will be realized in a destructive way. Besides, if the boundaries of multinational states are preserved for prudential reasons and not because they define political communities in the best possible way, safeguarding the internal organization of political communities within such states is all the more vital to give meaning to individual membership in the larger state. Hence, viable national communities need to be preserved in order to protect the equality of citizenship in a multinational state.

One may suggest that in the case of potential political cultures, the collective agency of the minority nation is not actualized, and, for this reason, truly belonging to the minority nation is not a real option. In the case of oppressed minorities, such an argument might conclude, the choice (autonomy) and the "equality of citizenship" arguments do not work. However, individual members of the group hold a set of beliefs about membership and attitudes toward the political culture of the dominating nation that certainly provides a framework for choice at the individual level. Even in a negative potential political culture, holding an attitude of non-acceptance of the political culture of the majority and *not* developing dispositions to behave based directly on officially promoted sets of beliefs is a choice that many minority members make. It is of course true that a group can mobilize according to a number of different scenarios; this does not mean, however, that the rules for the arrangement of multinational states ought to restrict the options for group mobilization in the hope that individuals who envisioned actualizing their group agency in a forbidden way will eventually become habituated to the result, even if it was not their preferred choice. A better set of norms can accommodate a number of developments, allowing individuals to choose group membership according to their preferences and even to change groups. For example, if some individuals from an irredenta perceive themselves to form a linguistic community and others perceive themselves to form a national community, in the end it is up to the members to organize one way or the other, but barring one of the options at the outset restricts individual choices. Moreover, those whose preferences are not satisfied are more likely to accept the outcome if both mobilization options are allowed. As I discuss in the next chapter, norms that are open to the changeability of identity and can accommodate all types of group mobilization make peaceful transitions to actualized political cultures more likely.

The Rawlsian Argument

Another argument supporting the conclusion that the self-determination claims of all groups should be given equal recognition is based on a modified version of the "original position"—Rawls's device modeling the conditions of fair agreement.[10] Here is an outline of this argument: The parties in the original position select basic norms of justice from a list. They do not know whom they represent and hence how the outcomes of their decisions will affect them; therefore, they are likely to decide on the outcome most likely to be acceptable to all.[11] Since in matters of basic political justice citizens are equal in all relevant respects[12] and their national identity is relevant in describing the limits and the meaning of "society" and the corresponding meaning of "cooperation," representatives of national groups would be included in the original position. Next, we add a norm of equal treatment for national groups to one of the principles of justice on the list from which the parties choose. Although it would be unfair for a national group to expect everyone else to accept a basic structure favoring the group, it is fair to appeal to the importance to individuals of beliefs about membership in what they perceive as their own political communities in order to endorse norms that equally favor all such groups in a multinational state. This makes it likely that the principle of justice, including, among other things, the equal treatment of national groups, would be chosen from the list by the representatives in the original position.[13]

This argument based on Rawls's original position is meant to demonstrate that if the minority national group's self-determination is not respected, the terms of membership in the larger state for the members of the minority are not just. I do not argue that respect for individual rights implies respect for group rights. I discussed why groups cannot be protected solely on the basis of respect for individual rights in Chapter 2. Allen Buchanan states that authority is legitimate when it is morally justified in the attempt to make, apply, and enforce general rules within a jurisdiction;[14] he grounds his criterion of minimal justice for states in respect for individual human rights alone, and he does not connect the realization of national self-determination claims to the legitimacy of multinational states.[15] I agree that legitimacy and justice are connected, but I disagree that the meaning of just authority as it applies to multinational states can be captured on the basis of respect for the individual rights of citizens alone. Political institutions of a multinational state that do not promote the self-determination of national minorities in the state's territory are not legitimate in the eyes of national minorities' members: these individuals associate legitimate authority with what they consider to be their own political communities. If we argue that the presence of an authority is beneficial, regardless of whether it reflects individuals' sense of the limits of legitimate political power, why would a state authority that did not acknowledge a national group's claim to self-determination be morally justified to rule the group? Its authority would be only as legitimate as the national group's government or the government of a state with randomly drawn boundaries. The legitimacy of political power is largely based on its support by a political community whose self-determination this power promotes, and it cannot be considered in isolation from the constitution of the corresponding group agent.

Pragmatic Arguments

One pragmatic consideration I have just mentioned is that a prohibition on the exercise of self-determination—provided the prohibited group has a corresponding political culture—frequently leads to the group's adoption of militant mobilization strategies in order to attain self-determination, which are detrimental to the group's and others' existence. In the face of unfulfilled hopes of national self-determination, it is not productive to insist that these hopes should be abandoned or changed for the sake of universal peace: the group agent's constitution simply cannot be changed without the group's participation.

While I have established that self-determination is an important shared good for a particular type of agent, the right to define the boundary of a political community meaningful to its members can also be supported pragmatically, as follows: Self-determination is highly valued in the international system, but its allocation is limited and unequal. Claims to self-determination are so commonly and persistently advanced that some solution other than an outright prohibition on the exercise of the right to self-determination must be found. If the regulation of relations concerning self-determination is not conceived of merely as damage control, it should be based on a background principle that specifies the mutual standing of the parties advancing self-determination claims. A critic might say that we can make decisions for such regulation on a case-by-case basis rather than by defining the status of non-state groups in advance, but this approach would be a compromise, the logical result of failure to establish a unified principle. Even in each particular decision procedure, some principle would define the status of the parties with respect to one another, if only for the purpose of that decision. If it is possible to establish such a principle, compromise will not be necessary. In this chapter, I argue that there is at least one principle—equality with respect to self-determination—that can be employed in most political decisions to define the status of national groups. Hence, even if the reason for the regulation of self-determination claims is purely pragmatic, such regulation requires an underlying moral principle—a universal principle describing the proper standing of all parties in relation to one another—and thus defines legitimate reasons for the agents' imposing limitations upon one another's behavior within this context.

Addressing self-determination claims is pragmatically useful also in the context of transitional and oppressive societies. We need to deal with groups of individuals that organize around the shared good of self-determination, even if we are not sure whether they are mistaken concerning the claims they are entitled to advance. If they are mistaken, it is probably the case that their mobilization as a collective agent is impeded: they may be unsure about the beliefs of all other members of their collective due to restrictions on public expression of their identity, or they may not have appropriate access to procedures for decision making and goal setting of the type required of a collective agent. Outright refusal to consider them as national groups plays into their mythology and encourages their mobilization, whereas providing tools for the proper actualization and democratization of their political community may help to assuage unwarranted claims. Once it is clear what all members conceive as their shared good, some group agents may come to realize that the identity expressed in their potential political culture does not correspond to their shared goals. We cannot know whether they are wrong unless their political culture acquires proper expression. The answer to the conundrum posed by potential political cultures is to let the corresponding agents actualize while limiting their behavior in a way that is efficient in controlling aggressive and destabilizing behaviors. Thus, for groups whose identity is stable enough to be sociologically distinct, we need to have norms to regulate their claims and corresponding behaviors.

Substate groups are capable of setting goals and acting in accordance with them if they possess some form of collective reasoning, even if it is partial and constrained. Unlike physically identifiable individual agents, collective agents are less tangible, especially if they possess no (or very limited) institutions of self-government and have little access to the public sphere, but in conflict situations many have proven to be destructive and uncontrollable. Such a group's claims cannot be done away with by means of simple prohibitions. Nations are groups that perceive themselves as political agents and operate on this basis, whatever tools of effective agency they have (and the fewer they have, the harder it often is to verify and civilize their national expression). Their self-understanding does not immediately entitle them to a right supporting this understanding, but treating them in such a way as to deny their self-understanding is not helpful if their cooperation is needed. Failing to provide them with fair conditions for inclusion in their host states or a legal framework that allows them to engage in negotiations on the terms acceptable to all parties encourages them to resort to illicit means to redress their grievances. As I mentioned in Chapter 2, acknowledging that the exercise of self-determination constitutes an important aspect of the well-being of national groups associated with the actualization and proper functioning of their group agency should convince us to grant them the right to self-determination *only if* we assume that national groups ought to be allowed to continue to exist. In the pragmatic context, however, it seems that the existence of national groups is a fact of the present international system that needs to be dealt with. It is unproductive not to provide national groups with the conditions of freedom that can allow then to function as a group agent in accordance with the members' shared intentions. It may be objected that substate national groups will actualize *because of* the rules I am advocating, but in this case, no harm would be done, because a controlled transition to nationhood would replace militant and destabilizing responses to the potentially frustrating refusal to attend to their claims.

In Chapter 3, I defined nations and explained why the presence of a political culture associated with self-determination with which members self-identify is a sufficient criterion for treating a group as a national group. The corresponding right to self-determination ensures that national groups are free in relation to other such agents. Members of national groups in oppressive and transitional societies often lack the effective capacity to exercise their agency, and I discussed a strategy for approaching such societies in the previous chapter. This strategy requires a formulation of the right to self-determination that promotes the proper actualization of group agents in both democratic and transitional or oppressive societies. I will now define and defend this right.

The Modified Right to Self-Determination

The Formulation of the Right

The current international system, which is based on statehood, places practical restrictions upon the implementation of the right to self-determination. Self-determination, however, does not require statehood but instead requires the proper actualization of a group's corresponding collective agency. We would not have to deny the exercise of the right to self-determination to national groups altogether if we eliminated the undue emphasis on the connection between statehood and nationhood and severed the link between the exercise of the right to self-determination and the acquisition of independent statehood.

The political and legal implementation of a principled moral relationship among various national groups, while distinguishing between self-determination and statehood, cannot ignore the status of states in the international system. At present, it is states that have the required institutional support to effect the change required by the moral principles that I advance for determining the status of substate groups. Relying on states to implement the equality of self-determination but making a state's entitlement to territorial integrity conditional upon its respect for the self-determination of substate groups increases the chance that state boundaries would not be changed too easily without the consent of all substate national units and before the proper standing of all corresponding groups within a state is defined and assured. Thus, the first step toward the ideal of equal self-determination is to establish that substate national groups ought to be equally treated within their host states. In this case, secession would no longer be a threat because the norms that require nations' equal status also require their proper behavior toward other groups, and unilateral secession is not a permitted behavior. The regulation of secession, therefore, falls under the regulation of substate national relations informed by the norm of equality of self-determination. Secession in cases of vast abuses of human rights—a present practice of the international community—will continue to check the abusive behavior of state authorities, while the norm of equality I propose will add to the set of circumstances under which legitimate secession is allowed, as I explain below.

Thus, we can retain the general meaning of "self-determination" as a group's control over its own political future but redefine the idea of self-determination as it applies to state institutions. This can be done if the basic organizational principles of multinational states and the basic principles for conflict resolution recognize, first, that self-determination does not require statehood, and, second, that all national groups deserve equal status with respect to self-determination by virtue of what they are.

These two elements define the modified right to self-determination, which states that all national groups have an equal right to self-determination provided that the realization of self-determination does not require the acquisition of independent statehood. A claim to self-determination advanced by a substate group be first and foremost a claim to equality within the boundaries of its host multinational state. Hence, national groups should be given an opportunity equal to those of other members of their host multinational states to determine their future political status within these states. The right to secede (or the right to independent statehood), then, results only from a host state's continuous noncompliance with the equality principle or from the mutual decision of all the national groups in a state after their equality has been achieved. The equality of status of national groups provides conditions of inclusion in a viable multinational state or, when this is impossible, a basis for negotiation among state-endowed and non-state national groups in conflict situations.

Substate groups may engage in a number of interactions with the host state that are beneficial to them, like economic cooperation or sharing in the maintenance of the military, but they are proper members of their host states only if they have been offered and accepted fair conditions of inclusion. The institutional arrangements of a multinational state need to include provisions assuring that the state cannot encroach upon a national group's power to control its political future. Such provisions could include but do not need to be limited to the following: The group is formally recognized as a national group in the constitution of the state. It has not only representatives in the central government, who are elected on a proportional basis, but also a number of seats in a higher chamber of the government or in a special nationalities council that represents national groups equally, with the questions that can be decided by each chamber divided between them. It has a significant power over changes to the state's constitution, such as a veto over any change that affects the group's vital interests. Ideally, the terms of its participation in state-level institutions, such as the legislature, the courts, or the civil service, should define areas of exclusive and shared competence to delineate the boundaries of the group's political power.[16] As long as the division of powers is negotiated among all affected parties and accepted voluntarily, an institutional scheme reflecting this division is adequate for the equal recognition of national groups' self-determination within the territory of a multinational state.

Different groups will seek different rights and institutional provisions to promote their particular interests. The degree of control a national group has over citizenship, foreign policy and trade, defense, customs, the budget, natural resources, education, and so forth should be negotiated in each case. A group may have exclusive control over its natural resources, for example, or it may share control with the state. The outcome of negotiations over degrees of control is valid only if it is acceptable to the group that has a prima facie claim to the resources, but the group may have to honor the contributions made by other groups or by the state to the development of those resources.[17] While different groups can hold and yield different powers—a national group may even opt to have only a set of cultural rights—their self-determination claims are respected as long as any political power they yield is relinquished voluntarily and can in principle be restored.[18] Although having the constitutionally or internationally recognized right to secede is linked to self-determination, it has significant qualifications and restrictions in the modified right and cannot be straightforwardly considered a safeguard of the group's self-determination.

If different groups in a multinational state have different powers, in what sense is their status equal? The requirement of equality protects their freedom as agents in a negative way by defining what cannot be denied to them. The application of the modified right to the arrangement of multinational states results in a number of mutual restrictions the members can place upon one another. In this sense, the modified right, as a general right of its subjects to be equally free, translates into a corresponding special right within each multinational state that allows the state's members to require of one another compliance with the voluntarily accepted rules of inclusion. The agents can interfere with one another's freedom due to the special relationship created by their joint membership, but the limits of this interference are determined by the principle of equality that underlies the general right. In the current international system, for example, equal sovereignty among states is merely formal, with no regard to their political role in international relations. Their formal equality, however, defines what ought not to be denied to any state actor under normal circumstances—its territorial integrity, for example—irrespective of its size. Similarly, the modified right determines what cannot be done to national groups, regardless of their size. It requires that no national group be deprived of its ability to negotiate the powers it needs to relate to other groups in the state. And if all other means fail, it grants national groups the right to secede. Thus, the modified right protects national groups from being interfered with by others who wish to control their future.

It may still be said that national groups in multinational states, even if they enjoy the modified right to self-determination, are worse off than those that presently have a state of their own. The current international order both grants a more privileged standing to groups with states and excludes most substate groups from the acquisition of this presently attractive status. But under the modified right, statehood does not carry with it a higher standing with respect to self-determination and is not singled out as the most attractive option for achieving self-determination. The modified right does not require equal statehood for all, but rather equal self-determining status. Self-determination is never unconditional: even state-endowed groups possess it only in relation to other such groups within a given territory. They mutually limit their capacity to self-determination based on the recognition of every state's equal entitlement. The European Union, for example, imposes many limitations on its members' powers, but the member states remain self-determining, because they join voluntarily and can maintain their self-determining status in relation to others. According to the draft treaty establishing a constitution for Europe, the union respects their equality before the constitution and their national identities.[19] The member states can challenge any decisions of the union they deem unjust or restrictive of their ability to control their separate political futures.[20] They can also submit proposals for the amendment of the treaty, and there is a procedure for its amendment. Finally, the member states have the right of exit.[21] Their diminished control over items traditionally understood as necessary for state sovereignty does not indicate the diminution of their self-determination. Similarly, the national groups' diminished control in a multinational state, does not preclude them from exercising self-determination limited only by the equal right of other self-determining groups.

A national group from a multinational state may seem to have less of a chance of entering into relationships with national groups outside of the state it belongs to than does a nation with its own state. A substate national group will relate to others via its state, which represents all groups within its territory equally, but is this mediated relationship an adequate substitute for direct contact, unrestrained by the terms of inclusion in the host multinational state? Let's begin to answer this question by remembering that there is nothing in the modified right itself that proscribes a group's direct contact with other national groups. Moreover, in the reality of international relations, as I have pointed out, even state-owning national groups' relations with others are mediated by their membership in regional structures and international organizations. The mediation of relationships with others by other national groups within one's state does not need to prevent groups from engaging in direct contact with communities outside of the state. Their equal self-determining status also increases the likelihood of the sort of willing cooperation within a multinational state that would allow groups to negotiate their privileges with others, including international relations, and result in a degree of discretion being permitted to the groups comparable to that of state-owning groups presently incorporated into regional structures or other kinds of alliances.

The changes to the international moral norms implied by the modified right will be in line with what Daniel Philpott terms the present status of the "constitution of international society." By the constitution of international society, he means a set of norms mutually agreed upon by polities who are the members of the society that define the holders of authority and their prerogatives and specify who constitutes legitimate polities, the rules for becoming one of these polities, and their basic prerogatives.[22] The most recent changes to the constitution of international society include global membership in it and the loss of state sovereignty in cases of states' violations of human rights (due to these states' subjection to outside enforcement of human rights standards). He also points out that within the European Union the states are no longer sovereign in the areas specified by EU law.[23]

The modified right provides a framework for the realization of two important ends. First, self-determination achieved in accordance with the right becomes a constructive rather than a destructive project. The goals of national groups change from competing for a state to cooperating within a state. Second, the modified right limits the aggressive behaviors of those groups that do not respect the rights of others. Means of satisfying self-determination claims that aim to diminish the self-determination of others, even if incidentally, are not compatible with the right, because they undermine the expected equality of status among national groups. The modified right does not allow state and non-state groups to enjoy their freedom at each others' expense.

The modified right aims at safeguarding the territorial integrity of states for more than purely pragmatic reasons. First, it advocates the self-determination of substate groups with limited sovereignty not only because independent statehood for all groups is not practicable but also because a system that links nationhood and statehood is historically contingent and unjust. The modified right sets up a norm of legitimacy that defines the moral circumstances under which a state can retain its right to territorial integrity: Only legitimate states have a moral right to territorial integrity. A legitimate multinational state treats its citizens equally. It cannot treat them equally if it ignores their national identities. Therefore, unless a state respects national identities of its citizens, it does not have a moral right to territorial integrity.[24]

One may object that although the modified right to self-determination is very important, it is secondary in importance to the right to territorial integrity that is an integral part of international law. It is presently customarily recognized, however, that illegitimate states do not have the right to territorial integrity—their borders can be crossed, for example, to establish a peacekeeping operation, or they can be blocked in the imposition of sanctions. I have been arguing that the legitimacy of multinational states depends not only on their respect for their citizens' human rights but also on their respect for national groups' self-determination rights within their territory. If the territorial integrity of states depends on whether they are legitimate in the light of international moral norms, multinational states would need, among other things, to comply with the modified right to self-determination to continue enjoying their right to territorial integrity.

It remains to be seen, of course, whether self-determination will retain its value in the eyes of national communities if it is not associated with independent statehood. There are reasons for thinking that it will, for not only is self-determination a constitutive shared good for national group agents, but, in the world with more than one political community, it also represents an important element of freedom for such communities. If the modified right is implemented and self-determination loses its present value associated with state sovereignty, national groups may still want to pursue statehood for reasons other than the realization of their self-determination claims. The modified right ensures, however, that their quest to acquire statehood will not be justifiable on the basis of their rightful claim to self-determination. I will explain how to address claims to statehood in cases like this below.

The modified right defines a framework for the other-regarding behavior of different national groups that requires a background guarantee of the mutual standing of all sides and aims at a more equitable distribution of power among them. The international institutional arrangements that would result from its implementation will be more just, because by treating similar groups similarly with respect to their entitlements, they will reflect the moral equality of different national groups outlined in the UN Charter. They will be also more stable, because they will aim at safeguarding the territorial integrity of multinational states through addressing competing self-determination claims within their territory.

Territorial Integrity

All things being equal, an approach to reforming international legal norms is likely to be more viable if it conforms with the right of states to territorial integrity: it is more likely that the norms advanced by the approach will be accepted by existing states, which perceive territorial integrity as supporting their vital interests. Besides, it is prudential to obey the principle of territorial integrity when possible, since the disintegration of states could significantly disrupt the functioning of political communities within their borders. I will elaborate in this section on why the modified right does not undermine—but, on the contrary, facilitates—the exercise of the right of states to territorial integrity, which is one of the fundamental principles of international law. I will compare the approach to territorial integrity of multinational states based solely on human rights to the nations approach I propose based, in addition to the norm of respect for human rights, on the modified right to self-determination, which does not require secession and aims at preserving multinational states.

Allen Buchanan argues that territorial integrity protects the self-determination of political communities by safeguarding control over the territory they occupy, furthers the most basic morally legitimate interests of the individuals and groups that states are empowered to serve, and gives individuals and groups an incentive to invest themselves sincerely and cooperatively in the existing political process. I will consider in turn under what circumstances each of his points supports the protection of territorial integrity.

First, the territorial integrity of a multinational state does not safeguard national groups' control over territory if they do not have proper institutions for the exercise of this control in the first place. To evaluate various autonomy arrangements, we need to clarify whether the existing or proposed terms of power sharing with the state satisfy the general norms of fair treatment. Buchanan does not consider groups' entitlements in determining the terms of organization for multinational states, and he ties the exercise of the right to secession to a number of situations in which the requirement of remedial justice applies, one of which is the restoration of broken autonomy arrangements. Without a broader normative framework specifying what norms should guide the fair treatment of substate national groups, we cannot evaluate whether a broken autonomy arrangement was just in the first place and on what conditions it ought to be restored.

The Kurds are a case in point: it was a problem that their autonomy was threatened by Saddam Hussein, but on the basis of Buchanan's model it is not clear what they were entitled to and whether their initial autonomy arrangement was just. We need to weigh the options available to minorities, including the restoration of their autonomy, secession, and the formation of an independent state with other minority groups bordering them (which is a possibility in the case of the Kurds) against a normative perspective that helps us evaluate the justifiability of each option from the point of view of fairness. Putting a stamp of approval on existing autonomy arrangements does not create such a perspective. The territorial integrity of the host state enhances the self-determination of national groups in its territory only if these national groups are capable of participating meaningfully in the political sphere and are given the opportunity to do so by having access to power structures more or less equal to those of the other groups in the state. Thus, we need to supplement Buchanan's statement about the benefits of preserving territorial integrity with an explanation of what constitutes the normative basis for groups' interaction within a state.

The inclusion of the right to self-determination in the norms for interaction of group agents assists in the creation of a constructive framework for conflict resolution. This cannot be achieved by a set of restrictions on the actions of national groups that does not take their legitimate interests into account. My approach both supports the well-being of political communities aspiring to self-determination and defends the territorial integrity of states that support the equality of national self-determination in their territory along with human rights. This conforms with the norm of legitimacy for states that I put forward, which requires a state to respect both human rights and the self-determination claims of substate groups in order to be considered legitimate.

Turning to Buchanan's second point, if a multinational state does not respect the self-determination claims of its substate groups, the stability provided by the preservation of such a state's territorial integrity will always be partial, because it will be accompanied by the presence of dissatisfied minorities who see no prospect of their unequal status changing, and the presence of such political communities is known to destabilize their host states and lead to conflicts. The objection that stability, even if slanted, may still be important for individuals' well-being can be met by pointing out that persistently denying individuals respect as members of a national political community interferes with their life choices and thus decreases their liberty and well-being while compromising the conditions of their membership in the larger community.

Finally, regarding Buchanan's third point, territorial integrity promotes the cooperation of national minorities if they can envision the fulfillment of their expectations within the state. Locking national minorities into a multinational state without satisfying their demands for respect of their group identity does not inspire them to participate in the political life of the state, while the lack of proper institutions for the actualization of this identity eliminates means of participation acceptable to the minority. If minorities are securely locked in, the majority has no motive to participate in a dialogue with them about self-determination or to opt for a change that would imply some power sharing, since it can avoid doing this while still respecting human rights. Hence, the political process could exclude minorities while providing means for the full participation of the majority. The principle of territorial integrity promotes cooperation among national groups only if it is accompanied by a norm of legitimacy that includes not only human rights but also equality of self-determination for national groups. Such a norm gives minorities more incentive to cooperate, because it does not associate states with nations, and it encourages the revision of international law to support the equality of national groups' self-determination within multinational states. It gives the majority more incentive to cooperate, because if the majority's behavior does not allow the state to achieve the status of being minimally just, the minority will have a legitimate claim to separate.

Thus, the approach to self-determination I advance supports the conclusion that none of the benefits of territorial integrity Buchanan lists can be achieved if the arrangement of a multinational state does not respect, in addition to human rights, the equality of national groups on its territory. In failing to specify whether protection of territorial integrity applies to states dominated by majorities that do not violate human rights but perceive the state as their own and wish to have the state border intact, the human rights approach ignores an important question that needs to be answered.[25] The human rights approach advances a limited ideal of legitimacy, which falls short when applied to multinational states because it ignores the moral status of groups and its importance for equal citizenship. My approach demands that territorial integrity should be enjoyed by those states that are shared by a number of national groups under a just arrangement, which should provide equal respect for the groups' self-determination, along with respect for individual rights.

A theory that makes the preservation of territorial integrity contingent upon respect for human rights alone is consistent with upholding the territorial integrity of states that are inherently unstable—states with one leading nation in which other national groups' claims to self-determination are disregarded and the majority is privileged by default. This approach does not seem to offer national groups much more than the existing international principles with respect to self-determination. The current interpretation of the right to self-determination allows secession by occupied national groups. Those states that systematically perpetrate human rights abuses are punished by international sanctions.[26] These are right solutions, but they cover only extreme cases. My approach aims at regulating relations among national groups systematically, rather than providing solutions only for extreme cases. Being inclusive of all national groups and protecting their basic interests, it minimizes incentives for substate groups to mobilize aggressively and thus promotes territorial integrity by offering the background principles for long-term stability.

Answering Objections

The major objections to a project like mine have to do with a concern that the modified right might create more problems than it solves: it might give national groups unreasonable expectations and hand them a justification for destructive behavior by legitimizing their claims to self-determination. I believe that the modified right would curb rather than encourage destructive behaviors. The introduction of the modified right is an effort to reconcile the two major principles presently influencing international relations: self-determination and territorial integrity. Distributing international status according to the universal legal right to self-determination is destabilizing only if self-determination is associated with statehood, as it is currently. Since the modified right does not consider statehood to be a necessary condition for self-determination, it protects the self-determination of national groups and stimulates their cooperation while preserving the territorial integrity of multinational states. Territorial integrity is a morally important principle only if it protects, or at least does not interfere with, the well-being of all those governed by the authority that is entitled to the preservation of the boundaries of the territory under its control. By providing a normative ground for the resolution of conflicts between stateless and state-endowed groups, the modified right would reduce the destabilizing effects of agitation by stateless national groups whose aim is to acquire international status equal to that of state-endowed groups.

It may be said that non-state groups, if their claims to self-determination are endorsed, will try to gain even more power by acquiring a state of their own. In the end, providing them with equal status may encourage destructive behaviors. The modified right, however, permits dealing with any type of secessionist claim only after the equality of standing of all national member groups is assured, and only with their consent. Under these circumstances, a national group can put forward its request and try to achieve its goals through peaceful negotiations that respect the requirements of distributive justice and the rights of other groups on the territory of the host state. If a substate group's members want to be recognized as a self-determining people, they have an opportunity to satisfy this demand: they receive a guarantee of equal self-determination within the state and of a right to secede either if their status is not persistently respected or by mutual agreement with other national groups. If it is a state that the group is after and it decides to secede unilaterally, disregarding all the regulations in place for the procedure, this destructive and unreasonable behavior can be justifiably punished. To resolve the conflict, the group's illegal behavior would be suppressed, but the group should still be guaranteed equal self-determining status within a multinational framework. National groups in this situation might justify some of their actions as acts of self-defense, a right now given to any state actor. It would not be possible, however, for them to claim—as they can now—either that the very existence of their community was in peril due to the international community's failure to recognize their rights or that they did not have legitimate means available to them of solving their problem.

The modified right can be said to have a reverse: that a group that is not being treated by its state as if it has the right may employ extreme means, such as terrorism, to get the entitlement specified by the right. Such a national group, however, may have a right to secede under the modified right, and thus to change its situation using lawful means. In order to establish its right to secede, the group has to show that the state it belongs to does not provide for the equal recognition of its self-determination. The group also has to show that it has not rejected reasonable suggestions put forward by the host state or refused to participate in negotiations with that state.[27] The host state can defend its entitlement to territorial integrity by showing that it respects both the self-determination of national groups on its territory and the human rights of their members, or at least that it has made reasonable efforts to initiate a process of change in this direction. It is necessary that special international agencies, possibly courts, be established to deal with self-determination claims. What would need to be shown in such courts in order for a group's claim to the right to secede to be dismissed is that equal participation is in principle available for the national group: that the group enjoys reasonable equality within the state's borders and has an opportunity to question and contest the state's decisions, while the state has demonstrated its willingness to change. Thus, relationships among national groups are better understood in the context of a long-term political process guided by the norm of equality, not as a one-time, drastic settling of accounts. That the modified right allows for secession in some circumstances provides the best motivation for host states to respect the national groups within their borders. Admittedly, some states may gamble, using force to suppress national minorities, but in doing so they will be violating the modified right.

Irredentist groups present a special case of claims to change borders. They can appeal to the idea of nationhood as political culture associated with the meaningful limits of political authority and claim that such a culture exists across the borders of their host states and that the territories separated by the borders ought to be permitted to join to satisfy the corresponding national group's right to self-determination. Hence, it may appear that although the modified right can deal with the claims of substate groups that are primarily localized within the borders of a multinational state by providing means to achieve equal self-determination within it, the right cannot help to resolve conflicts that may erupt over secession initiated by irredentist groups to reunite their national group. Nevertheless, if an irredentist part of a multinational state was acquired through occupation, that part of the state can legitimately secede. If not, giving the members of such a group equal status within their multinational state tests their commitment to secede and join the remainder state. If they qualify as a nation (that is, if they possess the required kind of political culture with which their members identify), it may be the case that in the end they will not define their self-determination project as one of unification with their remainder state, as was the case in Moldova. If an irredentist group does not qualify as a nation without the remainder state, the problem ought to be solved between the remainder state and the host state. But it is not immediately clear how, given the geographical border separating them, it can be established with certainty that the irredenta and its remainder state share the same political culture and thus are really members of the same nation. In any case, the irredentist group itself does not have a claim and a right to secede according to the modified right, and its relationship with the host state should be regulated and negotiated in the same way as are the state's relationships with other national groups in its territory. An international court would be a good place to resolve any disputes, and the existing regional structures would be helpful in providing institutional support for any cross-border arrangements.[28]

Kymlicka argues that a state may consider that granting its minorities special rights including self-governing rights is ill-conceived if these minorities also have kin groups that are majorities in neighboring states with whom the host state has poor relations. "...In most parts of the world minority groups are still seen as a fifth column, likely to be working for a neighbouring enemy. This is particularly a concern where the minority is related to a neighbouring state by ethnicity or religion, or, where minority is found on both sides of an international boundary, so that the neighbouring state claims the right to intervene to protect 'its' minority." In this case, relations between states and minorities are seen, "not as a matter of normal democratic politics to be negotiated and debated, but as a matter of national security, in which the state has to limit the normal democratic process in order to protect its very existence."[29] This "securitization" of minority rights presents obstacles for internationalizing these rights.

It is not clear, however, why giving minority rights to irredentist groups would endanger the state more than refusing to grant them such rights. When the latter policy is adopted, the neighboring enemy state has an excuse to interfere and the minority group is more likely to envision its future in the neighboring state. Since there is no chance that it will be properly accommodated in the host state, nothing attaches the minority to the state. The minority might think it more prudent to secede than to demand suitable terms of inclusion in the host state. Depending on the group's circumstances, its members may even give up demanding their rights peacefully and use militant tactics to advance their claims. Moreover, by denying rights to the minority, the state may appear to be settling a score with its neighbors; for, it may appear to be punishing those of the enemy group who are within the state's reach. It is hard to see what would motivate the minority or the neighboring state to hold back in their actions against the host state. It should be pretty clear that an uncompromising rejection of the modified right has the destabilizing effect of mobilizing minorities in ways potentially dangerous to the host state. Providing minorities with rights creates a framework of rules and limitations within which all parties are more likely to interact peacefully.

It may be said that a state that has a strategic or economic interest in the territory that its minority occupies may be willing to pay the high price of keeping the territory under control. The outcome of the acceptance of the modified right is that the state can still keep the territory, but in a more cost-efficient manner. And in case of secession according to the rules specified by the modified right, the state will negotiate the terms of secession acceptable to it, including economic compensation. It is likely that the cost of keeping the territory by force is much higher than the cost of economic cooperation in either of these scenarios. The modified right to self-determination makes both minorities and their host state better off and to accept it is a pragmatic and prudent move for a multinational state.

The modified right also takes away the incentive for minorities to seize power illegally and then demand the recognition of their de facto self-determining status, an historically common move noted by Kymlicka.[30] The inclusion of group entitlements in the constitutional arrangement of a state prevents such group actions by guiding the exercise of a national group's effective agency in the enjoyment of its self-determination in the host multinational state. The issue of the balance of power between a majority, minorities sharing territory with it and the neighboring kin-state is complicated, but it is not likely that it will be resolved through securitization and denial of minority rights.

Including the requirements of justice toward national communities within multinational states as a subject of international legal regulation might seem likely to require a degree of involvement that the international community is not able to provide. Establishing the norms of acceptable international behavior concerning national groups would be helpful in and of itself, however, for the following reasons: A state that violates the norms of fair treatment of minorities in its territory would cross the threshold of legitimacy in the international system and stop being a member in good standing. This alone could motivate some international actors to comply with the rules. The very existence of a just international norm can influence agents' behavior and assure their compliance; international agents normally want to be members in good standing, or at least to behave so as to not formally violate major norms.

Moreover, international intervention could take an indirect approach through the imposition of sanctions on a violator state, the suspension of important relations with this state, or the denial of some privileges previously afforded to it as a member in good standing. If a national group agitates after being given equal status within its host multinational state (or after the state has embarked on the process of change leading to the granting of such a status to the group), the state can justifiably penalize the group for its actions. In this case, extra international intervention is not required. I will argue that the norm of equality is not only just but also that it can be maintained by the subjects of the modified right in the next chapter, in which I deal with the practical impact of the modified right on international peace and consider how it ought to be implemented.

The modified right permits universal membership in a community of self-determining groups by redefining the institutional expression of the idea of self-determination. Hence, it can in principle be legalized. Recognition of the modified right would fill the void in international law created by the present lack of a proper regulation of relations among national groups and between states and national groups. It would reduce the split between the absolute entitlement of state actors to self-determination and the disentitlement of non-state actors to this same right. Although my approach does not provide a perfect resolution to the problem of the justice and stability of multinational states, it is an improvement over the status quo for both state-endowed and stateless nations: The modified right helps to improve the position of stateless groups with respect to power distribution in multinational states, and it is more just from their perspective than the status quo. It also improves the situation of state-endowed nations, because it helps make multinational states more stable. It is very likely that a group that was granted proper status within a multinational state would not want to secede. More often than not, it would be profitable for such a group to be together with other groups in a strong viable state rather than to strike out on its own, especially from an economic point of view.[31] Besides, even from the majority perspective, making a multinational state more just is a goal worth pursuing in and of itself.

I will say more about different ways to realize the norm of equality and discuss the probable effects of the introduction of the modified right to self-determination on the behavior of substate groups and their relations with their state-endowed counterparts in the next chapter.

Notes

1. An earlier version of the discussion of the consequences of the introduction of the modified right (now presented in parts of this chapter and of Chapter 6) was published in Anna Moltchanova, "Stateless national groups, international justice, and asymmetrical warfare," *The Journal of Political Philosophy*, 13(2), June 2005, 194–215, publisher: Wiley and Sons Ltd.
2. Jeremy Waldron, "Rights and Majorities: Rousseau Revisited," in *Liberal Rights: Collected Papers 1981–1991,* p. 400.
3. An authority external to a people and their political community can govern them legitimately on a temporary basis when it is an interim authority created and put in place for a period of transition.

4. According to Joseph Raz, a person may be said to have a right if and only if some aspect of his well-being (some interest of his) is sufficiently important in itself to justify holding other person or persons to be under a duty. See *The Morality of Freedom*, p. 166.
5. The notion that "equal consideration requires that all persons have the same fundamental status, as equal participants, in the most important decisions made in their societies" is defended by Allen Buchanan in his discussion of a human right to democracy. See *Justice, Legitimacy, and Self-Determination*, p. 143.
6. Moore argues that respecting collective autonomy is of moral importance. Institutional recognition of national identity is important for members' sense of identity and gives expression to their political aspirations. See *The Ethics of Nationalism*, p. 176.
7. This is so in part because a national group may be multicultural or multilingual, and different national groups may share the same language and culture.
8. Will Kymlicka persuasively argues that national assimilation is hard and, even on the utilitarian scale, is not a sacrifice we can require minorities to make, unless they choose its willingly. Immigrants, for example, willingly choose a different national culture and hence forfeit the option to remain in their initial culture; they can justifiably be expected to assimilate. Will Kymlicka, *Multicultural Citizenship*, Chapter 5.
9. Will Kymlicka demonstrates that minority rights can enlarge the freedom of individuals because cultural membership, including membership in a national, or "societal," culture, is a necessary condition for individual freedom. See *Multicultural Citizenship*, pp. 83–84. He also defends the distinction between immigrant and national minorities in chapter 5.
10. For a discussion of the original position in the context of multinational states, see Daniel Weinstock, "On Some Advantages of Constitutionalizing the Right to Secede," *Journal of Political Philosophy* 9, no. 2 (2001).
11. John Rawls, *A Theory of Justice* (Cambridge, MA: Harvard University Press, 1971), pp. 17–22.
12. John Rawls, *Justice as Fairness: A Restatement* (Cambridge, MA: Belknap Press/Harvard University Press, 2001), p. 18.
13. In his *Law of Peoples*, John Rawls proposes two original positions. The first is conducted within liberal states, and the second has as its parties representatives of peoples. In the second original position, the representatives do not choose among options from the list, they just approve of the set of the principles of justice that Rawls suggests. Rawls considers peoples as conceiving themselves to be equal and free. He extends international discourse to liberal and decent hierarchical peoples. I apply the technique of original position within a state, not internationally. See *The Law of Peoples* (Cambridge, MA: Harvard University Press, 2001), p. 34.
14. Buchanan, *Justice, Legitimacy, and Self-Determination*, p. 187.
15. Ibid., p. 335.
16. Those individuals living in the territory of a national minority who consider themselves members of the majority are represented by the majority. It is precisely because all groups are self-determining within a state that all individuals can consider the state as their own. The "minority majority" can perhaps have a seat in the legislative assembly of the majority nation.
17. In 1996, for example, 64% of Tatars and 41% of Russians in Tatarstan thought that the republic should have exclusive control over its natural resources, while 23 percent of Tatars and 44% of Russians considered joint control by Tatarstan and the Russian Federation to be the right choice. Given the ethnic composition of the republic, there was popular support for the state's exclusive control, but there was also some room for the government of Tatrstan to negotiate shared control based on the minority mandate and the interest of the group in being included in the Russian Federation. See L. M. Drobizheva, ed., *Asymmetrichnaja federatsia: vzgliad iz tsentra, respoublik i oblastei. Kniga 2, 2-e izdanie* [*Asymmetrical Federation: A View from the Center, Republics and Districs*], book 2, 2nd edition (Moscow: Institut etnologii i antropologii RAN, 2000), p. 195.
18. A good account of "decentralization strategies" is offered by John McGarry in "Orphans of Secession: National Pluralism in Secessionist Regions and Post-Secession States," in

National Self-Determination and Secession, ed. M. Moore (Oxford: Oxford University Press, 1998), p. 226.
19. Article I-5.1 of the draft Treaty establishing a Constitution for Europe (CIG 86/04).
20. The European Parliament, the European Council, and the European Court of Justice provide forums for this.
21. Article I-59 of the draft Treaty establishing a Constitution for Europe (CIG 86/04).
22. Daniel Philpott, "Westphalia, Authority, and International Society," *Political Studies* (1999), XLVII: 566–589, p. 567.
23. Ibid., p. 578.
24. Allen Buchanan complements his theory of secession with the notion of recognitional legitimacy, which pronounces that only those states that are minimally just can be recognized as legitimate. The concept of recognitional legitimacy, therefore, is employed by Buchanan to judge whether an entity under consideration satisfies the criteria for being a member in good standing in the international legal system. The minimal requirement of justice that Buchanan introduces is respect for human rights by the state domestically and internationally. According to Buchanan, territorial integrity is a morally progressive principle of international relations if it is assigned to states that satisfy the criterion of recognitional legitimacy. Thus, minimally just states are entitled to territorial integrity, and national groups do not have a right to secede from such states; the only reasons Buchanan allows for secession are gross violations of human rights and unjust occupation. See "Recognitional Legitimacy and the State System," pp. 48, 55.
25. Majorities often engage in power-based rhetoric that presupposes that they perceive the whole of the territory as theirs. A good example is a question asked in Russia—"How can the Chechens want to take a part of Russia away?"—or Georgia's considering Abkhazia and Serbia considering Kosovo as their inalienable territory.
26. Buchanan offers examples of the international response to the treatment of Kurds and human rights abuses in South Africa under apartheid to demonstrate how his theory should work.
27. On the international adjudicative process, see David Copp, "International Law and Morality in the Theory of Secession," *Journal of Ethics* 2 (1998): 219–245.
28. John McGarry raises the problem of national pluralism in secessionist regions or newly formed states and points out that such states "are often as heterogeneous as their predecessors, as likely to abuse minorities, and, subsequently, as prone to conflict." See "Orphans of Secession," p. 215. I believe that my system provides a good answer to the "Russian doll" problem of secession by attempting to concentrate on the regulation of relations among national groups in multinational states to make these states more just and less unstable. As far as groups other than national minorities are concerned, they typically do not advance self-determination claims and are not included in my approach. Their rights are covered under the widely accepted rights of national minorities and may be protected on that basis. Moreover, it is often easier to control the implementation of these kinds of rights in smaller states, for they are more easily influenced by the international community.
29. Will kymlicka, *Multicultural Odysseys: Navigating the New International Politics of Diversity* (Oxford: Oxford University Press, 2007), p. 119.
30. Ibid., p. 237.
31. For a discussion of this point, see Will Kymlicka, "Minority Nationalism and Multination Federalism," in *Politics in the Vernacular: Nationalism, Multiculturalism, and Citizenship* (Oxford: Oxford University Press: 2001), pp. 91–119. Kymlicka acknowledges that multinational federations will face secessionist movements. But he thinks that a well-designed multinational federation provides a framework for negotiating differences and, consequently, gives national groups good reasons to reject secession. Multinational federations have a weak kind of national unity, Kymlicka argues, that is different from that which uninational states often possess. But because federalism is often the only way of accommodating national differences, multinational federations have proven themselves to be surprisingly resilient.

Chapter 6
The Implications of the Modified Right to Self-Determination[1]

In the previous chapter, I defended the modified right to self-determination, which establishes a norm for the just treatment of national groups. Pragmatism indicates, however, that if the modified right is to regulate the relations among state-endowed and stateless national groups, it has to have the capacity to become a legal norm with universal application within the present international legal system. I have already demonstrated that the modified right does not contradict the principle of territorial integrity, which is fundamental to this system. I will now discuss how an approach to self-determination and the corresponding international norms based on the modified right could help define fair terms for autonomy arrangements for substate national groups. I will first define the "nations approach" to self-determination and then discuss the implementation of equal self-determination for all substate national groups in a multinational federation and the corresponding challenges.

Next, I will argue that the employment of my approach, and especially the introduction of the modified right, will have positive consequences for international peace. I maintain that if this approach were accepted in the international legal framework, it would be useful for responding to the moral claims of non-state combatants. The modified right undermines the moral basis for the "just cause" and "last resort" justifications for asymmetrical warfare, provides incentives for non-state groups to participate in negotiations, and eases their transition into becoming responsible members of the international community. These likely positive effects of the nations approach provide a partial, teleological justification for it. But the success of this normative framework in addressing the challenges multinational states face will depend in part on whether the community of states both accepts the norms of the framework and has sufficient resources to enforce them. I demonstrate in the penultimate section of this chapter that since the set of norms I advance respects the privileges of existing states, these norms have a good chance of being accepted, and the status they afford to the members of the international community will facilitate these members' voluntary compliance. In the last section of the chapter I deal with some empirical considerations that apply to implementing the nations approach.

A. Moltchanova, *National Self-Determination and Justice in Multinational States*, Studies in Global Justice 5, DOI 10.1007/978-90-481-2691-0_6,

The Nations Approach

The nations approach is based on my definition of a nation as a collective agent organized around the good of self-determination. This approach includes the modified right to self-determination and the corresponding norm of legitimacy for multinational states and extends the regulation of national groups' behavior to transitional societies, albeit employing a cautious approach to self-determination claims in such societies.

A prima facie claim to self-determination is based on the existence of group agents of the kind I define as nations. It identifies qualifying groups through their possession of a political culture with the shared goal of maintaining or acquiring collective agency related to the meaningful limits of political authority. The modified right to self-determination requires that a national group's claim to self-determination be its claim to equal recognition of nationhood within the boundaries of a multinational state. A just multinational state ought to be based on a partnership of different national groups as equal self-determining communities, and hence as equal members sharing the state's space. The rules regulating relations among national groups in a just state specify conditions of mutual respect and partnership, as well as separation procedures. If a group is not a nation, it does not qualify for the right to self-determination, but even those national groups that in principle qualify for the right may not be allowed to exercise it if they do not comply with the norm of equality prescribed by the nations approach.

The nations approach to self-determination upholds respect for human rights as a basic moral norm of international behavior, but it also requires the recognition of a moral entitlement of all national groups to equal status. The conditions of membership in the international community for stateless national groups ought to be considered an important issue of global justice. The nations approach maintains that the norm of legitimacy is not satisfied by political authority in a multinational state if it does not provide fair conditions of membership for its substate national groups, including equality of status with respect to self-determination. In Chapter 2 I determined that there is a fundamental difference between self-determination and other group rights. Linguistic and other minority rights that do not directly relate to self-determination define fair conditions of citizenship within political communities, the justifiable boundaries of which are determined by the shared good of self-determination. I accept but do not argue in this book that respect for minority rights other than self-determination is required for the just arrangement of a multinational state. Thus, the provision of fair terms of individual inclusion in political units organized around self-determination is necessary for determining the justice and legitimacy of a state, multinational or otherwise. The nations approach holds, therefore, that respect for the human and minority rights of citizens as well as their national identity is required for the just arrangement of multinational states. If a state does not address claims to self-determination on its territory properly, it cannot be considered minimally just, even if it does not violate human rights.

Contested secession has received much attention in recent scholarship. Since contested secession is based upon the disagreement of two or more national groups concerning their self-determination within particular boundaries, the nations approach considers secession as merely one aspect of the regulation of relations among national groups in their host multinational states, which ideally has to be done on a continuous basis according to the norms advanced by the nations approach. It prioritizes the terms of organization of multinational states over those of their dissolution, because the latter are implied by the set of principles guiding just arrangements for multinational states. Unilateral secession is not permissible in a state that satisfies the norm of legitimacy: after the will of the people of a national group is expressed (in a referendum, for example), this gives the group's representatives a mandate to either negotiate the group out of the state or renegotiate its position within the state. If a group is offered fair terms and rejects them without good reason, it does not have the right to secede.[2] Does substate self-determination allow group agents to be excessively influenced by political and economic circumstances external to their constitution? The nations approach assists with the maintenance of agents' constitutions and aims to shape their interactions in the best way possible to achieve equality of control over their political futures within the state.

In extending legal regulation to those self-determination claims that are now beyond the scope of the right to self-determination, the nations approach aims to minimize secessionist attempts in multinational states. It increases the range of possibilities for the satisfaction of self-determination claims by allowing and encouraging the exercise of self-determination within existing state borders, thereby reducing the potential instability of multinational states, as I demonstrate in this chapter. One of the goals of the nations approach is thus to ensure the stability of host states by securing their compliance with the ideal of just treatment afforded to all group agents on their territory with verifiable claims to self-determination.

The nations approach both acknowledges that it is important to preserve the territorial integrity of states and draws no necessary conceptual connection between nationhood and statehood. The consequence of the principle of equality of national self-determination for the domestic politics of multinational states is that national groups are not accorded a mere partial redistribution of power that is still vested in the main nation, but rather are given equality of status with other national groups, which is reflected in the constitutional and institutional organization of the state. A state entitled to territorial integrity should fairly represent all the national groups on its territory without giving only one group (or only some groups) privileged access to state power.

Three aspects of the legal system of a multinational state ought to comply with the nations approach in order for a state to satisfy the norm of legitimacy: (1) the general norms of the system, such as the state's constitution, bill of rights, or initial agreements determining the mutual status of the parties; (2) norms governing autonomy arrangements between the state and each national group; and (3) norms that categorize the entitlements of various subjects in mixed federations (federations with both national and territorial subjects). Bringing these norms into compliance with the nations approach is necessary to provide acceptable terms for the organization of the political institutions of a multinational state.

The nations approach requires that the conditions of equal discourse in a multinational state be satisfied or sufficiently well approximated. The conditions of equal discourse protect the equal freedom of the parties. Agreements made under the conditions of equal discourse are binding on all parties involved, regardless of the type of arrangements made in each particular case. Moreover, norms accepted in order to promote and maintain these conditions in the future are legitimate. The approval of a federal constitution by only the majority national group, for example, does not satisfy this requirement: federal laws ought to be approved by all affected groups, and no changes ought to be made to the initial agreement without all national groups' consent.

It is often acknowledged that the right to self-determination has two dimensions: an external dimension refers to "the international status of a people concentrated on a specific territory and the relations of this entity with the surrounding states," while an internal dimension has to do with the institutional organization and legal regulations of a multinational state designed to accommodate different national groups in the state's territory.[3] If only state-endowed national groups can enjoy the external aspect of self-determination and non-state groups are limited exclusively to the exercise of internal self-determination without freely consenting to be, their differential treatment does not comply with the nations approach, because state-endowed and non-state groups are constituted around the same shared good of self-determination but are being treated unequally. From the point of view of the nations approach, then, the fair inclusion of a substate group into a multinational state involves granting all groups—minorities and the majority—a similar degree of control over their political futures and thus involves the assurance that all groups can share in both external and internal self-determination.

Compare the following two accommodation strategies. A strategy that has an external institutional dimension presupposes that there ought to be at least one tool for the resolution of claims to self-determination, such as a referendum; requires international as well as internal supervision of conflict resolution; and allows minority national groups to enter external relationships with subjects beyond the borders of the host state. Although it is good if this strategy is supplemented by rules for long-term interaction among self-determining substate agents, the tools it proposes comply with the nations approach. The strategy of consociation, on the other hand, allows a national group to participate in the state parliament, but only on the basis of proportional representation, and it permits cultural but not political self-government.[4] The rules put forward by this strategy do not comply with the nations approach, although they can be used if a national group chooses to approve them under the condition of equal participation in discourse, and thus freely. The nations approach, however, would require that the group not be prevented from the exercise of self-determination in the future if it so chooses.

Thus, the principles of federal institutional design should reflect the prima facie equality of the moral entitlement of different national groups. There ought to be a set of norms, procedures, and institutional structures guaranteeing the possession and exercise of discursive control to each group. In general, the norms of participation for national groups in a federal legislative power, when based on the equal freedom of collective agents, ensure that the agents have the means to protect their interest in self-determination. This is essential to promote their cooperation within a multinational state. Various autonomy settlements defining the shared and exclusive powers between the federal state and each national group, which I discuss in the second part of this chapter, can express the national groups' equal status in decision making at the federal level of legislative power and thus satisfy the general standards regulating the proper status of national groups with respect to one another.

What criteria of assessment are available for the international community to judge whether a state satisfies the norm of legitimacy, or whether it is minimally just? Such a state should at least satisfy the following necessary conditions: First, basic discrimination should not be included in the constitution or institutions of a state, as would be introduced, for example, by a statement that the state represents one nation. Hence, no one group should have preferential access to a set of rights, powers, and institutional accommodations promoting its self-determination. Second, it has to be possible for a national group to question the justice of the constitutional layout of the state and to contest any provisions included in the internal arrangement of the state that it deems unjust and considers an imposition on its ability to determine its future political status. This assures that the group has at least minimal conditions for preserving its equal freedom. Third, the tools for exercising discursive control have to be available to all groups, including forums for discussion and the possibility of a referendum or some other procedure that allows individual members to make public their shared goal of acquiring and maintaining the effective exercise of their collective agency associated with self-determination. The presence of such tools allows the international community to discern the existence of a substate national group with sufficient accuracy. Finally, there has to be some legal recourse available for national groups. They have to be able to voice their grievances internationally in, for example, an international court or the UN, and the corresponding international agency must have a normative framework that allows it to pass judgments upon the status of the group. Ideally, there would also be some international institutional devices available for monitoring a group's situation and working to protect minorities' basic claims by various means.

I do not want to interpret equality in such stringent terms, however, that I make my theory irrelevant to the current processes of international relations. The scope of the notion of equality allows for a variety of arrangements, from states with the de facto equality of national groups to those that closely enough approach equality not to be considered unjust to those that are not in principle unjust and have demonstrated willingness to embark upon the process of negotiations and reform. It is important that, in each case when a state claims to be in the process of achieving the standard set by the norm of legitimacy, the international body responsible for the enforcement of the modified right establishes an acceptable time limit for a desired change toward equality to take place, after and only after which the state would be considered to have failed to satisfy the norm. If a country is a true democracy where in principle the equality of nations is possible, it is unlikely that it will be called unjust: in Canada, for example, even if at the present moment the equality of nations is not acknowledged constitutionally, a process exists that allows national groups to express their opinions and be heard. The nations approach's norm of legitimacy indicates, however, that such states should think about initiating the process of change from above.

Since secession is not only destabilizing but also in most cases impracticable, it is a priority of the nations approach to accommodate the self-determination claims of national groups in relation to one another within their host states. The recognition of their basic entitlements as a particular kind of actor allows national groups to share the state on the "right" grounds from their own and others' perspective.

Multinational Federations and the Nations Approach

In this section, I consider how the equal self-determination can be realized within the borders of a federation. The federations I discuss contain national or both national and territorial, but not exclusively territorial, units. Thus, they are either multinational or mixed (asymmetrical) federations. I first consider general organizational principles for such states and then deal with a number of challenges that a theory of multinational federalism needs to answer.

Equality of Self-Determination in Multinational States

One cannot approach a society that houses several national groups without paying attention to allegiances with respect to self-determination, because they denote the limits of political communities meaningful to their members. Given that federations ought to treat their citizens equally as citizens of the larger state and that they must respect human rights, they cannot discriminate on the basis of national origin. The central state can equally belong to all substate national groups in a number of ways, but it cannot justifiably create a hierarchy of national groups with a constitutionally entrenched difference in access to political power. Thus, there cannot justifiably be a "title" nationality, either at the state or substate level, that hosts within its territory other national groups that do not directly belong to the federal state (unless they choose mediation by the host republic voluntarily and have the option to change their mind). Thus, there has to be an established procedure (which may require a corresponding institutional structure) that allows all national groups to jointly determine the policies deemed to be within the jurisdiction of the federal power. There also has to be a division of powers between a central government and its national subunits that allocates enough power to national groups to allow them to control their political futures.

The central government can be delegated by subunion groups in a number of ways, but it is advisable to have a chamber in which all of the subunion national groups are represented equally. The federal constitution can only be amended in consultation with all subunion national groups and needs to be passed by this level of the legislature. Each subunit can have its own legislature and can, within the limits of compliance with the federal constitution, unilaterally amend its own constitution. There could also be a chamber that has proportionate representation if this is required by the type of authority that the joint government wants to exercise.[5] Such a federation is similar to a typical federal state in that the authority that is devolved is not immediately revocable, but the terms of membership are more relaxed than in a typical federal state: a federation that complies with the nations approach ought to have a set of rules that define when a group can exit the union and a set of corresponding procedures. Nevertheless, the federal state in my model will not be quite as relaxed in the rules of its formation as a confederation, in which two or more sovereign countries agree to coordinate economic and military policy and devolve the power to administer these policies to a supranational body composed of delegates of each country. In a confederation, the authority devolved upward is voluntary and revocable, because a state devolving its powers retains the right to unilaterally reclaim them.[6] A national group in a multinational federation, on the other hand, cannot unilaterally secede except in exceptional circumstances.

For an analogy that clarifies power sharing in a multinational federation in compliance with the nations approach, consider the distinction between joint and collective ownership of property drawn by Mathias Risse. Decision making at the federal level concerning federal laws and the corresponding powers of national groups can be likened to the terms of joint ownership of property: such ownership requires that a collective decision-making process be concluded to the satisfaction of each of the "owners."[7] Decision making at the level of each group, considered from the point of view of their membership in the federal state, is akin to the terms of collective ownership of property: each owner in this case enjoys equal entitlement to use of their part of the property within constraints. This means that each group has power to control its own constitution so long as it satisfies the norms of relating to other state members and conforms with the federal-level norms that regulate its relation to its citizens.

The constitutionally entrenched division of powers between each nation and the state need not be uniform; every national group can have its own arrangement with the state. Every national group is likely to have a different list of issues it considers important to its control over its political future. Its needs must be reflected in the norms of political power sharing with the state and the legal rules governing the group's territorial autonomy. The rules defining shared and exclusive areas of competence cannot give the majority group or the federal government fundamental priority unless the substate group agrees to this division under fair conditions of deliberation.

A range of existing accommodation strategies satisfy the norm of equality. In the Russian Federation, for example, some basic norms ensure the minimal level of entitlement in the relationships of all national republics with the center: the status and territory of the republics cannot be changed without their consent, federal authorities coordinate international relations jointly with the republics, and the republics hold their land and resources as the property of their peoples.[8] Under this general norm of equality, however, models of inclusion are envisioned by different republics on the basis of their constitutions: Tuva's constitution states that the republic is included in the Russian Federation on the basis of the federal treaty and that the republic has a right to self-determination and exit.[9] The republic of Sakha, on the other hand, acknowledges as superior on its territory only those laws of the Russian Federation that concern powers that the republic has voluntarily surrendered to the federation.[10] It delegates its powers through agreements and treaties and has the right to suspend federal laws when they contradict the federal treaty and the laws and constitution of Sakha. To acquire force in the territory of Sakha, federal laws that affect joint affairs need to be ratified by the legislative body of the republic. And Tatarstan's constitution states that Tatarstan is a sovereign state subject to international law; it is associated with the Russian Federation on the basis of the treaty determining the mutual delegation and separation of powers.[11]

Challenges to Multinational Federalism

The Charge of Inconsistency

One common criticism of multinational federalism is that it forbids dominant national groups from claiming ownership and control over public institutions at the central level but allows smaller national groups to make such claims at the substate level. The control of public institutions should be considered with respect to other national groups as well as to non-self-determining minorities and nationals of other groups as private citizens.

The major problem with the dominant group's claiming ownership over the public institutions of a state is that it prohibits other primary political communities from functioning properly within the borders of the state. We need to make sure that this problem is not reproduced at the substate level. My model of federalism certainly prohibits any group from exercising exclusive and unreciprocated control of public institutions at the central level. According to my plan, all national groups hold direct and equal membership in the state at the federal level of authority. In this model the state does not belong to any one group, but to all of them equally. Thus, at the federal level it is not the case that the dominant national group is deprived of its ownership of public institutions and others are empowered to wield the political authority the dominant group no longer enjoys.

How can the organization of a multinational state that maintains the equality of self-determination prevent a national group from reproducing, at the substate level of power, the patterns of political control previously exhibited by the dominant group within the state at large? This question arises when national groups have a large number of members of another national group residing within the territory they govern or when a new national group emerges within this territory.

The form of political control over a disputed territory populated by members of more than one national group needs to be decided based on negotiations mediated by the federal-level authority. The territory can be allocated to one group with special rights for members of the other; the corresponding groups may be able to share control over the territory (besides the shared control over the territory they already exercise, together with other groups, concerning the aspects of government relegated to the federal level of authority, which gives them a certain degree of control over the territory). Groups can govern jointly or they can divide spheres of influence, but no national group can exercise power over all or part of a substate territory that contains territorially concentrated members of another national group unless the latter give consent under fair conditions of agreement. An agreement is fair if the group retains equal status with respect to self-determination and its equal membership in the federal level of authority and has transferred some of its powers over its members within the territory of the other group to that group voluntarily. I will deal with the problem of the locus of self-determination for all national groups and the division of territory in more detail when I explain how to deal with the equality of self-determination of groups some members of which form minorities, and not necessarily territorially concentrated, in other substate units.

What should be done when a nation appears in the territory of an already defined national subunit that enjoys self-determination within the state? According to my account, none of the properly formed groups should be disadvantaged or disregarded, and each needs to be given membership in the state at the federal level. If there is a group that qualifies as national on the territory of one of the substate national groups, it is withdrawn from the authority of the "host" group and acquires a status equal to it within the federation. For example, some of the national republics in the Russian Federation contain, along with their title nationalities, national minorities. Since every national group deserves similar treatment within the federation, the participation in the federation of these national minorities cannot be mediated by their current host republics; the minorities ought be considered immediate and equal federal subjects. According to the modified right, the basic equality of status of each group with respect to self-determination has to be the guiding principle for regulating their relations. They have to be included in the federation equally with other national groups and not be treated as "minorities within" the recognized national republics precisely so as to not reproduce the hierarchical patterns of access to self-determination, in which one group controls another or is privileged over another. The larger group does not in any case have legitimate reach over a political community of self-determination that has located the source of authority within its own community without the consent of this community.

Treatment of newly formed units in a way that complies with the nations approach and aims to be consistent with the treatment afforded to already existing units in the multinational state certainly prevents substate groups from exercising excessive control over substate political institutions. What needs to be explained in this case is why I propose to keep state boundaries (previously associated, perhaps, with the power of the formerly dominant group) intact when the boundaries of national units within the state may be changed. The problem here concerns substate groups' being too deprived rather than too empowered. It is certainly true that the state does not belong to any particular group, but this may be a good reason to allow an equal right to secession from the state to all national groups. Whether this kind of solution is pragmatically destabilizing is a separate question that does not directly relate to the question of whether my approach offers a principled basis for multinational states' arrangement. I do not claim that state boundaries cannot be changed, but I do maintain that states should not be pulled apart until the status of their national subunits is established as equal and is regulated. Then national groups can secede by mutual agreement, and the process will be regulated by the legal and institutional framework that maintains their mutual standing.

Provided that national identities are accommodated fairly across the borders of substate units, what remains to consider is whether substate groups will exercise control prohibited to the formerly dominating national group over those minority groups—linguistic, religious, or cultural—that do not fall under the arrangement concerning substate national identities. All citizens in the federation are also citizens of the larger state and deserve the basic protection of their rights that is ideally guaranteed to all the residents of the federation's territory by the federal level of authority. The terms of substate groups' membership in a federation therefore ought to include compliance with basic federal guidelines for the protection of individual and group rights within their territory. Thus, the transfer of power to the substate level will not alter the conditions governing national groups' behavior toward minorities. Ultimately, the protection of individual and group rights depends on the organization of the federation, and the nations approach includes respect for minorities, as is required for the legitimacy of states.

Their mutual and reciprocal control over the federal level of government safeguards all groups' basic interest in self-determination but leaves certain areas up to them so long as they do not control or influence others in illegal ways. This prevents national groups from controlling public institutions at the substate level in a way that would be offensive to members of other national groups or that would violate their rights or the rights of other types of minorities.

There are several questions that need to be answered to demonstrate that my approach to federalism does not run into a different set of problems. In brief, they involve the possibility of endless and destabilizing division along national lines within a state, the treatment of groups that are not territorially concentrated, the justification for keeping state boundaries intact while changing the substate units' boundaries, the benefits of the substate type of self-determination, and the issue of the allocation of territory. I will answer these questions in the order in which I have listed them.

The Nations Approach and Dynamic Group Identities

It may seem that my approach to nationhood increases the possibility of minorities mobilizing along national lines and aspiring to acquire a status at the level of the federal state equal to that of already existing national groups, which presents a problem for the stability of multinational states. The destabilizing effects of dynamic identities that the nations approach accommodates can be controlled by the terms of nations approach in at least two respects.

First, division into national units—at least into those recognized as such by the nations approach—will be limited by the size of a viable national unit. The nations approach requires that only a group capable of creating and maintaining effective agency, and thus a group that is viable in terms of its relations with other groups, can be considered a nation. A group of two people who decide to become a nation and claim that they have a corresponding political culture would not qualify. A viable political culture, nevertheless, can come in many different forms short of sovereignty. Many indigenous peoples, for example, cannot form their own states. Their political culture is viable, however, if they can fulfill important functions of authority within their territory to safeguard their identity and membership.[12]

Second, the nations approach does maintain that if a group is formed in the right way, it is a national group and is entitled to be treated as such, with equality of self-determination provided at the substate level. But the nations approach also guards against strategic mobilization, thereby controlling what is considered an acceptable mobilization of a group agent. The nations approach, moreover, defines the means that groups which qualify as national can employ to realize their self-determination. It does not allow for unilateral secession from minimally just states: the recognition of the equal status of all national groups ought to happen, first and foremost, at the substate level, supported by appropriate federal institutions. That the approach does not promise complete sovereignty may also reduce the number of strategic mobilizations. The nations approach also requires that a federal constitution be drawn so as to provide procedures for changes in group status and the criteria that groups need to satisfy to qualify for such a change. Thus, if the nations approach were adopted, multinational states would have to accommodate shifting group identities, but they would also be provided with means for the controlled accommodation of changing national identities. Thus, the nations approach increases the probability that multinational federations will stay together.

Groups that Are Not Concentrated in One Territory

When defining the terms of organization for a particular multinational federation, we need to identify all national groups within the proposed territory, determine the terms of their inclusion, and make provisions for the accommodation of newly formed national groups. Determining the status of national groups is easier if national groups are territorially localized. There are two demographic patterns of distribution, however, that complicate the consideration of possible terms of group inclusion in a federation. Some groups that claim to be national may not have acquired adequate institutions for the realization of their self-determination in the past and may have members scattered over a number of territories governed by the political institutions of other national groups. Considering the constitution of the group agent and its shared goals, we can determine how to accommodate such a group. If it does not qualify as a national group, it can be protected by a set of minority rights, but not by the right to self-determination. If the group qualifies as a nation, it needs to be provided with means to realize its substate self-determination.

The group can be given a territory, especially if historically it had one. I discuss this kind of situation at greater length later in the chapter.

Other minority groups may have institutions of government with control over a certain territory within a multinational state but also have a large number of individuals who consider themselves to be members residing within a territory governed by another national group. Such a situation seems to present a challenge in accommodating their national identities. Here is one possible solution in accordance with the nations approach.[13] If national minority A resides within the territory of national republic B, and if A considers itself to be part of a national group that has its own national republic A elsewhere, minority A has its national identity represented in the federal state through its title republic A. The minority members may be entitled to some special cross-border arrangements to relate to their nation, subject to negotiations between the title and the host republics. In some cases, boundaries can be redrawn if it is expedient—for example if the minority populates a compact territory adjacent to the host republic. This accession procedure, however, has to comply with the modified right, which would mean that national subjects have to be given an equal possibility of exercising discursive control and thus equal freedom in having a say about the procedure. A number of factors, such as stability and historic entitlements, need to be taken into consideration. In some cases, minorities, even numerous ones, have appeared in the territory of other national groups as a result of population moves executed by an oppressive regime that disregarded the host group's right to self-determination, as is the case of the Russian population in the Baltic Republics. Overall, the nations approach prevents aggressive mobilization through the norm of equality and utilizes a cautious approach to mobilization in non-democratic states. Finally, if minority group A in the territory of republic B ceases to identify with the political culture of its corresponding national republic A and decides that it is a separate national group, it ought to be approached as one.

For example, in the Russian Federation, which ought to recognize Russian national identity and other national identities equally, Russians are often a minority in other national republics. It may be a good idea for the Russians to have their own parliament alongside the federal parliament. In the republics where they are a minority, the Russians would be able to relate to the Russian national political culture. They could even have a seat in the Russian (not the federal) parliament, which would allow those away from the "main" Russian nation to have a say in the nation's affairs. There are some existing non-territorial arrangements of this kind. A non-territorial group such as the Italian diaspora in Canada, for example, relates to already existing territorial nations—Canada and Italy, in this case. They relate to Canada as citizens and as an ethnic minority, and they relate to Italy as citizens who comprise an extraterritorial voting district.

Although the Russian-speaking minority can relate to its title nationality beyond the boundaries of the host national republic, which can in part determine the terms of its membership in the host republic, within the host territory the Russian minority members are a linguistic/cultural/religious minority and not a national group. If the Russian minority is territorially concentrated, its members could have certain political powers and a degree of self-government to fulfill their ethnic and other minority interests and enjoy adequate representation as this kind of group in the host national republic's parliament. The Russians would not have the right to annex parts of other national groups' territory, however, even if they felt that the Russian minority was numerous enough to warrant such an action.

Thus, we can institutionalize self-determination through models of multinational federalism that do not reproduce the patterns of exclusion exhibited by nation-states that contain minority nations. The modified right to self-determination and the corresponding organization of multinational states that I suggest withdraw national minorities from under the control of other national minority groups and require that other minorities (linguistic, religious, and cultural) be protected within the territory of each national group.

Benefits of Substate Self-Determination

While substate self-determination is a legitimate form of exercising national groups' power to control their political future, one may ask whether substate self-determination brings tangible benefits to national groups in multinational states. That their self-determination is mediated by their joint membership in the state, which stands between the groups and the rest of the world (because they ought to act in concert and be represented internationally as a "cluster"), seems to diminish the benefits that self-determination brings to substate national units. Traditionally the enjoyment of self-determination has often been tied to privileging the status of one group over others, and since I insist that national groups can enjoy the constitutive good of self-determination only while respecting the rights of others, this may appear to deprive national groups of the benefits of self-determination they aspire to.

In Chapter 2, however, I argued that being recognized as a self-determining group is a significant benefit for national groups because self-determination is their constitutive good. The argument in this book implies that those groups that enjoy the benefits of self-determination unjustly do not exercise their freedom properly, in accordance with their moral right. As I discussed in Chapter 5, moreover, the kinds of limitations that group membership in a federal state of this sort imposes on the self-determination of a national group are not all that different from those imposed by a membership in a regional structure. Ideally, there should be a forum for the international representation of all national groups, like a "United Nations," literally understood.

Finally, granting "reduced" self-determination to substate national groups is a way of equalizing the enjoyment of self-determination, which is presently unequally distributed. Equality within a state is still self-determination. In the next section, I argue that this form of self-determination is better than alternatives in its consequences. One may ask whether in this case self-determination cannot just be reduced to some other forms of membership in the larger state. What does substate self-determination allow groups to do that they otherwise could not in a democratic society that respects individual and minority rights? Talking about the good of self-determination precisely allows us to determine how to fairly treat individuals from substate national units as members of the larger state. In the previous chapters, I explained how the receipt of even a broad spectrum of linguistic, religious, and cultural rights does not amount to the satisfaction of the shared interest of groups organized around self-determination. Thus, if national minorities are not granted self-determination rights within their host society, the host society is not fully respecting the minority rights of their members. The proper actualization of a substate national group agency helps to maintain the equality of the national minority members' citizenship in the larger liberal state. If minority rights include self-determination rights and self-determination is not sovereignty, a liberal society that respects individual and minority rights will provide for the equality of national groups' substate self-determination. What does the satisfaction of the right to self-determination involve compared to other rights? Minority groups enjoying self-determination can control the parameters of their political futures and negotiate as equals with other similar groups concerning the limits of their powers over their political life and the territory they control. These features of self-determination clearly set it apart from other minority rights. I will now move on to the role of territory in the enjoyment of the substate right to self-determination.

Dividing the Territory of a Multinational State

A non-territorial right to self-determination, though incomprehensible in the present international system, is perhaps not inconceivable in the future and would be compatible with my notion of nationhood.[14] However, as I discussed in Chapters "Collective Agents and Group Moral Rights" and "A Definition of Nationhood", when the condition of equal freedom in controlling a group's political future is fleshed out in terms that pertain to the present international system, the modified right to self-determination requires that a national group enjoying self-determination control a territory.

The Roma, for example, claim that they are a non-territorial nation. As I argued in Chapter 3, satisfying the definition of nationhood is a necessary condition to qualify for the right to self-determination. The Roma, in their desire to be determined by the conditions of their internal life, would possess a political culture of self-determination and thus qualify for the corresponding right only if they conceive of self-determination in the forms currently available for being equally free with other group agents organized around self-determination. The members of the Roma residing within territories under the administrative control of other political communities will have to interact with these communities regarding their group interests, and the terms of these interactions they envision as ideal determine what type of group they aspire to be. To be constituted as a collective agent with the right to self-determination, the Roma would have to conceive of their interactions as allowing them to have a say about their political future in a form compatible with existing national units. If there is an area in which some Roma can and would want to form a national unit to exercise self-determination and to which the rest can relate, they will be able to exercise their right to self-determination based on this home territory. Or, each group of Roma within a particular state can have its own political and territorial arrangement to protect its self-determination. If the Roma prefer to retain their form of organization and remain non-territorial, which would prevent them from relating to other national groups in terms of equal freedom, they cannot be accommodated via an equal right to self-determination, though they can be granted other minority rights to accommodate them within their host states.

My approach to territorial distribution proposes a very general strategy of treating all national agents as equals and evaluating their entitlements and types of claims they can advance based on this criterion. Existing national groups can negotiate their boundaries within the constraints of the modified right and accommodate irredentas and other minorities along the lines suggested in the next section. Determining who controls the territory of Kosovo, for example, cannot be the unilateral task of Serbia: according to the modified right, Serbia cannot claim that Kosovo is a part of the Serbian state without negotiating with the Kosovars as a national group concerning the arrangements of the shared state. National groups certainly differ in their size and power, and the dominant group in a state will have more political, institutional, and even military resources to pressure others. But this is precisely why we need the tools to identify who qualifies as a political unit that is morally equal to them and to assess their interactions from a moral point of view.

When the territorial boundaries of a national group are not disputed, figuring out how to accommodate a group usually requires determining its status within the multinational state. When boundaries are disputed between two or more national groups, the situation seems to be more complicated, but the modified right still provides the general background principle for the settlement of disputes of these types. It establishes that national groups are entitled to equal status within a multinational state and requires that groups maintain discursive control in negotiations. One example of an existing territorial problem of this sort is the disputed territorial boundary between Ingushetia and North Ossetia in the Russian Federation. A number of the Ingush people live within the territory of North Ossetia's Prigorodny District. That district was part of the Chechen-Ingush autonomous Soviet republic until it was dissolved following the deportation of Chechens and Ingush to Central Asia in 1944. At that time, the district became part of the North Ossetian autonomous Soviet republic. Ingush self-determination can presently be advanced within the restored republic of Ingushetia, but not throughout the extent of its pre-1944 borders. The problem, then, is to fairly determine the territories of North Ossetia and Ingushetia.

We cannot simply use the pre-1944 boundaries of these two republics as the standard guiding the resolution of this dispute; neither can we refer to the republics' status within the former Soviet Union as reflecting their national identity. First, the known institutional structures corresponded to vacuous political cultures: the merged Checheno-Ingush territory did not reflect the groups' ideal of membership, as expressed in their potential political cultures. Second, the expulsion of the Chechens and the Ingush from their territory changed the geodemographic landscape of the area and influenced the composition of their potential political cultures.

Finally, although the vacuous nature of official political cultures at the time of displacement should signal the uncertainty concerning the nature of group agents whose members were displaced, the displacement was clearly addressed to the two particular peoples, and regardless of what shape their self-determination is to assume, this historical event created an additional dimension of the present-day problem. In terms of the territory, it can be posed in the following way: even though pre-1944 boundaries do not reliably demarcate the Ingush territory, given the vacuous nature of the official expression of their identity in the past, does the group's past suffering entitle it to compensation via the accession of the territory adjoined to North Ossetia in 1944?

My answer to this problem, based on the nations approach, is that historical facts may be brought up in the context of negotiations between the two groups, but that these facts have to be viewed from the perspective of the constitution of the present-day group agents pursuing self-determination. Thus the status of the district can be only resolved by considering the composition and location of the two—the Ingush and the Ossetian—group agents now and only if the equality of their status at the federal level is assumed. The equality of status applies to the group's entitlement to equal self-determination, but not within a specific set of borders. It should be acknowledged at the federal level that the two peoples have an equal right to self-determination but not an unqualified right to safeguard the territory the groups presently occupy or to secure the territory they aspire to occupy before a settlement concerning the territory is concluded to the satisfaction of both sides. Thus, what cannot be assumed or ruled out prior to negations between them is the following: The possibility that the Ingush people can exercise self-determination within their present borders should not be excluded, but it cannot be concluded that they should confine themselves to this territory. Thus, it should not be excluded that the locus of self-determination for the Ingush people is the present boundaries of their republic, with special arrangements made for the Ingush individuals living in North Ossetia. It should also not be assumed, however, prior to the outcome of fairly conducted negotiations concluded to the two peoples' mutual satisfaction, that the Ingush ought to entirely give up on their claims to a portion of North Ossetia. This is especially so because thousands of the Ingush lived there, and their situation was aggravated in 1992 when they were forced to flee from their homes as the result of fighting in the district. While the Ingush cannot participate in the negotiations fairly if their only demand is that Prigorodny District be returned to them, Ingush refugees should not be forced to entirely give up the prospect of residing in North Ossetia. The fate of the refugees should be subject to negotiations between North Ossetia and Ingushetia, and the refugees can be considered as citizens of Ingushetia protected by that republic. The possibility that the Prigorodny District will be returned to the Ingush people also cannot be excluded. If the majority of the population there is Ingush, the district can qualify as part of their territory based on the composition of the group agent. If the district's ownership was not disputed before 1944, this fact is only a weak contributing factor to Ingushetia's claim to ownership because of the vacuous nature of the prior political culture.

Negotiations can only be concluded when both sides are satisfied, and they will undoubtedly assume a complex form. If it appears that no resolution is possible within the confines of this process, there ought to be a procedure for arbitration that will determine the fate of the territory based on the present constitution of group agents within it and will take into consideration acts of unlawful accession of the territory in the past without unreasonably disadvantaging its present inhabitants, as Gans recommends. The territory can be given to one of the republics. Both groups can be asked to relinquish their claims to the territory and it can be granted a special status in which the citizens of the two republics coexist under the aegis of the federation without being directly governed by any one republic. Or the territory can be divided between the two republics, with a peacekeeping federal force put in place to control the area during the transitional time. In all of three cases, the modified right should govern the process.

How can we provide institutional and territorial accommodation to an emerging unit if an existing unit has already received a territory that should rightfully belong to (or at least be shared with) the emerging unit? If the territory of a national group includes a newly appeared minority that claims to be another national group, and if this identity is verified, according to the modified right, this minority should refocus its membership in the state through a direct relation to the central state, at this stage as an equal to the host national group. The territorial entitlement of the host group would seem to present a problem under these circumstances. To remedy this, the constitution of the federal state can include the provision that the territorial boundaries of its political units remain open to revision under certain circumstances and specify a procedure for this process. This provision should introduce strict criteria to be satisfied by sub-unit groups to qualify for nationhood.

Gans's defense of the sub- and inter-statist conception of self-determination of nationhood offers a number of important suggestions concerning the division of territory by national groups. He argues that each group that qualifies for the right to self-determination has to be given a package of privileges, normally within a state that coincides with its homeland, including self-government rights, special representation rights, and rights to cultural preservation. He also does not see territory as tied to its present occupants. Gans argues that partial ceding of territory is sometimes justified based on the following moral argument: Given territorial scarcity, national groups are to be granted self-government rights in at least one geographical location, and other nationals living outside of their territory will relate to that location.[15] Both first occupancy (the presence of the group in the territory historically prior to other groups who presently live there) and formative territory (a territory of primary importance in forming the historical identity of the group) ought to play a role in determining the location in which a national group can exercise its self-determination.[16] If some other group occupies this territory, it will have to share it with the group whose self-determination is being promoted, because no group qualifies for total sovereignty over a territory, and two or more groups can share one territory to realize their self-determination. Gans argues that if a group is required to cede some territory, "People will only have to pay the price of being excluded from specific areas." He continues, "These areas would not be any larger that those from which they would in any case be excluded, if the territorial rights accompanying self-determination were justly distributed among national groups."[17]

What happens when two national groups lay a claim to the same territory? Surely they have to share the territory, but how many individuals from each side ought to be located there, and what parts can they settle on? Answering these questions is especially difficult if members of the group who cede the territory view this act as giving up the part of their homeland. Gans maintains that we can determine how to resolve such a case on the basis of how much harm the removal of some individuals would cause to the functioning of the community. I agree with this reasoning but would add that the determination of harm requires us to view the parties involved as equal agents with similar claims. Otherwise the group that occupies the territory is privileged, and thus the formative territory argument does not seem to work. Furthermore, the solution to the problem cannot be imposed by a third party; only the two groups, considered as equal agents, can, through a carefully regulated process of negotiation, determine the conditions for the division of the territory. I have demonstrated that the modified right limits aggressive behaviors by setting limits to the acceptable modes of exercising self-determination. It is possible that under some circumstances, a national group will be so hostile that it will not be able to conceive of a future in which it shares a territory with another group. In this case, the function of the modified right is limited to the determination of the entitlement to self-determination and of acceptable and unacceptable group behaviors (the latter of which will include the hostile behavior of the group in question). The modified right cannot always be enforced peacefully, but it presents a standard of justice that can justify some interventions by the international community which, combined with the recognition of the prima facie equal right to self-determination of the groups in question, creates the possibility of turning the hostile group into a cooperative member of international community.

I will demonstrate that Gans needs to make explicit the constitutive structure of group agents to explain why formative territory is important to the exercise of self-determination. Why should a group have the locus of its self-determination in the region its members perceive as a formative territory? Why can it not be satisfied with territory somewhere else (perhaps with the right to visit the "formative" territory free of charge)? Why was Birobidzhan not a proper site of Jewish self-determination? It had formal structures of self-government, preservation of culture, and representation. Why did its vacuous political culture not turn, with all the means of actualization available after Perestroika, into a real political culture of the Jewish republic? The important fact here is not that the Birobidzhan political culture could not in principle have corresponded to the Jewish national culture because it was not the formative territory, but rather that Jewish community members do not consider Birobidzhan to be their formative territory. If one day they change their minds, the territory will become a "formative" one. It is the group agent's shared set of beliefs and shared intentions that turn a territory into a potential site for self-determination. Considering national groups as collective agents also clarifies why formative interest requires some control over the territory in question—why polyethnic rights (rights that enable groups of common national origin to express their original culture while integrating with another culture and living at least their political and economic lives within that other culture)[18] with access to land through membership in the state of another nation is an arrangement that does not accommodate the national group properly. I agree that polyethnic rights protect an interest different from that protected by the right to self-determination, but Gans's account requires clarification concerning group entitlements based on their constitution. In this case, he would be able to determine the numbers sufficient to populate the territory to provide the national self-determination of both groups.

The idea of a formative territory may allow groups to lay claim to territories they have no relation to solely for strategic and power-grabbing reasons. If the Russians were to claim that Kiev and the surrounding part of the Ukraine is their "formative territory," should they execute their shared self-determination with the Ukrainians there? Would it matter if the Russians mobilize along these lines and self-identify with the belief that Kiev is their formative territory, or would an elite claim that Kiev is Russia's formative territory suffice? Or, given the per capita argument for the morality of territorial redistribution that Gans advocates, should the Russians give up parts of Siberia to the Chinese in accordance with distributive justice? To deal with these kinds of claims, we need the checks and balances provided by the nations approach, which pays attention to the constitution of group agents and determines their entitlements based on their equality of status safeguarded by the modified right enjoyed by the qualifying agents. Only if the Russians and the Chinese come to an agreement acceptable to both sides can they decide how many citizens from each nation must live in Siberia to fulfill their self-determining functions in the region. Or, if it is established that the Russians are entitled to share self-determination with Ukranians within what presently are the boundaries of Ukraine, they can determine the number of Russians who are allowed to move to satisfy the shared right and the territories on which they will reside for this purpose only by mutual agreement. Such an agreement will be based on the acknowledgment of equal status in the discourse of national group agents and the corresponding prohibition of aggressive behaviors and strategic mobilization, and it will attend to the uncertainly of national identities in transitional and non-democratic environments. My account of the possibilities for change is not as sweeping as Gans's. Groups may end up, following a process of negotiation, sharing a territory. However, this outcome is not guaranteed simply on the basis of a notion of the locus of groups' self-determination prior to the period of negotiation between equal group agents.

Also, given that Gans allows people to move to formative territories, his statement that groups without the potential for self-government should be afforded polyethnic rights needs to be qualified. If he has in mind a group that does not aspire to self-determination, it is not clear why he evaluates such a group in terms of self-government. More importantly, if the group in question is an agent whose interest requires self-determination and no geodemographic conditions to exercise it presently exist but these conditions can be created in principle by the group's relocation, Gans still needs to explain why we should not satisfy the group's claims by moving a group or changing state boundaries. I agree with the general spirit of his project of advancing sub- and intra-state self-determination, but his discussion of the geographical location of the right to self-determination is not as strong as it could be unless he uses the idea of group agency to distinguish between the types of groups and their entitlements and to help limit the effects of the territorial claims of groups that both infringe upon the interests of others and lack a moral ground. The enjoyment of the modified right to self-determination is territorial, and the conditions of territorial division are determined based on the equal status of qualifying group agents.

Mixed Federations

I will now briefly discuss some general guidelines for the organization of a multinational state with mixed subjects—territorial and national—that conform to the nations approach. Territorial units without separate national identities, such as different oblasts in the Russian Federation, belong to the same national group, even if the group is composed of a large number of such units. A territorial unit can become a national group if it mobilizes accordingly. As the unsuccessful agitation by political elites in the Ural region demonstrates, however, territorial units normally have regional, not national, identity. The people of the Ural region consider Russia (although not the Russian Federation, perhaps) to be their political community.[19] All national groups, on the other hand, given their nature as collective agents of a particular kind, need to be recognized as the same type of subject at the federal level and must have equal status in relation to one another in their ability to control their political futures. This may mean that several territorial units are represented by only one national group, which (as is the case for the Russians in the Russian Federation) can be much larger than other national groups. So long as each national group has a say about its political future in a form satisfactory to it, its agency and self-determination are respected. An oblast or a province cannot be a member of the federation at the same level as a national group, because territorial-administrative units normally perceive their powers (even if they have regional parliaments) to have been delegated by the respective national units in which these powers are ultimately vested. Territorial-administrative units can, however, have equal representation in a separate chamber within their own national group's legislature in addition to proportional representation (there are no national subunits within the territory of the sub-state national group). They would be able thus to have access to the federal legislature both through their national group and through federal-level proportional representation.

A Teleological Justification of the Nations Approach

The nations approach deals with both the equal treatment of individuals within multinational states and global justice with respect to political communities that advance claims to self-determination. In this section, I demonstrate that its implementation would provide for a more peaceful relationship between substate and state-endowed national groups and that its norms stand a good chance of being upheld by the subjects it would regulate because they serve their interests. This section provides a teleological justification of my approach.

Asymmetrical Warfare

Asymmetrical warfare in all of its forms is a growing concern for the world community. Controlling conflicts of this type is important for world peace. The introduction of the nations approach, and the modified right in particular, would have a mitigating effect on some justifications for asymmetrical warfare and especially for terrorism enacted in the name of self-determination. The implementation of the nations approach and the modified right cannot eliminate all justifications for the actions of non-state combatants, but it renders invalid those that have to do with claims to self-determination and demands for the equality of status of substate and state-endowed groups.

A military action is acceptable, according to just war theory, if it is waged by a legitimate authority, has just cause (such as a response to aggression), and is a last resort (such as a pre-emptive strike in light of an imminent threat to the very existence of a political community). A war should be waged so as to avoid the use of excessive force and to minimize harm to noncombatants, who must not be intentionally targeted. Although in the current international paradigm the right to wage war belongs only to states, stateless national groups that wage asymmetrical wars often justify their goals and their means in terms of just war theory. Many theorists agree that the just cause criterion can apply to non-state groups and that there are cases in which non-state actors have de facto legitimate authority.[20] Asymmetrical warfare can also be viewed, in certain circumstances, as the last resort of stateless groups. A national minority dissatisfied with its subordinate status and denied both means for the improvement of its situation and the right to secede may consider asymmetrical warfare as the only remaining option for obtaining the political status members perceive their community deserves. In the absence of legitimate means to address their claim to self-determination, they can argue that they are waging a war in self-defense, as a last resort to protect their political community.

Many theorists also agree that freedom fighters can attack military targets provided the fighters represent a de facto legitimate authority and have just cause. While few theorists would argue that targeting civilians to advance political goals satisfies the criteria of justice in war, in some cases, terrorists may use the rationale of supreme emergency to justify their tactics. Such a justification for targeting civilians or otherwise breaking the war convention applies, according to Michael Walzer, when either the survival or the freedom of a political community is in question. He considers the survival and freedom of political communities—whose members share a way of life, developed by their ancestors, to be passed on to their children—to be among the highest values of international society. The violation of these values in the absence of other means to protect them is a sufficient reason to adopt a supreme emergency response, Walzer explains, due to the rule of necessity.[21] The good of the survival of a political community under extreme circumstances, however, does not mitigate the moral wrong of targeting innocent people; it merely overrides it. Walzer argues that Churchill's order to bomb German cities at the early stages of World War II (but not later) was justified.[22] He does not apply his justification to terrorists who advance claims to self-determination on behalf of a non-state group. The supreme emergency justification plausibly applies to their actions as well, however, if there is an imminent danger of the total deterioration, paralysis, and ultimate disintegration of their political community because its way of life and the will of its people to self-govern are severely disrupted, as happened in Chechnya.[23]

Non-state combatants justify their tactics by the need of their political community to survive, by the inequality of the power relations they are involved in, and by the lack of avenues for the realization of their goals. If the nations approach were accepted in the international legal framework, it would be useful for responding to the moral claims of non-state combatants. With respect to non-state combatants' advancing the right to self-determination of their national groups, the nations approach, as I argue below, undercuts just war justifications for asymmetrical warfare, provides incentives for stateless groups to participate and to avoid using pressure tactics in negotiations, and creates additional responsibility on the part of these groups.[24] I demonstrate that the guarantees provided by the modified right create conditions for both state and non-state agents to satisfy their goals, which creates prospects for the modified right's being voluntarily maintained by its subjects.

The granting of equal status with respect to self-determination to all of the sides in a conflict underscores which legal norms ought to define legitimate avenues for the achievement of self-determination, and one of them is participation in a justly arranged multinational state. The nations approach reflects the self-perception and aspirations of non-state groups because it recognizes them as they want to be recognized. A national group may claim that it resorts to asymmetrical warfare as the only means to attain equal status. Its goal of equal freedom with other national communities is the just cause that the group seeks to advance through its belligerent actions. The implementation of the nations approach, however, provides a national group with the means to achieve self-determination peacefully. If such an avenue for the realization of self-determination is open to the national group, its "just cause" justifications for asymmetrical warfare would be negated. If the nations approach is followed by set of international legal norms and corresponding practices that reflect the modified right of all national groups to self-determination, this will provide stateless national groups with a framework in which they can ensure their existence through legitimate and peaceful means. Thus, the survival of their political communities will no longer be threatened, and their "supreme emergency" justifications of terrorism based on the threat to the political community's survival or limitation and destruction of any self-government would not apply. If the nations approach is established as an international practice, a non-state group may have the right to secede if its host state persistently rejects the norms of the nations approach and denies the group the enjoyment of the modified right within its borders. The group would not, however, acquire the right to engage in war.

Where does this leave the international community with respect to its response to asymmetrical warfare, and in particular to terrorism? The moral force of retaliating against terrorism is diminished if terrorists have some moral justification for their actions. The same reasons that outweigh (but do not eliminate) the moral wrong of the means employed by terrorists in the supreme emergency justification can weigh in as independent reasons in determining the international community's response. This can then result in conflict between a duty to punish and a duty to support the justice of the international order. Other things being equal (including, of course, the means by which it is carried out), the more just the cause, the greater the chance that it will outweigh the moral wrongs of a terrorist act. This fact can partially or completely discredit the international community's response, assuming that terrorism is not defined in some question-begging way that makes it always unjustified a priori.[25] The implementation of the modified right hence eliminates a possible moral conflict for the international community in its responses to terrorist action. If terrorists have no normative justification for their acts, they can unquestionably be held fully responsible for killing civilians and be treated as what they have become—mere international criminals.

The means for the resolution of disagreements among national groups provided by the nations approach limit the kinds of claims that can be legitimately put forward in the settlement of disputes. The threat of unilateral exit would not work as a bargaining tool, for example, partly because unilateral secession is an outlawed action and partly because negotiated exit is permitted if other attempts at negotiation do not work. If there is a reason for a national group to be dissatisfied with the recognition of its self-determination in a just state, the state will be likely to resolve the problem internally or to negotiate a peaceful separation, which would then fall under the category of "separation by mutual agreement."

Basic principles that might bring the warring parties together and basic terms upon which they can negotiate are more effective if they define the status of the parties with respect to one another, not only in the context of negotiations but also in principle. Then, the moral status of non-state groups in international relations is not negotiated but instead is assumed as a starting point. That the nations approach grants the modified right to all national groups provides such a moral status for non-state groups. The recognition that minority groups' entitlement to self-determination is equal to that of state-endowed groups both in and after negotiations secures not only a better negotiating position but also a better chance that the provisions they agree upon will be followed through on after the negotiations are over. In the absence of such recognition, a minority group may fear that even if the negotiations are successful, little can deter the other party from violating agreements afterward. Granting an acknowledged international status to substate national groups assures that they have recourse to the international agencies in such cases of noncompliance. A non-state group's equal entitlement to self-determination designates its international status regardless of the outcome of negotiations and creates additional assurance for the group that the international community will back its legitimate claims if the other party fails to treat it as an equal.

The acknowledgment of the stateless national group's equal international status as a particular type of group agent with corresponding entitlements ensures that the protocol for negotiations will reflect its standing. This will diminish the desire of the group to use pressure tactics in negotiations to counteract what it perceives as the unfair advantage of state-owning groups.[26] A lack of proper international recognition, on the other hand, is often what the militant actions of national minorities aim to rectify in the first place. If a non-state national group is not recognized as a self-determining political entity or even respected as such in negotiations, it may resort to terrorism and other destructive strategies as a means of leveling the playing field with its state counterparts. The group's members will not be willing to give up what they perceive as their only bargaining tool: being dangerous. Although it is impossible to guarantee equality for a stateless national group in all respects, the recognition of equal status defines the group's basic entitlements and the corresponding obligations of the international community in assisting the group to secure them. Without such recognition, it will appear only prudent to the members of the group to maintain a level of political violence necessary to sustain continuous pressure on its opponents and to push for its demands to be satisfied while its members are armed.

In the Palestine-Israel conflict, for example, demands that the Palestinian side disarm prior to any settlement of the conflict and without any background guarantees of equal standing upon doing so have not seemed to work. Equal standing can be granted to Palestinians either through equal substate self-determination within the Israel-Palestine territory by the Israelis and the Palestinians or through the formation of a Palestinian state. The latter is a more viable option for granting Palestinians equal status with respect to self-determination, given that one of Israel's basic principles is that it is a Jewish state. Perhaps the militants would continue their struggle even if equal international standing was afforded to Palestine. But in this case, they will have no justification for such activities, or at least not the justification that their actions are required for the survival of their political community. The Palestinian state and the international community will be able to employ all means possible to eliminate terrorists without being held back by the supposed justice of the terrorists' cause, because this cause will no longer be just. If the Palestinian state aims at the destruction of the state of Israel and uses state terrorism and other means to employ political force, the international community would have a clear reason to intervene and deal with the situation, as it legitimately can in any case of aggression.

Turning non-state national groups into equal international actors by recognizing their status makes it more incumbent upon them to exhibit appropriate international behavior. If they are equal subjects of international law and parties to the war convention, their responsibility is similar to that of all state-endowed subjects. As recognized international members that are expected to behave in accordance with international norms, which they accept by virtue of their membership, and they can be held responsible if they do not comply with the relevant norms.

Making a national group's behavior a condition of whether it is going to be included in the international community, on the other hand, is unproductive as a way of assuring its compliance with international norms. First, affirming one's equal standing through proper conduct is much more appealing than merely trying to qualify for such equal standing with the same behaviors. This is so because setting special conditions on a group's behavior prior to the recognition of its equal standing goes against the group's deepest moral claim that it is equal to other national groups.

It is unjust to hold national groups responsible as if they are members of the international community while denying them that membership and its privileges. If substate groups are to be held responsible, they have to be given the status of normally responsible members of the international community—members with the capacity for self-determination. Moreover, placing demands upon substate groups equal to those placed upon the members of international community implicitly acknowledges that they are a particular type of group agent—the same type as the members currently enjoying higher status within the international community. If a national group is unconditionally acknowledged and protected as a member of the international community, restricting the group's entitlements as punishment for its violation of international norms will be less threatening to the group, whose primary struggle is to realize its agency by achieving a proper international standing, than would be denying the group membership in the international community while demanding that it behave as a member would behave.

A stateless national group will be reluctant to change its conduct, furthermore, without guarantees that when it stops this conduct aimed at putting pressure on internationally accepted world actors, it will achieve its goals. If the international community refuses to acknowledge that the members of the group are members of a nation, as they claim to be, it suggests to the group that other, legally accepted members of the international community may not be truly committed to settling the group's conflict on terms acceptable to all parties. Moreover, when a national group's cooperation is needed, it is simply unproductive to refuse to address the group based on its self-definition. Finally, if attaining recognition as a self-determining group ceases to be a substate group's primary goal, it can direct its efforts to fulfilling the responsibilities of a normal member of the international society.

For transitional societies, defining the principles that qualify groups as rights holders and providing norms to regulate their behavior once their national composition is finalized should help to guide their transition peacefully. The availability of such a framework for the satisfaction of self-determination claims within a host state renders unnecessary and unjustified the resort to extreme measures to protect the existence of a national community. Moreover, substate groups are assured that if they comply with the rules they will avoid retaliation and be able to gain a significant degree of control over their political futures.

If we consider the actions of some groups to be governed by what Walzer calls "the war convention," with all the corresponding prerogatives of the use of force, the waging of wars, and the protection of their citizens, and if the actions of other groups are not governed in the same way, then this creates two classes of world citizens: those who have a legal right to defend themselves and who can, due to their properly institutionalized group agency, wage military operations and legally trade arms, and those who are denied this privilege. This outcome is wrong not in itself, but as a consequence of the unequal actualization of group agency, which I argue in this book is morally wrong.[27] It may appear that federal substate units, under the modified right, would be in a similar situation of not being able to unilaterally initiate a military offensive and thus being disadvantaged in relation to state-owning national groups. This is not the case, however, because these groups would have means to actualize their agency and a set of legal guidelines to regulate their military power. Unlike substate nations without an international status, in case of military emergency they would know what actions they are entitled to undertake and what other groups are in charge of the military cooperation. They would also, due to their acknowledged international standing, have an established set of procedures for appealing to international agencies as a group agent whose interests are in need of protection. The institutional structure that conforms to the modified right is superior to a system under which groups can only appeal to international agencies when their members' human rights have been abused.

Equal self-determination may appear difficult to harmonize with another consideration: that national groups that consistently use terrorist tactics or oppress some of their own members, such as women, do not have and should not be accorded equal moral standing with other national groups. This is a valid concern. The nations approach limits the aggressive behaviors of a national group toward others, however, both with respect to other equally self-determining subjects and with respect to the group's own members. It places restrictions on what qualifies as a valid claim to self-determination. Thus, the *exercise* of the modified right is conditional in part upon a group's goals and behavior, although the group retains its *status* as a national group regardless of its behavior. There are situations in international relations that allow a state's sovereignty to be violated. If a state unjustifiably attacks its neighbors and has to be invaded to arrest its advance, for example, its invasion does not compromise the fact that the state is *in principle* an equal international agent. Precisely because of its status as an equal international agent, it is held up to a standard of behavior expected of all such agents. A national group can be deprived of the *enjoyment* of its right to self-determination, however, if its behavior violates the equal right to self-determination of others.

While the nations approach protects national groups from unnecessary interference with decisions pertaining to their political futures, it also justifies restrictions imposed by the members of a multinational state or the international community on one another. As I discussed in Chapter 4, those groups that respect human rights within a multinational state have the right to demand a similar respect from others, lest everyone's international status be jeopardized. And if a national group exercises self-determination through the acquisition of its own state, it is expected to respect the standard of human rights.

Pragmatic Norms and Self-Interest

The modified right can realistically be maintained because both stateless and state-endowed members of the international community are motivated to cooperate to uphold it. The modified right helps them realize their respective goals of achieving self-determination and safeguarding territorial integrity. It maintains a situated standard of justice derived within the framework of practical limitations. As a theoretical illustration of a pragmatic normative approach, I would like briefly to consider Thomas Hobbes's derivation of the norm governing the interactions of free agents that aims to preserve their rights[28] and Immanuel Kant's explanation of why such a norm can be maintained by agents themselves.

Both philosophers agree that a community of free and self-interested agents can operate peacefully only on the basis of a system of norms that guides the agents' interactions in order to preserve what belongs to the agents naturally: their freedom. They disagree about whether such norms can be maintained by the agents themselves. In Chapter 14 of *Leviathan*, albeit in his discussion of individual and not group agents, Hobbes demonstrates that the "Right of Nature"—the right of each man to preserve his own life—requires for its maintenance a corresponding law that prescribes mutual limitation. The "Second Law of Nature," which is an important example of a pragmatically derived norm, states that "a man be willing, when others are so too, as farre-forth, as for Peace, and defence of himselfe he shall think it necessary, to lay down this right to all things; and be contented with so much liberty against other men, as he would allow other men against himselfe."[29] This law, though derived from the nature of the agents, cannot be maintained by them and requires a strong power to implement it. From a Hobbesian point of view, then, the prospects of the enforcement within the international community of the norms proposed by the nation approach are rather bleak. If we assume that mutual limitation of self-interested, free, and equal agents is the best law to follow, how can the proper operation of the international community based on this law be enforced?

Kant acknowledges that no sovereign could exist who was strong enough to maintain peace in international relations through political violence. Nonetheless, he is optimistic that the law of mutual limitation can be maintained by its subjects through their voluntary compliance, which is based partly on their self-interest. The members' voluntary compliance with the law offers the best prospect for peace. In complying, each member implicitly assumes that others also comply. This requires some limitation—but equal limitation—on the freedom of members. If the rules are not followed, the system breaks down, war ensues, and no one is free. The members' mutual compliance with the rules as a condition of the rules' successful implementation is therefore their best incentive to comply. Hence, if the members are free and self-interested agents, the best coordination game is one that maintains the equality of their status. Kant argues that the political form that can preserve and secure the freedom of each nation is a federation of nations, which does not aim to acquire any power like that of a state but rather aims merely to preserve and secure the freedom of each confederated state. [30]

Both Kant's and Hobbes's views call attention to the importance of the presupposition of equal freedom. For, according to them, individuals are willing to accept limitations upon their powers if their freedom is preserved in some form (or relinquished no less than that of others). Overall, a pragmatically derived norm, although relying on presuppositions about agents' nature, is mainly based on regulation of the agents' interactions in order to preserve the agents' aims. Although the enforcement of such a norm relies upon the agents' willingness to comply, their interests make it likely that they will comply.

Presently, the lack of a coherent rule of membership in the international community contributes to tensions among members and non-members, because in some cases non-members believe that they are agents of the same kind as members and that they are being denied membership unjustly. This belief in the particular character of their agency sustains them over time as precisely that type of agent, but without the means for proper exercise of their agency. The international community aims at sustaining peaceful relations among its member states. Stateless national groups that are not members of the international community, however, are capable of initiating war within or with member states. Moreover, since membership carries with it certain privileges and protections, non-members are required not to interfere with the freedom of members, while their own freedom is restricted. Attempts to keep in check dissatisfied non-members who have become or are about to become aggressive often increase the volatility of an already tense international situation. The international system will have a better chance at stability when all similar world actors enjoy equal status and when the maintenance and enjoyment of this status in itself serves as an incentive for members to comply with the rules of membership. It is easier to enforce the rules of civil international behavior if it is more profitable for stateless national groups to obey the rules than to break them. Membership in the international community, with its corresponding rights and obligations, is more attractive than being outlawed, creating the motivation for national groups to respect international legal regulations.

Hence, to lay the groundwork for peace, the international community needs to involve non-state national groups in the regulation of relations among its members by recognizing that such groups have a claim to self-determination equal to that of others. Creating a special league of stateless nations would include them into such a regulation, but as second-class groups, not as equal participants. Other solutions short of acknowledging them as self-determining group agents, such as giving them a set of consultation rights or another form of group protection, would be inadequate for the same reason. Self-determination is their constitutive shared good, and it warrants the inclusion of non-state groups in the international community on an equal basis due to their organization. Their inclusion would ensure that they have a chance to actualize their collective agency properly. National groups' claims to self-determination may equitably be satisfied on a case-by-case basis or according to an additional set of international principles, but in any case their satisfaction should be based on acceptance of the basic norms that regulate the other-regarding behavior of substate groups offered by the nations approach.

The right to choose among a set of options and not let some dominate in this choice does not guarantee that disputes about options will not arise. The nations approach helps to resolve disagreements, however, through negotiations between participants. The basic framework for the negotiations safeguards the participants' equal freedom in the discourse. This, in the end, assures that all sides have a chance to acquire control over their political futures based on principles acceptable to everyone involved. Thus, by defining the conditions for membership in the international community for both state-endowed and stateless groups, the nations approach relies in part for the enforcement of its norms, and of the modified right in particular, on members' voluntary compliance with those norms, which is possible because the norm of equality promotes members' chief interests.

In addition to the benefits of following the nations approach for the subjects it regulates, other aspects of the approach improve its chances of being successfully enforced. First, it introduces an ideal norm that does not create tensions between moral and legal principles and utilizes a definition of nationhood clear enough to be applied to a wide range of cases. Second, it defines what constitutes the just treatment of susbstate groups regardless of who enforces it, and it is compatible with a variety of international arrangements.

The Former USSR Republics as a Real-World Example

It may be objected that my conclusions about the impact of the equality principle on the stability of multinational states and the behavior of both state-endowed and stateless groups are merely speculative. Since there are currently no rules regarding relations among these groups, however, it would be unconvincing to claim that regulating relations that are not presently regulated will make them worse. This is especially true if the proposed regulation is specifically designed to address the issues that cause or exacerbate tensions in international relations. Indeed, there is some evidence in the case of the former Soviet republics that the norm of equality, when implemented and maintained, even only formally, frames collective agents' actions and mutual perceptions in such a way that they are more likely to attempt a peaceful resolution to their conflict. The former Soviet republics nominally retained their sovereignty in the union through the constitutional right of exit.

The former USSR was dissolved relatively peacefully at the level of the union republics, using a process based on the constitutionally recognized equality of the separating units. The question of how to deal with national groups, however, is still looming within former republics' territories. The norms regarding the agents' status present in the constitution of the former USSR shaped the collective agents' self- and mutual understandings in very important ways. In the Georgia–Abkhazia conflict, for example, Abkhazia, a former autonomous republic, was, under the Soviet regime, unequal in status to its host, Georgia, a former union-level republic. The national groups in the Chechen-Russian conflict also belonged to two different levels in the former Soviet hierarchy of nationalities, with the complication that Chechens used to share an autonomous republic with the Ingush people (Checheno-Ingushetia). The constitutionally recognized inequality of status of different national groups within the republics certainly contributed to instability. The ranking of groups disregarded the moral entitlements of the groups, and the whole idea of the hierarchy was clearly arbitrary. The ranking shaped republican and sub-republican groups' mutual thinking in such a way that their relationships, after the fall of the Soviet Union, often ended up as a standoff between minority groups, which were trying to gain what they felt they morally deserved, and the majority, which was protecting what it had. When the status of two national groups is unequal, it reassures the higher-ranked national group that it, and not the minority, has a special connection to the state. While there is nothing inherently problematic about legitimizing the majority's desire to safeguard its boundaries, sanctioning its disregard for claims to self-determination on its territory does not contribute to stability, because it defends the territorial integrity of the state for the wrong reasons. Had the relations among national groups been regulated on the basis of equal status with respect to self-determination, the various national groups would have perceived their relations differently. And shared beliefs of group members about desired political status and its relation to the existing norms are crucial in the formation of group strategies for action. Thus, once recognized as valid and entrenched in the constitutional and institutional design of multinational states, the norm of equality is likely to guide group members' collective decision making and actions, because the agents' goals in the realization of their agency would be formulated with this norm in mind.

It may be objected that the Abkhazian and many other minority nationalisms are kept alive by external factors (such as Russia's alleged assistance with weapons). But it would be hard to imagine that the Russians created Abkhazian national identity and claims to self-determination where there were previously none. The often-voiced perception and criticism of the nationalist ideal as an effective ideological tool that leads to strategic mobilization points to an important feature of this ideal: since other methods seem to be less effective in mobilizing the populations of transitional societies than the nationalist slogans purportedly used by elites to preserve their power, it may be that nationhood and national identity correctly reflect an important aspect of the popular will and represent groups' desired relation to political power. Trying to forge "St. Petersburg" or "Ural" national identity where no corresponding political culture existed has not proven to be effective. The claim that the Abkhazians have less of a right to preserve their control over their political future than the Georgians do is unsubstantiated at least because it runs contrary to the moral entitlement of the corresponding collective agents. There is nothing mysterious and primordial about claims to self-determination and national identity: a collective agent's political culture can be created, manipulated, and changed over time. But precisely because it can be engineered, we should be concerned about how to guarantee it actualizes while it is not under duress of any kind, and we should also try to ensure that the widest possible public sphere is available to its participants for the development and expression of their national culture. The equality principle, if implemented, either results in the improved stability of multinational states—when national groups learn to live together and appreciate a joint possession of their host state—or provides good background conditions for peaceful separation.

The Implementation of the Nations Approach

The Enforcement of the Nations Approach

Some of the already existing mechanisms used to enforce international norms could support the implementation of the nations approach. The same types of international sanctions that exist now could be employed to secure the compliance of states that do not satisfy the norm of legitimacy with the principle of equality and the modified right to self-determination. Their compliance could be monitored through the international court, for those groups that were able to apply to the court, and through international observers for groups in oppressive countries.

Overall, what outsiders can do to help a people is often limited by what they can do to help build the people's institutions, as Risse points out in the context of global economic justice.[31] I think this applies to justice with respect to self-determining group agents overall. If the international community helps to safeguard the peace within and territorial integrity of an inherently unstable state without changing the state's internal organization, the effort is often wasted because it does not address the source of the problem. Extra resources are spent on bolstering a government that is not fully in control because it overrides the will of the member collective national agents while constantly meeting their resistance. A lesser or similar amount of resources can yield better results by bringing member groups' own authorities to properly govern their territories. This is achieved if the division into self-governing units reflects the beliefs of the population concerning the meaningful limits of political authority over them. When national groups are in control of their political futures, the likelihood that they will govern themselves more efficiently increases. David Miller argues, for example, that promoting the self-determination of national groups is a way to help the needy in their corresponding countries and thus to improve international distributive justice. This is so because proper authority helps in distributing aid efficiently and allows the population to take care of itself better than it otherwise would. Miller argues that international justice comes into play when we encounter people whose lives are less than decent (in the sense that they cannot engage in the range of human activities that are common across culturally varied societies and are therefore central to human life).[32]

I have argued that being a member of a national community is a good that is basic to the proper political inclusion of individuals into their societies and, moreover, that respect for human rights and the maintenance of basic freedoms are necessary to national groups' proper actualization and exercise of their group agency. It is always possible, nevertheless, that self-determining national groups will disrespect the standard of human rights within the territory they govern. Some groups, for example, oppress women. The existence of such groups is a problem, but it can be better approached if the group agent has a government that conforms generally to group members' expectations concerning the bounds of their political community. Such an agent has political institutions with discernible decision-making procedures, which facilitates communication with the group and increases the number of ways in which group practices can be influenced by the international community. A national unit's possession of an identified and internationally accepted government ensures that the group can be held responsible for violating the standard of human rights. International engagement with national groups may take any of several acceptable forms, and it should be considered a prerogative of international bodies to monitor violations of human rights and issue a verdict concerning national groups' standing. International support for the group or protection of the group's interests in the international arena or within its federal state, for example, ought to be conditional on the group's respect for human rights. National groups that form federal units can belong to the international society either directly or via their joint membership in a federal state. They are not out of reach of international institutions. If substate groups are not assisted in actualizing their agency and thereby remain without an institutionalized set of rules for self-government and political decision-making, they will be much harder to influence.[33]

This raises the question of what type of membership in the international community national groups should have to make it easier to protect the human rights of their members. Perhaps, as I suggested, a "Modified UN" or some other international body could serve as a forum for national groups. National groups have to be able to air their grievances and receive support for their rights internationally.

The Acceptance of the Nations Approach

Even potentially effective norms need to be first accepted by the world community, which is made up of existing states, in order to be useful. Is it plausible that the set of norms I propose could be adopted in the near future? Any proposal to reform the international legal system faces the following difficulty: A principle needs to be proposed for a vote in such a form that the number of states sufficient for its acceptance will vote in its favor. If the norm of legitimacy turns too many world actors into outlaws, it is not likely to be accepted. Buchanan, for example, opts for a notion of minimal justice based on human rights in the hope that it will be accepted because it does not run against the interests of existing states.

The claim that states will not decide in favor of a rule that is against their interests, such as their interest in territorial integrity, however, represents an oversimplified version of how the voting process takes place. Strategic voting to support alliances or influence adversaries must also be taken into account. States may also be inclined to accept a morally progressive principle in order to continue being members of international community in good standing, which would entitle them to receive some sort of reward (such as loans from international financial organizations) or help them avoid sanctions. Moreover, the pragmatic hurdles to enforcing a principle in international society may mitigate the consequences of accepting it for those states that do not wish to comply with it. Therefore, although the acceptance of international norms by states is interest-based, the complexity of the voting process and the influence that some well-entrenched international norms and practices have on the behavior of member states loosens the seemingly straightforward connection between the acceptance of a proposal put for a vote and the voters' immediate interests involved with respect to the proposal. The Universal Declaration of Human Rights was accepted at a time when many countries violated human rights to some extent. Countries like the former USSR signed it not from a desire to safeguard the intrinsic goodness of human rights but rather to satisfy some other, more remote interests connected to their membership in the world community, and in doing so they condemned on paper practices that they accepted in reality. As I discussed in the previous chapter, in pragmatic terms, the rejection of the modified right is more costly for a multinational state than its acceptance even if the cost is calculated from the state's internal political perspective, regardless of the implications for its international standing. The rejection of the modified right has the destabilizing effect of mobilizing minorities in the state's territory, and its acceptance provides a framework for negotiations that benefits all parties.

One may object that even states not directly affected by the modified right may hesitate to accept it out of a concern for the protection of citizens of legally unstable transitional multinational states. They may agree that the modified right expresses more legitimate and just conditions of inclusion for minorities than the status quo, but conclude that, in practice, the modified right cannot be enforced peacefully and efficiently. They may believe that to be the case because, in transitional states, neither the minority nor the majority can rely on effective legal institutions and an impartial police to ensure the protection of human rights.[34] In response to these skeptics, I would say that political stability and the rule of law are more likely to emerge if it is stipulated in the rules of transition that the state institutions cannot belong to one group, majority or minority; this discourages various groups in the territory of the state from mobilizing so as to monopolize the state institutions. The modified right prohibits the association of the state power with one single group and shapes the transitional state's institutions so as to reduce the amount of power a group can exert over non-members. This decreases the chances of discrimination against non-members and, consequently, makes it less likely that the group would violate the human rights of non-members. The modified right also stipulates the equality of all nations within a state, which allows groups to monitor the treatment that other groups afford to their members. This reduces the chances of discrimination against a group's own members and, consequently, makes it less likely that the group would violate the human rights of its members. The concern that the modified right will lessen individual security in transitional states is not justified.

It is true that claims by minorities can emerge before a state's institutions are fully functional, but this is precisely why the modified right needs to guide the transition to such institutions and provide the norms for their formation: we need to avoid the crystallization of the typical "well-functioning" state institutions that associate one national group with the state and become the source of governmental bias leading to political tensions.

Kymlicka discusses the worry that, if the international community endorses a right to culture or a right to self-determination, this prejudges internal debates within a group that is not decided on how to mobilize; thus it treats one notion of the group as essential. Hence the endorsement of the modified right may be perceived as a form of interference.[35] In response to this worry I would say that the acceptance of the modified right is needed to counter an already existing form of interference with group identity that the present legal rules create: as far as self-determination is concerned, international law promotes ethnic groups with states while leaving all other groups in a legal limbo: no matter how they are going to mobilize, the process is not regulated by international rules except for the prohibition of self-determination in the majority of cases. Hence, ethnic majorities are "essentialized" by the international legal rules as entitled to a state. This prejudges the majority's political status and pushes it to a very specific type of mobilization. The modified right deals with entitlements of a certain type of group agent but it doesn't prescribe which groups should be included under its regulation prior to their mobilization, and thus it doesn't predetermine their future. The terms the right offers for the regulation of relations among groups within a territory are provisional and general for any transitional state. This hardly incites one definite type of mobilization; but the modified right can control certain types of group agents' mobilization within a territory by offering the parameters that the corresponding multinational state's political institutions ought to meet for the state to be legitimate and just. Hence, members of an international forum have good reasons to accept the modified right; this is especially true if the forum is specifically designed to deliberate about international norms. The pressure to explain why some groups are entitled to the right to self-determination while others, similarly constituted, are denied the right, in the absence of clear pragmatic counterindications, makes it more likely that the members of the forum will be inclined to strive for the coherence of its approach to establishing international norms.

Furthermore, the nations approach conforms to recent developments in international practice. Examples of developments that dissociate state and nationhood and aim at the recognition of the equality of national groups within multinational states include the establishment of the Scottish Parliament; the introduction of the European Framework Convention for the Protection of National Minorities, which presupposes that states should adhere to a system of protection of national groups on their territory; and the organization of a multinational state with equality of founding national groups in Bosnia-Herzegovina as a means to resolving the conflict there peacefully.

As we have seen, the nations approach safeguards the territorial integrity of multinational states by offering a solution for stability: by conforming to the norm of legitimacy, states can keep national groups within their boundaries and minimize potential and existing conflicts. The interest of states in stability—and the prospect of being protected by the territorial integrity principle—would give them a good reason to accept the condition of minimal justice. In addition, states known in the past for breaking the rules of international law may be guided by self-interest to maintain their status with respect to the world community, while international law—abiding states are likely to accept the "enhanced" condition because it both conforms to the normative presuppositions of international law and is consistent with recent developments in international practice.

If a norm is insincerely accepted but is not followed by a number of states, does any benefit derive from its acceptance? Its insincere acceptance indicates that the perpetrator states want to appear to be playing by the rules and thus indirectly acknowledge the validity of the rules. Their acceptance of the norm thus helps with the norm's reinforcement, because they can be held accountable to norms they have agreed to in writing or by voting. The fact of their acceptance thereby reinforces the moral judgment of other parties to the agreement concerning the rule-breakers' behavior and creates the possibility of a legal judgment binding on the party to the agreement that breaches the norm. Moreover, is a norm is accepted, it becomes part of international practice and discourse and even those who did not vote for it or sign an agreement concerning it guide their actions and phrase their justifications of actions with the norm's validity in mind.

Judgments by International Agencies Concerning Transitional Societies

Passing judgments on claims to self-determination requires a delicate balancing act. National groups have to express their claims to self-determination; the international community should not pass judgments and impose sanctions upon a state that is not considered minimally just to its national minorities if those minorities do not want national self-determination and are satisfied with their cultural minority status. A claim to self-determination needs to be verified as genuinely representing a collective agent's shared aspirations in order to eliminate strategic claims and those associated with vacuous political cultures. The nations approach requires that a claimant possess the right kind of political culture to qualify for the consideration of its claim. A national group may not be able to make a self-determination claim, however, if it is severely oppressed. This is why I suggested the cautious approach to nationhood in oppressive states. Approaching transitional and oppressive societies with caution does not mean that international regulations should not apply to such states or that the relations of national groups—even formally acknowledged national groups—should not be regulated. The cautious approach simply warns the international community to be alert to the emergence or revelation of new national identities and to not take the claims of vacuous political cultures regarding nationhood at face value. It also implies that the international community should pressure oppressive and transitional states to improve human rights and allow freedom of expression.

The use of the cautious approach permits employing the modified right in cases of the emergence of new nations. Used together with the cautious approach, the modified right requires that, while equality of status with respect to self-determination for those groups that can nominally be considered nations should be affirmed for the time being, a provision should also be made to include other nations that may appear in the territory of the state under the principle. The provisional inclusion of newly formed nations should also be guaranteed by the existence of international agencies that monitor the process and pass judgments about the claims to nationhood advanced by national groups. This assures that when and if new national groups appear they will be included under the regulation. In addition, the equality principle defines the terms of negotiations national groups ought to follow.

A national group can be mistaken about the stability of its identity. As long as this identity is minimally expressed, however, and the group members are convinced that this expression reflects their preferences, the group can be considered a national group. Non-democratic societies provide a good reason to establish and maintain an international legal standard for dealing with changing and emerging national identities based on the norm of equality of national groups. Promoting the equality of status of all national groups—those which are emerging as well as those already established in the territory of a transitional state—may help to make periods of transition less tumultuous.

The Liechtenstein Draft Convention on Self-Determination through Self-Administration,[36] which speaks of the self-determination of non-state groups in its external meaning, is a significant achievement in the direction of formulating a framework for the protection of national minorities. One of the goals of the draft convention is to properly transfer self-determination from the international realm into the realm of internal state politics, where it can be mediated by the rules and organizations of the international legal system. This is especially important given that borders are changing, in Europe in particular, from the nation-state to a more "soft, porous" reality.[37] The basic notion that the draft convention uses to identify self-determining units is "communities." It could profit, however, from identifying basic features of nationhood, which is the leading notion now associated with self-determination. Engaging the idea of nationhood in the context of self-determination would help to specify to whom a state belongs, which kinds of groups are associated with states, and how to divide powers when self-determination claims conflict.

Empirical Considerations

One may argue that whether my account to self-determination will bring about more peace is an empirical question. If it is an empirical question, the approach needs to be tested, because it has never been applied. Yet, as an earlier section in this chapter showed, there is some evidence that equal status with respect to self-determination makes relationships among national groups more peaceful: the former USSR fell apart along union republic lines peacefully, but the hierarchical status of national groups within each union republic has contributed to a number of armed conflicts. The conflict in the former Yugoslavia was also in part prompted by the breach of the constitutionally entrenched equality of the constitutive republics.

Michael Hechter agrees that a particular federalizing strategy will work in containing nationalism. He argues that nationalist conflict can be contained by institutions providing decentralized decision-making within multinational states.[38] He arrives at this conclusion by considering three types of conditions that can decrease such conflict. First, we can increase the costs of collective action. This strategy is not specific to nationalist conflict and is not readily available, according to Hechter. I would add that this strategy can work, but it is unjust according to my approach. Second, we can reduce the salience of national identity. Hechter thinks that national identity is not likely to wane. I agree with this assessment, given my account of the constitution of group agents organized around nationhood. Finally, we can decrease demands for national sovereignty.[39] This is the strategy that can work, according to Hechter. I agree with his approach. He suggests that institutions that increase the central state's accountability to national minorities should reduce the demand for sovereignty and hence the potential for nationalist conflict.[40] While federal decentralization can mobilize minorities by providing them with greater resources to engage in collective action, such as protesting the federal state's policies, such decentralization erodes the demand for sovereignty, according to Hechter, while too much centralization engenders fragmentation.[41]

Ted Robert Gurr does not see any discernible patterns of connection between equalizing the enjoyment of self-determination by various national groups and reducing ethnopolitical conflict. He studies groups that experience political or economic discrimination and have taken political action in support of collective interests and notes the difference between national and other types of minorities: national peoples seek separation or autonomy from the states that rule them; minority peoples seek greater access or control.[42] He acknowledges that demands for secession or autonomy are driven by the desire to protect group identity.[43] But he does not observe either more or less stability associated with multinational federalism. Jack Snyder disagrees that more stability would result from equalizing the enjoyment of self-determination. He thinks that supplanting an archaic empire by nation-states with a new world order is bound to be a bloody process, especially when the preconditions of any statehood, let alone democratic statehood, are shaky.[44] I disagree with this assessment, given the experiences of the former USSR. If anything, the conflicts that emerged on its territory suggest that the set of norms I advocate is absolutely necessary to regulate substate groups' relations, including those of transitional societies. What is more, self-determination does not need to be exercised as state sovereignty, and if this becomes an international norm, it will lead to more stability. The lack of norms for the regulation the relations among potential national group agents is harmful. What the conflict on the territory of the former USSR demonstrates is that when a people is not allowed the proper institutionalization of its group agency, its modes of actualization will deteriorate and become detrimental to its own members and other peoples around them. Moreover, the denial of the possibility of self-determination as one mode of group actualization may turn national identity from a contingent and merely possible form of group organization into a highly desired formative goal around which a group whose identity is suppressed will choose to mobilize.

The lack of evidence that proposals like mine will lead to instability disarms arguments against giving substate groups the right to self-determination, which often hinge upon the claim that preserving the status quo is less damaging than introducing changes in the norms regulating self-determination. Such "realist" arguments commonly state that moral considerations, though important, are not relevant to the formulation of international norms, simply because the cost of implementing norms based on moral precepts is too high. I have argued that an approach to self-determination that aims to change norms so as to introduce fairness into the treatment of substate groups and preserve the territorial integrity of multinational states can be accepted by the community of states and has a good chance of being enforced. Moreover, moral justifications of the rights of state-endowed national groups, such as the rights to territorial integrity, sovereignty, and self-defense, are routinely advanced by and on behalf of states in the realist scheme, at least to enhance the pragmatic considerations of preserving the status quo. Such moral rights need at least to be weighed carefully when it comes to the rights of stateless groups.

An important consideration in pragmatic arguments is world peace. World peace, however, is created not only by peace in relations among states but also by peace within states. A pragmatic limitation on the universal ideal of self-determination may be imposed to preserve world peace, and such a limitation may require that some peoples give up their self-determination claims. Nevertheless, the commonly recognized prerogatives of self-defense and the preservation of territorial integrity for state-endowed nations often allow them to wage war. Thus, to advance or protect their self-determination, state-endowed groups are allowed to use political violence, while stateless groups are denied self-determination for fear of political violence. If existing states have the right to preserve their territorial integrity by keeping stateless nations at bay, often by use of force, then world peace is threatened by wars within state boundaries. It may be as reasonable to require, for the sake of universal peace, that host states let their minorities secede. In addition, the costs associated with breaking up existing states can be outweighed on the "peace scale" by the consideration that it is easier to ensure the compliance with international legal norms of smaller state units with respect to both these states' international and their domestic policies. Now, this is not the approach I advance in this book, but this thought experiment concerning hypothetical changes to state boundaries reveals an important deficiency in the status quo, which denies equal respect to stateless groups that are not different in principle from the state-endowed groups favored by present arrangements. Continuing with this line of reasoning, considerations of principle require that stateless groups be at least entitled to be compensated for giving up the exercise of their self-determination, especially since it is hard to justify the denial of their right to self-determination as a measure to preserve peace. Taken to its logical conclusion, such a line of reasoning would require some redistribution of power within the host multinational states, and it seems that the implementation of the scheme of equality of self-determination within such states would provide the most stable and morally appealing arrangement due to its inclusiveness and fairness.

Notes

1. An earlier version of the discussion of the consequences of the introduction of the modified right (now presented in parts of this chapter and of Chapter 5) was published in Anna Moltchanova, "Stateless national groups, international justice, and asymmetrical warfare," *The Journal of Political Philosophy,* 13(2), June 2005, 194–215, publisher: Wiley and Sons Ltd.
2. On the other hand, if a systematic genocide was organized in the past by the members of one national group against another, it provides a good reason for secession, even if the harmed national group is offered fair terms to remain within the multinational state.
3. Henrard, K. *Devising an Adequate System of Minority Protection: Individual Human Rights, Minority Rights and the Right to Self-Determination* (The Hague: Kluwer Law International, 2000), p. 281.

4. See John McGarry, "Introduction: The Comparable Northern Ireland," *in Northern Ireland and Divided World: Post-Agreement Northern Ireland in Comparative Perspective,* ed. J. McGarry (Oxford: Oxford University Press, 2001), pp. 15–16, and Brendan O'Leary, "Comparative Political Science and the British-Irish Agreement," in ibid., p. 57.
5. For an exhaustive discussion of federalism and confederalism see: Will Kymlicka and Jean-Robert Raviot, "Living Together: International Aspects of Federal Systems," *Canadian Foreign Policy*, Volume 5, No. 1 (Fall 1997): 1–50. Federalism and confederalism are both different from administrative decentralization, where a central government establishes basic policy in all areas, but then devolves the power to administer these policies to lower levels of government, typically regional or municipal governments. Ibid., pp. 8–9.
6. Ibid., pp. 8–9.
7. Mathias Risse, "How Does the Global Order Harm the Poor?" *Philosophy and Public Affairs 33*, no. 4 (Fall 2005): 349–376, pp. 359–360.
8. There is a disagreement over what determines the legal status of the national republics in the Russian Federation—the federal treaty or the constitution. Here, I discuss only the norms put forward by the documents, not the status of the documents in relation to one another.
9. L. M. Drobizheva, A. R. Aklaev, V. V. Koroteeva, and G. U. Soladtova, *Democratizatsiia i obrazi nationalizma v Rossiiskoi Federatsii 90-x godov* (Moscow: Misl', 1996), p. 169.
10. Ibid., p. 171.
11. "Sovereign" here has a less drastic meaning in comparison with international law. It does not appear contradictory to state, in the Russian context, that a republic is "sovereign" within the federation's territory.
12. The same question in a historical perspective would be something like the following: The nation of Beothuk of Newfoundland was extinct by 1829. Under my scheme, could the last known Beothuk, Nancy Shanawhdit, have claimed that she had the right to self-determination equal to that of the British settlers? She was a representative of a political culture that had vanished. Had she still wanted to be considered a nation, there should have been a proper arrangement made for a symbolic recognition of her nation's past existence, but since it was not a viable agent in relation to others any longer, its political culture could not have been given institutional arrangements similar to those of the settlers.
13. A similar solution is suggested by Gans's approach to substate self-determination.
14. Perhaps in the future there can be a non-territorial nation communicating via the Internet, for example.
15. Gans, p. 167
16. Ibid., pp. 101, 107, 115.
17. Ibid., p. 108.
18. Ibid., p. 40.
19. V. A. Mikhailov, *Natsional'naja Politika Rossii: istoria I sovremennost* (Moscow: Pusskii mir, 1997), p. 408.
20. See Haig Khatchadourian, "The Morality of Terrorism," in *Contemporary Moral Problems: War and Terrorism,* ed. J. E. White (Belmont, CA: Wadsworth Thomson Learning, 2003), p. 39; Laurie Calhoun, "The Terrorist's Tacit Message," Ibid., pp. 46–53; and Andrew Valls, "Can Terrorism be Justified?" in *Ethics in International Affairs,* ed. A. Valls (New York: Rowman and Littlefield, 2000), pp. 65–80.
21. Michael Walzer, *Just and Unjust Wars: A Moral Argument with Historical Illustrations*, 3rd edition (New York: Basic Books, 2000), p. 254.
22. Ibid., pp. 255–261.
23. As the 2003 elections orchestrated by the Russian government demonstrated, the political community of Chechnya is kept alive rather artificially, and its foundation is deeply shaken. Walzer says that self-determination "is the right of a people 'to become free by their own efforts' if they can." Ibid., p. 88. Since the deterioration of self-determining communities can bring them past the point when they are capable of being self-determining, they may want to try any means to safeguard their potential for being a political community before any prospect

of success is gone and their militant action serves no purpose except the expression of their desperation.

24. I bracket the question of whether the recognition of the modified right as a *legal right* as opposed to a widely shared understanding of the meaning of self-determination and its universal status, is required to achieve the effects I discuss below. The modified right has the potential of being realized as a legal right, and this is what is important for my argument here.
25. Compare J. Angelo Corlett, *Terrorism: A Philosophical Analysis* (Dordrecht: Kluwer Academic Publishers, 2004).
26. On the underdog's use of unconventional tactics to counteract the unfair advantage of its opponent, see Shannon E. French, "Murderers, not Warriors: The Moral Distinction between Terrorists and Legitimate Fighters in Asymmetric Conflicts," in *Terrorism and International Justice*, ed. J. P. Sterba (Oxford: Oxford University Press, 2003), p. 34.
27. This outcome is similar to the one that Gans notices exists if we consider self-determination in statist terms. Gans provides four arguments against the statist conception of self-determination as creating injustice. First, statist self-determination creates two classes of citizens within each state (those to whom the state belongs as the members of the state-owing group and the rest). Second, it creates two classes of national groups—those with and those without their own states. This argument of course rests on the premise that there is a prima facie case for moral equality of certain groups we call national, which I defend in this book. Third, his type of self-determination advantages nation-state group members over citizens in diasporas. Finally, the statist conception that advocates a one-to-one correspondence of nations and states is not compatible with the freedom of migration and pluralism. Gans, pp. 69–70.
28. One caution regarding the use of Hobbes's norm is that it applies to subjects that are roughly equal physically, and national groups possess different resources and influence. Hobbes argues, however, that agents are equal, because the weak can always kill the strong by forming factions or using weapons. In the age of powerful weapons, the weak—including substate national groups and terrorists operating on their behalf—can cause significant damage, and thus they are somewhat "equal" with those who are stronger.
29. Thomas Hobbes, "Of the First and Second Naturall Lawes, and of Contracts," in *Leviathan* (New York: Penguin Books, 1986), pp. 189–190.
30. Immanuel Kant, "Perpetual Peace: A Philosophical Sketch," in *Political Writings* (Cambridge: Cambridge University Press, 1991), p. 105.
31. Risse, p. 376.
32. David Miller, "National Responsiblity and International Justice," in *The Ethics of Assistance: Morality and the Distant Needy*, ed. Deen K. Chatterjee (Cambridge: Cambridge University Press, 2004), pp. 130–131.
33. Miller argues for communal values and ties as having special importance and thus for modifying the form in which the standard of international justice is expressed. Miller's bundle of goods universally necessary for decent life does not include the right to political participation, for example. However, we need some sort of democratic environment for the proper actualization of groups and for making sure that they are receiving help on a principled basis. (For example, it is not the case that the international community should actively lobby for self-determination rights for a linguistic group if it lacks information concerning the group's constitution.)

    Miller poses an interesting question concerning the difference in how cultures attach importance to shared goods, such as religious participation. Do liberal members of the international community have an obligation of justice toward members of a community if they are deprived in relation to cultural values that the liberal countries do not share? Miller concludes that when we deal with a society in which even the oppressed seem to be content, we need a more objective approach to determining whether the society satisfies the standard of minimal decency. But then he falls back on the minimal standard of democratic values and support for individual autonomy. Ibid., pp. 127–129.
34. This concern is discussed by kymlicka in Multicultural Odysseys, p. 183.

35. Ibid., p. 240.
36. See *The Self-Determination of Peoples: Community, Nation, and State in an Interdependent World*, ed. Wolfgang Danspeckgruber (London: Lynne Rienner, 2002), pp. 382–92.
37. Wolfgang Danspeckgruber, "Self-Determination and Regionalization in Contemporary Europe," in *The Self-Determination of Peoples: Community, Nation, and State in an Interdependent World*, ed. Wolfgang Danspeckgruber (London: Lynne Rienner, 2002), p. 196.
38. Michael Hechter, *Containing Nationalism* (Oxford: Oxford University Press, 2000), p. 33.
39. Ibid., p. 134.
40. Ibid., p. 136.
41. Ibid., p. 146, 152.
42. Ted Robert Gurr, *Minorities at Risk: A Global View of Ethnopolitical Conflicts* (Washington, D.C.: United States Institute of Peace Press, 1993), p. 6, 15.
43. Ibid., p. 316.
44. Jack Snyder, "Introduction: reconstructing politics amidst the wreckage of empire," *Post-Soviet Political Order: Conflict and State-Building*, eds. Barnett R. Rubin and Jack Snyder (London and New York: Routledge, 1998), pp. 2–3.

Conclusion

The current state of affairs with respect to substate groups' self-determination and the corresponding international legal norms contradict the moral norm of equal self-determination for national groups stated in the UN Charter. I propose a treatment of minority nationalism that preserves the stability of multinational states while granting the moral claims to self-determination that substate groups advance. My approach maintains that careful attention to the definition of concepts and categories, and to the formulation and justification of normative principles that apply to group agents is very important pragmatically. Moral justifications need not be in conflict with pragmatic limitations nor sacrificed to satisfy these limitations. Most skeptics who argue against a normative theory like mine warn of the possible consequences of accepting an approach that grants self-determination to all national groups. They point out the negative effects that the expansion of self-determination may have on the state as the main forum of justice and democracy, or on the existing statist world system, which is perceived as necessary to peace and stability. This reasoning, nevertheless, rests on the acceptance of a particular philosophical account of the nation and of the existing set of norms as valid. This choice of what norms to privilege is not without consequence to the very political stability and justice a consequentialist account aims to protect.

Mainstream acknowledgements of a stateless group's entitlements are rarely, if ever, construed in a manner that satisfactorily captures that group's organization and intentions. It is undeniable that international norms influence how groups mobilize and act, and the defense of the privilege of state-endowed groups proves, in the end, to be destabilizing. What happens when international norms distort the moral status and entitlements of group agents? If these group agents are constructed around beliefs of membership that conform to these international norms, they would interact with other groups in a framework that maintains unjust inequality. This is detrimental to peace among nations, and the more the distortive ideology defines a group, the lower on the downward spiral of worsening relations with its neighbors it is likely to find itself. Since norms are something in relation to which or in opposition to which groups define themselves, international norms that do not promote coherent assignment of international status to group agents are politically explosive. This is why clear and philosophically coherent articulation of ideas on minority nationalism is important. The norms of interaction for national groups should equitably take

A. Moltchanova, *National Self-Determination and Justice in Multinational States*, Studies in Global Justice 5, DOI 10.1007/978-90-481-2691-0_BM2, into consideration the reasons for which and the manner in which the groups are constituted. If norms like these accompany the groups' mobilization in transitional environments from the start, it will be more likely that all groups will act within the limits acceptable to all participants.

Some national groups have gained the dramatic advantages that come from being in possession of independent states. Claims to self-determination by substate groups within the territory that a state-endowed group controls are treated by the international community as undermining the sovereignty of the host state. But this sovereignty advances the self-determination only of the state-endowed nation and runs contrary to the fact that substate groups are morally entitled to self-determination based on their constitution as group agents. While substate national groups are not afforded the same entitlements as state-endowed groups by international law, they are asked to behave in accordance with the norms that privilege state-endowed groups. A remedy to tensions caused by substate nationalism is offered by the modified right to self-determination extended fully to all national groups and exercised primarily within the territory of existing states. The central contention of the nations approach is that a theory of federalism based on the modified right can eliminate the fundamental inequality between stateless and state-endowed nations proposing an effective solution to rival claims to self-determination. I support the preservation of the existing state boundaries for a large number of cases of self-determination: justice requires separation of state and nation and it is an issue of injustice to redraw boundaries unnecessarily.

My goal in the book was to develop an internally coherent philosophical approach to the issue of national self-determination. My approach maintains, along the traditional line of liberal nationalism, that states are not tied to nations, that states should treat nations with equal respect based on the acknowledgment that national groups hold the right to self-determination, and that how nations are treated is an issue of justice (and therefore of injustice if a state adopts coercively integrated nation-building policies). My approach goes beyond traditional liberal nationalism in that I do not maintain that the world is largely constituted by existing stable nations. I consider nationhood as a function of group agency; this makes the notion of the nation attentive to the dynamic nature of national identity, especially in transitional societies. The nations approach can accommodate the fact that national identities may change; it doesn't give up, in the absence of stable group agents in a given political environment, either the notion of group entitlements or the norms for group agents' interactions. Thus, it can deal with unstable national identities in transitional societies. The nations approach includes a set of guidelines for approaching claims to self-determination in such societies to facilitate peaceful changes in their political landscape. It considers states legitimate only if they protect individual and group rights of their members, including the right to national self-determination within their borders. The idea of political legitimacy it promotes if realized would ensure that, in the world in which both "globalization" and "nationalism" are important, individuals can be governed by political authority they consider their own and allow this right to others.

Bibliography

Arinin, A. N. *Issledovania po prikladnoi i neotlozhnoi etnologii*, no. 105 (Moscow: Institut etnologii i antropologii RAN).

Brian Barry. *Culture and Equality: An Egalitarian Critique of Multiculturalism* (Cambridge, MA: Harvard University Press, 2001).

Belitser, Natalya and Orlyk, Pylyp. *The Constitutional Process in the Autonomous Republic of Crimea in the Context of Interethnic Relations and Conflict Settlement* (Kyiv, Ukraine: Institute for Democracy, 2000).

Brilmayer, Lea. "Secession and Self-Determination: A Territorial Interpretation," *Yale Journal of International Law* 16, 1991: 177–202.

Brown, Archie, ed. *Political Culture and Communist Studies* (Houndmills and London: The Macmillan Press Ltd., 1984).

Brubaker, Rogers. *Nationalism Reframed: Nationhood and the National Question in the New Europe* (Cambridge: Cambridge University Press, 1996).

Buchanan, Allen. "What's So Special About Nations?" in J. Couture, K. Nielsen, and M. Seymour (eds.) *Rethinking Nationalism* (Calgary, Alberta: University of Calgary Press, 1996).

Buchanan, Allen. "Self-Determination, Secession, and the Rule of Law," in Robert McKim and Jeff McMahan (eds.) *The Morality of Nationalism* (New York, Oxford: Oxford University Press, 1997), 301–323.

Buchanan, Allen. "The International Institutional Dimension of Secession," in Percy B. Lehning (ed.) *Theories of Secession* (London, New York: Routledge, 1998), 227–256.

Buchanan, Allen. "Recognitional Legitimacy and the State System," *Philosophy and Public Affairs* 28(1), Winter 1999: 46–78.

Buchanan, Allen and Golove, David. "Philosophy of International Law," in J. Coleman and S. Shapiro (eds.) *The Oxford Handbook of Jurisprudence and Philosophy of Law* (Oxford: Oxford University Press, 2003), 868–934.

Buchanan, Allen. *Justice, Legitimacy, and Self-Determination: Moral Foundations for International Law* (Oxford: Oxford University Press, 2004).

Calhoun, Laurie. "The Terrorist's Tacit Message," in J. E. White (ed.) *Contemporary Moral Problems: War and Terrorism* (Belmont, CA: Wadsworth Thomson Learning, 2003).

Canovan, Margaret. *Nationhood and Political Theory* (Cheltenham, UK, Brookfield, US: Edward Elgar Publishing limited, 1996).

Carens, Joseph H. "Liberalism and Culture," *Constellations* 4(1), April 1997.

Cassese, Antonio. *Self-Determination of Peoples: a Legal Reappraisal* (Cambridge: Cambridge University Press, 1995).

The Charter of the United Nations

Cobban, Alfred. *The Nation State and National Self-Determination* (London: Collins, 1969).

Connor, Walker. *Ethnonationalism* (Princeton: Princeton University Press, 1994).

Copp, David. "International Law and Morality in the Theory of Secession," *Journal of Ethics*, 2, 1998: 219–245.

Corlett, J. Angelo. *Terrorism: A Philosophical Analysis* (Dordrecht: Kluwer Academic Publishers, 2004).

Couture, Jocelyne, Nielsen, Kai, Seymour, Michel (eds.). *Rethinking Nationalism* (Calgary, Alberta: University of Calgary Press, 1996).

Dahl, Robert A. *Democracy and Its Critics* (New Haven and London: Yale University Press, 1989).

Danspeckgruber, Wolfgang. "Self-Determination and Regionalization in Contemporary Europe,"In Wolfgang Danspeckgruber (eds.), *The Self-Determination of Peoples: Community, Nation, and State in an Interdependent World* (London: Lynne Rienner, 2002).

De Wachter, Frans. "In Search of a Post-National Identiy: Who Are My People?" In Jocelyne Couture, Kai Nielsen, Michel Seymour (eds.), *Rethinking Nationalism* (Calgary: University of Calgary Press, 1996), 197–219.

Doppelt, Gerald. "Is There a Multicultural Liberalism?" *Inquiry* 41(2), June 1998: 223–248.

L. M. Drobizheva, A. R. Aklaev, V. V. Koroteeva, and G. U. Soladtova, *Democratizatsiia i obrazi nationalizma v Rossiiskoi Federatsii 90-x godov* (Moscow: Misl', 1996).

Dupre, John. "Sex, Gender, and Essence," *Midwest Studies in Philosophy*, XI (1986), 441–457.

The European Framework Convention for the Protection of National Minorities: Council of Europe, European Treaties, ETS No. 157 (Strasbourg, 1.II.1995), http://www.coe.fr/eng/legaltxt/157e.htm

Fleming, Margot. *A Critical View of Cultural Essentialism: the Native Women's Association of Canada, Problems of Inequality and Aboriginal Self-government* (Montreal: McGill University, 1995).

Fichte, Johann Gottlieb. *Addresses to the German Nation* (New York: Harper and Row, 1968).

French, Shannon E. "Murderers, not Warriors: The Moral Distinction between Terrorists and Legitimate Fighters in Asymmetric Conflicts," in J. P. Sterba *Terrorism and International Justice* (Oxford: Oxford University Press, 2003).

Gans, Chaim. *The Limits of Nationalism* (Cambridge: Cambridge University Press, 2003).

Geertz, Clifford. *The Interpretation of Cultures* (New York: Basic Books, 1973).

Gellner, Ernest. *Nations and Nationalism* (Oxford: Basil Blackwell Publisher Limited, 1983).

Gellner, Ernest. *Conditions of Liberty: Civil Society and Its Rivals* (London, 1994).

Giddens, Anthony. *The Nation-State and Violence: Volume Two of A Contemporary Critique of Historical Materialism* (Cambridge: Polity Press in association with Oxford: Basil Blackwell, 1985).

Giuliano, Elise. "Who Determines the Self in the Politics of Self-Determination? Identity and Preference Formation in Tatarstan's Nationalist Mobilization," *Comparative Politics*, April 2000.

Choudhry, Sujit. "National Minorities and Ethnic Immigrants: Liberalism's Political Sociology," *Journal of Political Philosophy* 10, 2002.

Graff, James A. "Human Rights, Peoples, and the Right to Self-Determination," in J. Baker (ed.) *Group Rights* (Toronto: University Toronto Press, 1994).

Gould, Carol C. "Group rights and social ontology," pp. 43–57, Christine Sistare, Larry May and Leslie Francis (eds.) *Groups and Group Rights* (Lawrence KS: University Press of Kansas, 2001), 44–45.

Green, Leslie. "Two Views of Collective Rights," *Canadian Journal of Law and Jurisprudence* 4(2), July 1991.

Gurr, Ted Robert. *Minorities at Risk: A Global View of Ethnopolitical Conflicts* (Washington, D.C.: United States Institute of Peace Press, 1993).

M. Guboglo, *Mozhet li dvuglavii oriol letat' s odnim krilom? Pazmishlenia o zakonotvorchestve v sphere ehnogosudarstvennikh otnoshenii* (Moscow: Russian Academy of Sciences, 2000).

Hall, John ed. *The State of the Nation: Ernest Gellner and the Theory of Nationalism* (Cambridge: Cambridge University Press, 1998).

Hannum, Hurst. *Autonomy, Sovereignty, and Self-Determination: The Accommodation of Conflicting Rights* (Philadelphia: University of Pennsylvania Press, 1996).

Hannum, Hurst. "Contemporary Developments in the International Protection of the Rights of Minorities," *Notre Dame Law Review*, 66, 1991: 1431–1448.
Hart, H. L. A. "Are There Any Natural Rights?" *Philosophical Review* 64(2), April 1955.
Hartney, Michael. "Some Confusions Concerning Collective Rights," in Will Kymlicka (ed.) *The Rights of Minority Cultures* (Oxford: Oxford University Press), 221.
Hechter, Michael. *Containing Nationalism* (Oxford: Oxford University Press, 2000).
Henrard, K. *Devising an Adequate System of Minority Protection: Individual Human Rights, Minority Rights and the Right to Self-Determination* (The Hague: Kluwer Law International, 2000).
Heyes, Cressida J. *'Back to the Rough Ground!': Wittgenstein, Essentialism, and Feminist Methods* (Ph.D. thesis, Montreal: McGill University, 1997).
Hobsbawm, Eric. "Introduction: Inventing Traditions," in Eric Hobsbawm and Terence Ranger (eds.) *The Invention of Tradition* (Cambridge: Cambridge University Press, 1983), 1–15.
Hollinger, David A. "Not Universalists, Not Pluralists: The New Cosmopolitans Find Their Own Way," *Constellations* 8(2), (2001).
Khatchadourian, Haig. "The Morality of Terrorism," in J. E. White (ed.) *Contemporary Moral Problems: War and Terrorism* (Belmont, CA: Wadsworth Thomson Learning, 2003).
King, Charles. *The Moldovans: Romania, Russia, and the Politics of Culture* (Stanford, CA: Hoover Institution Press, Stanford University, 2000).
King, Charles. *Post-Soviet Moldova: A Borderland in Transition* (Iasi: The Center for Romanian Studies, The Foundation for Romanian Culture and Studies, 1997).
Kingsbury, Benedict. "Claims by Non-State Groups in International Law," *Cornell International Law Journal* 25, 1992.
Kravchuk, Leonid. "We Will Live Together in the Ukrainian State," *Krimskii studii*, no.1, in *Turkistan Newsletter - Turkistan Bulteni* (March 7, 2000, ISSN:1386–6265).
Kukathas, Chandran. "Cultural Rights Again: A Rejoinder to Kymlicka," *Political Theory* 20, 1992: 674–680.
Kymlicka, W. *Multicultural Odysseys: Navigating the New International Politics of Diversity* (Oxford: Oxford University Press, 2007).
Kymlicka, Will. *Politics in the Vernacular: Nationalism, Multiculturalism, and Citizenship* (Oxford, New York: Oxford University Press, 2001).
Kymlicka, Will. *Finding Our Way: Rethinking Ethnocultural Relations in Canada* (Oxford University Press: Oxford, 1998).
Kymlicka, Will. *Multicultural Citizenship: A Liberal Theory of Minority Rights* (Oxford: Clarendon Press, 1995).
Kymlicka, Will and Raviot, Jean-Robert. "Living Together: International Aspects of Federal Systems," *Canadian Foreign Policy* 5(1), Fall 1997: 1–50.
Laitin, David. "Political Culture and Political Preferences," *American Political Science Review* 82(2), 1988: 589–597.
Laitin, David and Reich, Rob. "A Liberal Democratic Approach to Language Justice," in Will Kymlicka and Alan Patten (eds.) *Language Rights and Political Theory* (Oxford: Oxford University Press, 2003).
Larmore, Charles. "Political Liberalism," *Political Theory* 18(3), August 1990: 339–360.
Malcolm, Noel. *Bosnia: A Short History* (London: Macmillan/Papermac, 1994).
Margalit, Avishai and Raz, Joseph. "National Self-Determination," *Journal of Philosophy* 87(9), September 1990.
McMahon, Christopher *Collective Rationality and Collective Reasoning* (Cambridge: Cambridge University Press, 2001).
Mayall, James. "Sovereignty, Nationalism, and Self-Determination," *Political Studies* 47, 1999: 474–502.
McDonald, Michael. "The Personless Paradigm," *University of Toronto Law Journal* 37(2), Spring 1987.
McGarry, John. "'Orphans of Secession': National Pluralism in Secessionist Regions and Post-Secessionist States," in Margaret Moore (ed.) *National Self-Determination and Secession* (Oxford: Oxford University Press, 1998), 215–232.

McGarry, John. "Introduction: The Comparable Northern Ireland," in J. McGarry (ed.) *Northern Ireland and Divided World: Post-Agreement Northern Irelnad in Comparative Perspective* (Oxford: Oxford University Press, 2001).

V. A. Mikhailov, *Natsional'naja Politika Rossii: istoria I sovremennost* (Moscow: Pusskii mir, 1997).

Mill, John Stuart. "Considerations on the Representative Government," in *Utilitarianism, On Liberty, Considerations on Representative Government* (London: J. M. Dent & Sons Ltd, 1991).

Miller, David. *On Nationality* (Oxford: Oxford University Press, 1995).

Miller, David. "Secession and the Principle of Nationality," in Jocelyne Couture, Kai Nielsen, Michel Seymour (eds.) *Rethinking Nationalism* (Calgary, Alberta: University of Calgary Press, 1996), 261–282.

Miller, David. *Citizenship and National Identity* (Cambridge, U.K.: Polity Press, 2000).

Miller, David. "National Responsibility and International Justice," in Deen K. Chatterjee (ed.) *The Ethics of Assistance: Morality and the Distant Needy* (Cambridge: Cambridge University Press, 2004).

Miller, Seumas. *Social Action: A Teleological Account* (Cambridge: Cambridge University Press, 2001).

Moore, Margaret. "On National Self-Determination," *Political Studies* 45(5), 900–913.

Moore, Margaret. *The Ethics of Nationalism* (Oxford: Oxford University Press, 2001).

Nickel, James W. "Group Identity and Group Rights," in Ian Shapiro and Will Kymlicka (eds.) *Ethnicity and Group Rights*, NOMOS 39 (New York: New York University Press, 1997), 235–256.

Nickel, James W. "The Value of Cultural Belonging: Expanding Kymlicka's Theory," *Dialogue* 33, 1994.

Noonan, Jeff. "Need Satisfaction and Group Conflict: Beyond a Rights-Based Approach," *Social Theory and Practice* 30, 2004.

Nootens, Genevieve. "Liberal restrictions on Public Arguments: Can Nationalist Claims be *Moral Reasons* in Liberal Public Discourse?" In Jocelyne Couture, Kai Nielsen, Michel Seymour (eds.) *Rethinking Nationalism* (Calgary, Alberta: University of Calgary Press, 1996), 237–260.

Norman, Wayne. "Theorizing Nationalism (Normatively): The First Steps," in Ronald Beiner (ed.), *Theorizing Nationalism* (Albany: State University of New York Press, 1999), 51–66.

O'Leary, Brendan. "Comparative Political Science and the British-Irish Agreement," in J. McGarry (ed.) *Northern Ireland and Divided World: Post-Agreement Northern Irelnad in Comparative Perspective* (Oxford: Oxford University Press, 2001).

Parekh, Bhikhu. *Rethinking Multiculturalism: Cultural Diversity and Political Theory* (Cambridge, MA: Harvard University Press, 2000).

Pettit, Philip. *A Theory of Freedom: From the Psychology to the Politics of Agency* (Oxford: Oxford University Press, 2001).

Piper, Laurence. "Do I Need Ethnic Culture to Be Free? A Critique of Will Kymlicka's Liberal Nationalism," *South African Journal of Philosophy* 21(3), 2002.

Philpott, Daniel. "In Defense of Self-Determination," *Ethics* 105(2), 1995: 352–385.

Pogge, Thomas W. "The Bounds of Nationalism," in Jocelyne Couture, Kai Nielsen, Michel Seymour (eds.) *Rethinking Nationalism* (Calgary, Alberta: University of Calgary Press, 1996), 463–504.

Pohl, J. Otto. "The Deportation and Fate of the Crimean Tatars," a paper presented at the 5th Annual World Convention of the Association for the Study of Nationalities: "Identity and the State: Nationalism and Sovereignty in a Changing World," 13–15 April 2000, Columbia University, New York.

Pye, Lucian and Verba, Sydney (eds.). *Political Culture and Political Development* (Princeton: Princeton University Press, 1965).

Ratner, Steven R. "Does International Law Matter in Preventing Ethnic Conflict?" *International Law and Politics* 32, 2000: 591–642.

Rawls, John. *A Theory of Justice* (Cambridge, Massachusetts: Harvard University Press, 1971).

Rawls, John. *Justice as Fairness: A Restatement* (Cambridge, MA: Belknap Press, Harvard University Press, 2001).
Rawls, John. *The Law of Peoples* (Cambridge, MA: Harvard University Press, 1999).
Raz, Joseph. "Authority, Law and Morality," in *Ethics in the Public Domain* (Oxford: Clarendon Press, 1996), pp. 210–237.
Raz, Joseph. *The Morality of Freedom* (Oxford: Clarendon Press, 1986).
Réaume, Denise G. "Common-Law Constructions of Group Autonomy: A Case Study," in Ian Shapiro and Will Kymlicka (eds.) *Ethnicity and Group Rights*, NOMOS 39 (New York: New York University Press, 1997), 257–289.
Réaume, Denise "Individuals, Groups, and Rights to Public Goods," *The University of Toronto Law Journal* 38(1), Winter 1988.
Réaume, Denise "The Group Right to Linguistic Security: Whose Right, What Duties?" in Judith Baker (ed.) *Group Rights* (Toronto: University of Toronto Press, 1991).
Renan, Ernest ."Qu'est-ce qu'une nation?," in Tome I (ed.) *Œuvres complètes de Ernest Renan* (Paris: Calmann-Lévy, Éditeurs).
RFE/RL NEWSLINE Vol. 5, No. 34, Part I, February 19, 2001 (http://www.rferl.org/newsline).
Risse, Mathias. "How Does the Global Order Harm the Poor?" *Philosophy and Public Affairs* 33(4), Blackwell Publishing, 2005: 349–376.
Rubio-Marin, Ruth. *Language Rights and Political Theory*, Will Kymlicka and Alan Patten (eds.) (Oxford: Oxford University Press, 2003).
Schull, Joseph. *Russian Political Culture and the Stateless Intelligentsia* (Montreal: McGill, 1986).
Seton-Watson, Hugh. *Nations and States* (London: Methuen, 1997).
Seymour, Michel. *On Redefining the Nation*, in Cahier No. 97–01 (Montreal: Universite de Montreal, Faculte des arts et des sciences, 1997).
Simmons, A. John. *Moral Principles and Political Obligations* (Princeton: Princeton University Press, 1979).
Smith, Graham. "Sustainable Federalism, Democratization, and Distributive Justice," in Will Kymlicka and Wayne Norman (eds.), *Citizenship in Diverse Societies* (Oxford University Press: Oxford, New York, 2000).
Snyder, Jack. "Introduction: reconstructing politics amidst the wreckage of empire," Barnett R. Rubin and Jack Snyder (eds.) *Post-Soviet Political Order: Conflict and State-Building* (London and New York: Routledge, 1998).
Stalin, Joseph. *Marxism and the National Question: Selected Writings and Speeches* (New York: International Publishers, 1942).
Stoiciu, Andrei. *Fiction et Réalité Identitaire: Le cas de la Bessarabie.* (Montreal: Humanitas, 1995).
Subtelny, Orest. *Ukraine: A History* (Toronto: University of Toronto Press in association with the Canadian Institute of Ukrainian Studies, 1993).
Szporluk, Roman. "Thoughts About Change: Ernest Gellner and the History of Nationalism," in John Hall (ed.) *The State of the Nation: Ernest Gellner and the Theory of Nationalism* (Cambridge: Cambridge University Press, 1998), 23–39.
Tamir, Yael. *Liberal Nationalism* (Princeton: Princeton University Press, 1993).
Tamir, Yael. "The Right to National Self-Determination," *Social Research* 58(3), Fall 1991: 565–590.
Tanner, Marcus. *Croatia: A Nation Forged in War* (New Haven, CT: Yale University Press, 1997).
Tully, James. "Liberté et devoilement dans les sociétés multinationals," *Globe* 2(2), 1999.
Valls, Andrew. "Can Terrorism be Justified?" in A. Valls (ed.) *Ethics in International Affairs* (New York: Rowman and Littlefield, 2000).
Van de Putte, Andre. "Democracy and Nationalism," in Jocelyne Couture, Kai Nielsen, Michel Seymour (eds.) *Rethinking Nationalism* (Calgary: University of Calgary Press, 1996), 161–196.
Waldron, Jeremy. *The Right to Private Property* (Oxford: Oxford University Press, 1988).

Walker, Brian. "On the Very Idea of a Queer Nation," in Jocelyne Couture, Kai Nielsen, Michel Seymour (eds.), *Rethinking Nationalism* (Calgary: University of Calgary Press, 1996), 505–550.

Walzer, Michael. *Just and Unjust Wars: A Moral Argument with Historical Illustrations,* 3rd edition (New York: Basic Books, 2000).

Ware, Robert X. "Nations and Social Complexity," in Jocelyne Couture, Kai Nielsen, and Michel Seymour (eds.) *Rethinking Nationalism* (Calgary, Alberta: University of Calgary Press, 1996), 133–160.

Weber, Max. *Economy and Society: An Outline of Interpretive Sociology*, Guenther Roth and Claus Wittich (eds.), 2 vols. (New York: Bedminster, 1968).

Weinstock, Daniel. "On Some Advantages of Constitutionalizing the Right to Secede," Journal *of Political Philosophy,* 9(2), 2001: 182–203.

Welch, Stephen. *The Concept of Political Culture* (London: The MacMillan Press Ltd., 1993).

Wellman, C. *A Theory of Secession: The Case for Political Self-Determination* (Cambridge, New York: Cambridge University Press, 2005).

Wellman, Christopher H. "A Defense of Secession and Political Self-Determination," *Philosophy and Public Affairs* 24(2), Spring 1995: 142–171.

Wenar, Leif. "The Nature of Rights," *Philosophy and Public Affairs* 33(3), Summer 2005.

Young, Iris Marion. "A Multicultural Continuum: A Critique of Will Kymlicka's Ethnic-Nation Dichotomy," *Constellations* 4(1), 1997: 48–53.

Index

A. Moltchanova, *National Self-Determination and Justice in Multinational States*, Studies in Global Justice 5, DOI 10.1007//978-90-481-2691-0_BM2,

GPSR Compliance

The European Union's (EU) General Product Safety Regulation (GPSR) is a set of rules that requires consumer products to be safe and our obligations to ensure this.

If you have any concerns about our products, you can contact us on ProductSafety@springernature.com

In case Publisher is established outside the EU, the EU authorized representative is:

Springer Nature Customer Service Center GmbH
Europaplatz 3
69115 Heidelberg, Germany

Batch number: 10823959

Printed by Printforce, the Netherlands